First World War
and Army of Occupation
War Diary
France, Belgium and Germany

14 DIVISION
Divisional Troops
Royal Army Medical Corps
44 Field Ambulance
20 May 1915 - 30 June 1919

WO95/1892/1

The Naval & Military Press Ltd
www.nmarchive.com
Published in association with The National Archives

Published by

The Naval & Military Press Ltd

Unit 10 Ridgewood Industrial Park,

Uckfield, East Sussex,

TN22 5QE England

Tel: +44 (0) 1825 749494

www.naval-military-press.com

www.nmarchive.com

This diary has been reprinted in facsimile from the original. Any imperfections are inevitably reproduced and the quality may fall short of modern type and cartographic standards.

© Crown Copyright
Images reproduced by permission of The National Archives, London, England, 2015.

Contents

Document type	Place/Title	Date From	Date To
Heading	WO95/1892/1		
Heading	14th Division 44th Field Ambulance May 1915-1919 Jun		
Heading	War Diary Of No. 44 Field Ambulance From 20/5/1915 To 31/5/1915 Volume 1		
War Diary	Southampton	20/05/1915	23/05/1915
War Diary	Watten	24/05/1915	25/05/1915
War Diary	Zuytpeene	26/05/1915	26/05/1915
War Diary	Fletre	27/05/1915	27/05/1915
War Diary	Locre	28/05/1915	31/05/1915
Heading	14th Division 44th Field Ambulance Vol II June 1915		
Heading	War Diary Of No.44 Field Ambulance R.A.M.C. From 1st June 1915 To 30th June 1915 (Volume 2.)		
War Diary	Locre	01/06/1915	05/06/1915
War Diary	La Clytte	06/06/1915	14/06/1915
War Diary	Hilhoek	14/06/1915	14/06/1915
War Diary	Schoude	15/06/1915	17/06/1915
War Diary	Hilhoek	18/06/1915	28/06/1915
Heading	14th Division 44th Field Ambulance Vols III And IV July & Aug 15		
Heading	War Diary Of 44th Field Ambulance From July 1st 1915 To Aug. 31st 1916 (Volume 3 And 4)		
War Diary	Hilhoek	01/07/1915	17/07/1915
War Diary	P O P	17/07/1915	15/08/1915
War Diary	St Jan Der Biezen	16/08/1915	26/08/1915
War Diary	St Jan	27/08/1915	31/08/1915
Heading	14th Division War Diary Of 44th Field Ambulance From May 1st (Volume 3)		
War Diary	St Jan	01/09/1915	06/09/1915
War Diary	St Jan Der Biezen	07/09/1915	11/09/1915
War Diary	St Jan	12/09/1915	14/09/1915
War Diary	Hilhoek	15/09/1915	29/09/1915
Heading	No. 44 F.Q. Oct. 1915		
War Diary	Hilhoek	30/09/1915	31/10/1915
Heading	14th Division 44th F.A. Vol 7 Nov. 1915		
Heading	War Diary Of 44th Field Ambulance From November 1st To Novbe. 30th 1915 Volume 4.		
War Diary	Poperinghe	01/11/1915	17/11/1915
War Diary	P O P	18/11/1915	30/11/1915
Heading	War Diary of 44th Field Ambulance R.A.M.C. from December 1st to December 31st 1915 Volume 8		
War Diary	Poperinghe	01/12/1915	04/12/1915
War Diary	Pop.	05/12/1916	12/12/1916
War Diary	Poperinghe	13/12/1915	18/12/1915
War Diary	Pop.	19/12/1915	19/12/1915
War Diary	Poperinghe	19/12/1915	19/12/1915
War Diary	Pop	20/12/1915	31/12/1915
Miscellaneous	Nominal roll of Officers 44th Field Amb. R.A.M.C. 19th Dec. 1915	20/12/1915	20/12/1915

Miscellaneous	Nominal Roll of N.C.O.s & Men 44th Field Ambce. R.A.M.C.	19/12/1915	19/12/1915
Miscellaneous	Nominal Roll of N.C.O.s and men A.S.C. M.O. all Md 44th Fd. Ambu. 19th Dec 1915	20/12/1915	20/12/1915
Miscellaneous	Nominal Roll of the ASC attached to 44th Field Ambulance R.A.M.C. 19 Dec. 1915	20/12/1915	20/12/1915
Heading	14th Division 44th F.A. Vol 9 January 1916		
Heading	War Diary of 44th Field Ambulance From Jan. 1st to Jan 31st/16 (Volume 6)		
War Diary	Poperinghe	01/01/1916	02/01/1916
War Diary	Pop	03/01/1916	06/01/1916
War Diary	Poperinghe	07/01/1916	09/01/1916
War Diary	Pop.	09/01/1916	13/01/1916
War Diary	Popp.	13/01/1916	20/01/1916
War Diary	Poperinghe	21/06/1916	31/06/1916
Heading	War Diary of 44 Field Ambulance from 1st February to 29th February 1916 Volume 10		
War Diary	Poperinghe	01/02/1916	12/02/1916
War Diary	Annizelle	13/02/1916	22/02/1916
War Diary	Flersellen	22/02/1916	24/02/1916
War Diary	Doullens	25/02/1916	25/02/1916
War Diary	Sombrin	26/02/1916	29/02/1916
Heading	War Diary of 44th Field Ambulance From 1st March 1916 to 31st March 1916 Volume II		
War Diary	Sombrin	01/03/1916	01/03/1916
War Diary	Fosseux	02/03/1916	08/03/1916
War Diary	Fosseux Chateau	08/03/1916	31/03/1916
Heading	War Diary of 44th Field Ambulance for Period 1st to 30th April, 1916 Volume 12		
War Diary	Fosseux	01/04/1916	30/04/1916
Heading	War Diary of 44th Field Ambulance for period 1st to 31st May 1916 Volume 13		
War Diary	Fosseux	01/05/1916	09/05/1916
War Diary	Liencourt	10/05/1916	31/05/1916
Heading	War Diary of 44th Field Ambulance for period June 1st to 30th 1916 Vol 14		
War Diary	Liencourt	01/06/1916	30/06/1916
Heading	War Diary of 44th Field Ambulance July 1-31 1916 Vol 15		
War Diary	Liencourt	01/07/1916	31/07/1916
Heading	War Diary of No 44 Field Ambulance for the Month of August 1916 Vol 16.		
War Diary	Barly	01/08/1916	01/08/1916
War Diary	Gezaincourt	02/08/1916	08/08/1916
War Diary	Dernancourt	09/08/1916	12/08/1916
War Diary	In The Field	13/08/1916	31/08/1916
Heading	14th (Light) Div. War Diary of 44 Field Ambulance September 1st to 30th 1916		
War Diary	L' Arbre G' Mouche	01/09/1916	09/09/1916
War Diary	Dernancourt	10/09/1916	10/09/1916
War Diary	In The Field	11/09/1916	17/09/1916
War Diary	Field	17/09/1916	17/09/1916
War Diary	Dernancourt	18/09/1916	21/09/1916
War Diary	Grouches	22/09/1916	25/09/1916
War Diary	Barly	26/09/1916	30/09/1916

Heading	War Diary of 44th Field Ambulance 14th Div. from 1st October 1916 to 31st October 1916 (Volume 18.)		
War Diary	Barly	01/10/1916	27/10/1916
War Diary	Sombrin	27/10/1916	31/10/1916
Heading	14th Div. War Diary of 44th Field Ambulance for month of November 1916		
War Diary	Sombrin	01/11/1916	03/11/1916
War Diary	Ivergny	03/11/1916	10/11/1916
War Diary	Liencourt	10/11/1916	30/11/1916
Heading	14th Div. 44th Field Ambulance War Diary for Period- December 1 to 31 1916 Vol 20		
War Diary	Liencourt	01/12/1916	18/12/1916
War Diary	Wanquetin	18/12/1916	31/12/1916
Heading	14th Div. 44th Field Ambulance War Diary For Period January 1st to 31st 1917 Vol 21		
War Diary	Wanquetin	01/01/1917	31/01/1917
Heading	14th Div. War Diary of 44th Field Ambulance for Month of February 1917 Vol 22		
War Diary	Wanquetin	01/02/1917	08/02/1917
War Diary	Arras	08/02/1917	28/02/1917
Heading	War Diary of No. 44 Field Ambulance for Month of March 1917 Vol 23		
War Diary	Arras	01/03/1917	31/03/1917
Heading	14th Div. 44th F.A.		
War Diary	Arras	01/04/1917	06/04/1917
War Diary	Ronville	07/04/1917	12/04/1917
War Diary	Arras	13/04/1917	15/04/1917
War Diary	Berneville	16/04/1917	22/04/1917
War Diary	Barly	23/04/1917	24/04/1917
War Diary	Bellacourt	24/04/1917	26/04/1917
War Diary	Hercatel	26/04/1917	30/04/1917
Miscellaneous	B.E.F. Summary of Medical War Diaries For 44th F.A., 14th Divn. 7th Corps, 3rd Army. Western Front. April-May. '17		
Miscellaneous	44th F.A. 14th Divn. 7th Corps. O.C. Lt. Col. W. Egan. 3rd Army		
Heading	War Diary 44 Field Ambulance May 1-31.1917 Vol 25		
War Diary	Hercatel	01/05/1917	31/05/1917
Miscellaneous	B.E.F. Summary of Medical War Diaries For 44th F.A., 14th Divn. 7th Corps, 3rd Army Western Front. April-May '17		
War Diary	Medical Arrangements.	02/05/1917	02/05/1917
Miscellaneous	B.E.F. 44th F.A. 14th Divn. 7th Corps. O.C. Lt. Col. W. Egan. 3rd Army.	03/05/1917	03/05/1917
War Diary	Casualties	03/05/1917	03/05/1917
War Diary	Total Admissions	03/05/1917	03/05/1917
War Diary	Evacuation	03/05/1917	03/05/1917
War Diary	Casualties R.A.M.C.	04/05/1917	04/05/1917
War Diary	Decorations	04/05/1917	04/05/1917
War Diary	Casualties	06/05/1917	06/05/1917
War Diary	Moves Detachment	11/05/1917	11/05/1917
War Diary	Casualties R.A.M.C.	11/05/1917	11/05/1917
War Diary	Moves Detachment	14/05/1917	14/05/1917
War Diary	Moves Detachment	17/05/1917	17/05/1917
War Diary	Operations.	20/05/1917	20/05/1917
War Diary	Casualties	20/05/1917	20/05/1917

War Diary	Moves Detachment	26/05/1917	26/05/1917
War Diary	Medical Arrangements	02/05/1917	02/05/1917
Miscellaneous	B.E.F. 44th F.A. 14th Divn. 7th Corps. O.C. Lt. Col. W. Egan. 3rd Army.	03/05/1917	03/05/1917
War Diary	Casualties	03/05/1917	03/05/1917
War Diary	Total Admissions	03/05/1917	03/05/1917
War Diary	Evacuation	03/05/1917	03/05/1917
War Diary	Casualties R.A.M.C.	04/05/1917	04/05/1917
War Diary	Decorations	04/05/1917	04/05/1917
War Diary	Casualties	06/05/1917	06/05/1917
War Diary	Moves Detachment	11/05/1917	11/05/1917
War Diary	Casualties R.A.M.C.	11/05/1917	11/05/1917
War Diary	Moves Detachment	14/05/1917	14/05/1917
War Diary	Casualties R.A.M.C.	14/05/1917	14/05/1917
War Diary	Moves Detachment	17/05/1917	17/05/1917
Miscellaneous	B.E.F. 44th F.A. 14th Divn. 7th Corps. O.C. Lt. Col. W. Egan. 3rd Army.	20/05/1917	20/05/1917
War Diary	Casualties	20/05/1917	20/05/1917
War Diary	Moves Detachment	26/05/1917	26/05/1917
Heading	War Diary 44 Field Ambulance June 1917 Vol 26		
War Diary	Hercatel	01/06/1917	03/06/1917
War Diary	Agny	04/06/1917	11/06/1917
War Diary	Monchiet	11/06/1917	12/06/1917
War Diary	Larbret	12/06/1917	13/06/1917
War Diary	Vauchelles	13/06/1917	30/06/1917
Heading	War Diary 44 Field Ambulance July 1917 Vol 27		
War Diary	Vauchelles	01/07/1917	10/07/1917
War Diary	Beauval	10/07/1917	12/07/1917
War Diary	Boeschepe Farm	13/07/1917	31/07/1917
Heading	War Diary 44 Field Ambulance August 1917 Vol 28		
War Diary	Boeschepe Farm	01/08/1917	06/08/1917
War Diary	Hondechem	06/08/1917	16/08/1917
War Diary	Lyssenthoek Farm	16/08/1917	16/08/1917
War Diary	Waratah Camp	17/08/1917	31/08/1917
Heading	44 Field Ambulance War Diary September 1917 Vol 29		
War Diary	Bailleul	01/09/1917	03/09/1917
War Diary	Ravelsberg	03/09/1917	30/09/1917
Heading	War Diary 44 Field Ambulance October 1917 Vol 30		
War Diary	Ravelsberg	01/10/1917	06/10/1917
War Diary	Conquerors Camp	06/10/1917	09/10/1917
War Diary	Chippewa Camp	09/10/1917	11/10/1917
War Diary	Woodcote House	12/10/1917	24/10/1917
War Diary	Q. 23 C 65	25/10/1917	31/10/1917
Heading	War Diary 44 Field Ambulance November 1917 Vol 31		
War Diary	Q. 23 C.65.	01/11/1917	12/11/1917
War Diary	Sheet 36 D F 1 d 4.4.	13/11/1917	28/11/1917
War Diary	Hallines	28/11/1917	30/11/1917
Heading	War Diary 44 Field Ambulance December 1917 Vol 32		
War Diary	Red. Farm Brandhoek	01/12/1917	17/12/1917
War Diary	Red Farm	18/12/1917	25/12/1917
War Diary	Cormette	25/12/1917	27/12/1917
War Diary	Hallines	27/12/1917	31/12/1917
Heading	44 Field Ambulance War Diary January 1918 Vol 33		
War Diary	Hallines	01/01/1918	04/01/1918
War Diary	Sailly Le Sec	04/01/1918	22/01/1918
War Diary	Fresnoy	23/01/1918	23/01/1918

War Diary	Arvillers	24/01/1918	24/01/1918
War Diary	Tirlancourt	25/01/1918	25/01/1918
War Diary	Jussy	26/01/1918	31/01/1918
Heading	44 Field Ambulance War Diary February 1918 Vol 34		
War Diary	Jussy	01/02/1918	28/02/1918
Heading	War Diary 44 Field Ambulance March 1918 Vol 35		
War Diary	Jussy	01/03/1918	21/03/1918
War Diary	Beaumont	21/03/1918	22/03/1918
War Diary	Guivry	22/03/1918	23/03/1918
War Diary	Tirtancourt	23/03/1918	24/03/1918
War Diary	Noyon	24/03/1918	24/03/1918
War Diary	Lassigny	25/03/1918	25/03/1918
War Diary	Ressons	25/03/1918	26/03/1918
War Diary	Clairoix	26/03/1918	27/03/1918
War Diary	Beaupuits	28/03/1918	28/03/1918
War Diary	Cinqueux	29/03/1918	29/03/1918
War Diary	Nogent	29/03/1918	30/03/1918
War Diary	Airion	31/03/1918	31/03/1918
Heading	War Diary 44 Field Ambulance April 1918 Vol 36		
War Diary	Fay St. Quentin	01/04/1918	01/04/1918
War Diary	Hardivillers	02/04/1918	02/04/1918
War Diary	Fosse Manant	03/04/1918	03/04/1918
War Diary	Blangy-Tronville	03/04/1918	04/04/1918
War Diary	Fovilloy	04/04/1918	04/04/1918
War Diary	Aubigny	04/04/1918	05/04/1918
War Diary	Glisy	05/04/1918	07/04/1918
War Diary	St. Acheul	07/04/1918	10/04/1918
War Diary	Dargnies	11/04/1918	12/04/1918
War Diary	Crequy	13/04/1918	14/04/1918
War Diary	Crepy	15/04/1918	15/04/1918
War Diary	L'Oblois Wood	16/04/1918	21/04/1918
War Diary	Ecquedecques	22/04/1918	30/04/1918
Heading	War Diary 44 Field Ambulance May 1918 Vol 37		
War Diary	Ecquedecques	01/05/1918	28/05/1918
War Diary	Therouanne	28/05/1918	29/05/1918
War Diary	Lart	29/05/1918	31/05/1918
Heading	War Diary 44 Field Ambulance June 1918 Vol 38		
War Diary	Lart	01/06/1918	03/06/1918
War Diary	Bournonville	04/06/1918	04/06/1918
War Diary	Conteville	05/06/1918	10/06/1918
War Diary	Bournonville	11/06/1918	30/06/1918
Heading	War Diary 44 Field Ambulance July 1918 Vol 39		
War Diary	Bournonville	01/07/1918	06/07/1918
War Diary	Rety	07/07/1918	10/07/1918
War Diary	Le Brevil	10/07/1918	11/07/1918
War Diary	Helvelinghem	12/07/1918	12/07/1918
War Diary	Watten	13/07/1918	31/07/1918
Heading	44 Field Ambulance War Diary for Month August 1918 Vol 40		
War Diary	Watten	01/08/1918	20/08/1918
War Diary	Ambulance Farm	21/08/1918	28/08/1918
War Diary	Bollezeele	29/08/1918	31/08/1918
Heading	War Diary of 44th Field Ambulance From:- 1/9/18 To:- 30/9/18 Vol 41		
War Diary	Bollezeele	01/09/1918	15/09/1918
War Diary	L'Ebbe Farm 27/F 29 b. 9.4	16/09/1918	21/09/1918

War Diary	Vlamertinghe Mill	22/09/1918	22/09/1918
War Diary	Ouderdom	23/09/1918	30/09/1918
Heading	War Diary for month October 1918 44th Field Ambulance Vol 42		
War Diary	Long Barn	01/10/1918	03/10/1918
War Diary	28. S.17 a. 5.9	03/10/1918	05/10/1918
War Diary	Moat Farm	06/10/1918	09/10/1918
War Diary	Farm	10/10/1918	12/10/1918
War Diary	28 M 33 Cu 3	13/10/1918	16/10/1918
War Diary	Messines	17/10/1918	19/10/1918
War Diary	Wattrelos	19/10/1918	31/10/1918
Heading	War Diary 44 Field Ambulance November 1918 Vol 43		
War Diary	Wattrelos	01/11/1918	09/11/1918
War Diary	Chateau Espierres	10/11/1918	14/11/1918
War Diary	Torcoing	15/11/1918	30/11/1918
Heading	War Diary December 1918 44 Field Ambulance Vol 44		
War Diary	Tourcoing	01/12/1918	31/12/1918
Heading	14th Division. War Diary-44th Field Ambulance. 1st January 1919-30th January 1919 Vol 45		
War Diary	Tourcoing	01/01/1919	30/01/1919
Heading	14th Division. War Diary-44th Field Ambulance. Period:- 1/2/19-28/2/19 Vol 46		
War Diary	Tourcoing	01/02/1919	28/02/1919
Heading	War Diary of 44th Field Ambulance (R.A.M.C.) From: 1st April, 1919 To: 30th April, 1919 Vol 48		
War Diary	Tourcoing	01/04/1919	30/04/1919
Heading	War Diary of 44th Field Ambulance (R.A.M.C.) 1-31st March, 1919. Vol 47		
War Diary	Tourcoing	01/03/1919	31/03/1919
Heading	War Diary of 44th Field Ambulance. From: 1st May, 1919 To: 31st May, 1919		
War Diary	Tourcoing	01/05/1919	31/05/1919
Heading	44th F.A. June 1919		
War Diary	Tourcoing	01/06/1919	30/06/1919

WO95 1890/1

14TH DIVISION

44TH FIELD AMBULANCE

MAY 1915 - DEC 1916
1919 JAN

121/55/4.

May 1915.

14th Division
Confidential

War Diary
of
No 44 Field Ambulance

from 20/5/1915 to 31/5/1915.

Volume 1

Lt Col Kempton 121/55/4
121/55/4

O.C.
44 F. Amb. ae
½ G. Stenrson

Army Form C. 2118.

WAR DIARY

or

INTELLIGENCE SUMMARY.

(Erase heading not required.)

Instructions regarding War Diaries and Intelligence
Summaries are contained in F. S. Regs., Part II.
and the Staff Manual respectively. Title pages
will be prepared in manuscript.

Place	Date	Hour	Summary of Events and Information	Remarks and references to Appendices
	1915			
Southampton	20/5	6 p.m.	44th F. Amb. entrained at Tantology 6 in two trainloads. first at 7.15 2nd at 7.15. Entrained in 25 mins. Embarked in SS Princess at 7.30. Proceeded to Havre light ship. Slight fog. Ordered to return to S. hampton.	A1
	21/5	9 p.m.	Back again at 3.30 p.m. Uneventful journey	A2
	22/5	9 p.m.	Disembarked at HAVRE. Proceeded to Rest Camp No 1. arrangements excellent	A3
	23/5	9 p.m.	Entrained at 15 in one train. the 15 four seats attached for journey half 13 pas at MONTÉROULIER BUCHY and Attempted ABBEVILLE. Reported to R.T.O at Watten. ordered to detrain at ST OMER. detrained and marched back to WATTEN - billeted in château at LE NOUT.	A4
WATTEN	24/5	10 a.m.	Chateau (after D.D.M.S stage try) previous occupant (French troops) found motor to surround of château & to O.O. & of 1st Bde. reported to A.D.M.S in morning Offered one tent subalter for stay. Submitted orders to pass thro to dispose of such.	A5
	25/5	6.30 p.m	2 pm received order to be ready to move at short notice. Orders for 14 Fr. F. Amb. workshops the attached to this bunch	A6

WAR DIARY
or
INTELLIGENCE SUMMARY.

Army Form C. 2118.

2. O. 4th F. Amb'ce
  1st Cav. Division

Place	Date	Hour	Summary of Events and Information	Remarks and references to Appendices
	1915			
ZUYTPEENE	26/5	9.45 p.m.	Marched from WATEN at 9 a.m. transferred 1 Cur. to H.Q. 4 Staff Hosp. ARCQUES and 3 to H.Q Cav. A. Sgn. ST OMER & 4 to H.Q 10 Staff Hosp. STOMER. Billeted at LE BOIS PERDU - bad billets, had water supply for over 60 given fell out from 7th Rifle Bde 2 miles from H.Q. of Bde now from other regiments - was told by O.C. 7th K.R.R. that many men had visited Estaminets in evening. Met the Genl PLUMMER at 6 p.m. at H.Q. discussion re Preparations.	#1.
FLÊTRE	27/5	8 p.m.	Marched from ZUYTPEENE via OXELAERE - ST SILVESTRE - CAESTRE to FLÊTRE. good billets near Bde H.Q. Your admission Wanted ½ 1 mile to H.Q 10 Staff Hosp STONER 3 to H.Q 10 C.C. Staff HAZEBROUCK R.I.	
LOCRE	28/6	10 p.m.	Received orders at 12.15 a.m. to proceed independently to LOCRE for G.O.C. 6th Inf. Bde. Marched at 2.30 a.m. via BERTHEN - and WESTOUTRE to LOCRE met at LOCRE by Billeting Offr. who reported that unit was to be attached to H.Q 1/1st NORTH MIDLAND Fld Amb of 46th 1st Division. Billeted in Convent at LOCRE with above unit. Before leaving FLÊTRE	#2

Army Form C. 2118.

3.O.

44 F Ambulance
14th Div.

WAR DIARY
or
INTELLIGENCE SUMMARY.
(Erase heading not required.)

Instructions regarding War Diaries and Intelligence Summaries are contained in F.S. Regs., Part II. and the Staff Manual respectively. Title pages will be prepared in manuscript.

Place	Date	Hour	Summary of Events and Information	Remarks and references to Appendices
LOCRE	28.5	10 p.m.	Transferred one case of mineral to No 10 Stat's Hosp'l STONER. In the evening reported to 8vr of 139th Inf R'ee at KEMMEL. Saw arrangements for evacuation of wounded from trenches arranged with O.C. 1 N. Mid F A and O.C. 2 N.M.F amb'ce at DRANOUTRE for men to be attached for training. Detail as follows - One Officer daily as O.O. another as Collecting Offr to bring casualties straight from Reg'l dressing Stations. No 1 N.M.F.A. 4 Sergs. 28 orderlies for stretcher bearers. 2 NCOs & 4 men in pack store, 8 men on duty with Regts in trenches to relieve worry two days. I ordered 6 pack trench'rs & were brought for duty in Regimental dressing stations. No 2 N.M.F.A. - 5 Laundry men 5 in the mess - 8 men for nursing duties 2 men daily for duty in aid posts. 6 men in dressing station. 12 men in trenches. Instructed personally by D.A.D.M.S. that all casualties pass through Pte N. Ferris 37637. transferred to O. Cas. S. with testicles Pte V Zemrovich 4/3290? - infected bathing fluid - laundry & disinfector - attach'd	
LOCRE	29.5	10 p.m	Visited No 2 N.M.F.A. and are returned by them. One man...	

Army Form C. 2118.

U.O. 4th N. MID. F. AMB CE
Lt. Col. Fio a

WAR DIARY
or
INTELLIGENCE SUMMARY
(Erase heading not required.)

Instructions regarding War Diaries and Intelligence Summaries are contained in F. S. Regs., Part II. and the Staff Manual respectively. Title pages will be prepared in manuscript.

Place	Date	Hour	Summary of Events and Information	Remarks and references to Appendices
LOCRE	29.5		Brigade washed & given clean clothing by F.A. about every 8 days. Drew respirators - men detailed for trenches all examined & sent out with respirators. During the march from WATTEN to LOCRE the transport did admirably thanks to the energy of the transport officer Lt BROSTER & the instrument. The personnel of the A.S.C. are extremely bad - including the N.C.O.'s who are as ignorant of horse management as the men. The discipline at present leaves much to be desired. The animals are excellent.	#1
LOCRE	30.5	9 p.m.	Wind north - fine. We is detailed for training as follows No 1 N. MID. F. AMB Trenches 8 dressing station & dressing station 2 Sergt & 14 men - pack stor 1 off & 4 men - No 2 N. MID. F.A. Trenches 14 - laundry & baths 10 - nursing duties 4 adv. dr. staff 6 - aid posts 2 -	#2
LOCRE	31.5	9 p.m.	Details same as 30th. North wind - fine -	#3

12/5931

$\frac{12}{5931}$

amb.

14th Division

44th Field Ambulance

Vol: II.

June 1915

Confidential.

War Diary.

of

No. 44 Field Ambulance, R.A.M.C.

From 1st June 1915 to 30th June 1915.

(Volume 2.)

WAR DIARY
or
INTELLIGENCE SUMMARY.
(Erase heading not required.)

Army Form C. 2118.

Instructions regarding War Diaries and Intelligence Summaries are contained in F.S. Regs., Part II. and the Staff Manual respectively. Title pages will be prepared in manuscript.

Place	Date	Hour	Summary of Events and Information	Remarks and references to Appendices
	1915			
LOCRE	1.6	9pm	North wind - fine - details of duties the same as before. 3 sick horses sent to 28th Mobile Veterinary Station. At 3 o'clock am visited all trenches occupied by Notts & Derby (Territorial) in front of KEMMEL. Inquired of several officers who all very pleased to have RAMC orderlies in trenches to render first aid in casualties in trenches according to daily - sanitary arrangements excellent all urine & excreta buried at night - urine tins at frequent intervals all water used to make tea. Considered that the scheme of sending RAMC orderlies into trenches an excellent one - men in trenches like to feel that Expert first aid is handy and RAMC men feel they are sharing the same hardships & risks as their comrades. As equipment they take bare bottle & haversack - no option as required and 3 shell dressings and bottle of iodine placed in it.	
LOCRE	2.6	10pm	Fine warm - North wind - details of duties the same as before.	
LOCRE	3.6	9.30pm	Cloudy - West wind - nothing of importance to record.	

Army Form C. 2118.

WAR DIARY
or
INTELLIGENCE SUMMARY.
(Erase heading not required.)

Place	Date	Hour	Summary of Events and Information	Remarks and references to Appendices
LOCRE	4.6.	9 p.m.	Cloudy - South west wind - details as before	
LOCRE	5.6.	9 p.m.	Fine South west wind - details as before - Make plan of laundry & wash house of No 2 NORTH MIDLAND F.A. sent it to S.M.S.O. 4th Division with no Ordnance Equipment required. Received message from Division H.Q to proceed on 6th inst to LA CLYTE under orders of G.O.C. 41st High Bde to billets vacated by 43rd F.Amb.ce at LA CLYTE with advanced station at DICKE BUSCH	fs
LA CLYTE	6.6.	9.30 p.m.	Rode over to LA CLYTE in afternoon saw O.C. 43rd F.A. & went on to DICKE BOSCH - Staff's Lieut FLOOD to proceed to LA CLYTE at 7.30 and go round with collecting party & one ambulance to aid posts - Issued orders for tomorrows move. Proceeded to LA CLYTE at 9 a.m. and took up billets vacated by 43rd F. Amb - 21 sick left behind from by them they belonged to 3 different divisions - asked for terms for instructions for their disposal - all cases not suitable for	#s

WAR DIARY
or
INTELLIGENCE SUMMARY

Army Form C. 2118.

Instructions regarding War Diaries and Intelligence Summaries are contained in F. S. Regs., Part II. and the Staff Manual respectively. Title pages will be prepared in manuscript.

(Erase heading not required.)

Place	Date	Hour	Summary of Events and Information	Remarks and references to Appendices
LA CLYTE	6.6		Provisional rest camp WESTOUTRE to send out three ambulances at 11 pm to visit aid posts. Relief trenches - also one ambulance to proceed along YPRES road at 11 pm to be met by M.O. DCLI - trench digging. Admissions 23. Sick tr. to H.Q. P BAILLEUL 2.	
LA CLYTE	7.6	9.45	Fine warm N.W. wind. Transferred to C.C.S. BAILLEUL 34 Prot camp WESTOUTRE to - large numbers of former rest camp cases tried himself to trace whereabouts.	
LA CLYTE	8.6		Thursday - local shows - transferred to C.C.S BAILLEUL to Div rest camp. - For men of various TF units to rest from rest camps, from 1 N.M.F.A. LOCRE for distribution - Enquired of H.Q. 4 Div. 4th & 13th as to whereabouts of batty's H.A.C. could get no information returned them. Sent Sgt Major & A.D.M.S. for instruction in taking flox Anil is attach for treatment of sick certain walk points in training of personnel & Officer - N.COs + men	

1577 Wt.W10791/1773 500,000 1/15 D. D. & L. A.D.S.S./Forms/C. 2118.

WAR DIARY
or
INTELLIGENCE SUMMARY.
(Erase heading not required.)

Army Form C. 2118.

Place	Date	Hour	Summary of Events and Information	Remarks and references to Appendices
LA CLYTTE	8.6		quite ignorant of handling of sick. Serj. Major equally ignorant. Have to instruct all NCO's in each store office, ward master duties and supervise all detail of their work - Lack of second regular R.A.M.C. officer greatly felt. Such solution for sprayers in trenches to G.O.C. 41st Bde. DICKERSON saturated sol'n Hypo with 2½ handfuls Soda Carb: in each 2 gall petrol tin - sent 10 gas orders for 3 ambulances to go to Brasserie to N.W. to aid post D.R.R.R. & to call at aid post at Pioneer Farm beyond to evacuate wounded from. Sent instructions for keeping down flies in trenches to N.Q. 41st Bde. Transferred to O.C'S BAILLEUL — 25 [16 wounded] " " Div. Rest Camp WESTOUTRE — Ambulance to Pioneer Farm received message from M.O. J.R.B. to send ambulance to Pioneer Farm to-night - enquired from Signalling officer 43rd Bde whereabouts - not heard of was.	AL

WAR DIARY
or
INTELLIGENCE SUMMARY.
(Erase heading not required.)

Army Form C. 2118.

Instructions regarding War Diaries and Intelligence Summaries are contained in F. S. Regs., Part II. and the Staff Manual respectively. Title pages will be prepared in manuscript.

Place	Date	Hour	Summary of Events and Information	Remarks and references to Appendices
LA CLYTTE	9.6.9.45		Cloudy - wind N. West - Inspected well dug by men W. of village for animals - good supply in fair quantity. Reported by Lieut Broster that he had wandered about for 4 hours trying to find PIONEER FARM - sent message to M.O. 7th R.B. to double group on Cas B in arrears or send guide. Transferred to BALLIOL Sick 14 Wounded 8 " " Sick 4 Rest Camp. Wounded R 1 In afternoon inspected water dam in N.13.c. S.16 of LA CLYTTE with Sare Offr of Div. Suggested topping a stream higher up and piping it to dam - it also that concrete dam be made with wastage re required. Solution for sprinklers to Bde H Q. No 3 Motor convoy calls daily at 10 am for transport to BAILLEUL. Motor cyclist of convoy calls daily at 9am to get wounded - By stem works smoothly - Inspected detachment at dilution near DICKEBUSCH - Lieut AT. Mitced Lieut ATKINS.	

WAR DIARY
or
INTELLIGENCE SUMMARY.

(Erase heading not required.)

Army Form C. 2118.

Place	Date	Hour	Summary of Events and Information	Remarks and references to Appendices
LA CLYTTE	10.6.	9.30	Transferred to C.C.S. BAILLEUL sick 1 wounded 4	AJ
			" " Sta. R.C. " 4	
			Cloudy some rain - N. wind	
LA CLYTTE	11.6.	9.45	Wind N. some rain - arranged to take over lath house buildings of Sto Bge at LA CLYTTE for F. Aubé - Secured 7 4 carts & three boiling tanks.	AJ
			Transferred to C.C.S BAILLEUL sick 1 wounded 2	
			" " Sto R.C. WESTOUTRE " " " nil	
			Following went to DICKEBUSCH & saw Bde Maj. D.A.D.M.S. & arranged about Collecting wounded - Same arrangement as 41st Bde	
LA CLYTTE	12.6.	9.30	Cloudy, wind mod to fresh -	AS
			Transferred C.C.S. BAILLEUR sick 4 wounded 10	
			" " Sta R.C. " 2 " 1	
			Officers.) RR. Capt Fairlie E. G.S.W. Took his with him.	
			8 R 13. Lieut Walter A. Lawton. Kit sent by servant	
			1 Div Cyc Coy " Baumgarten G.S.W. Haversack pistol & case taken by Col Edwards to Bailleul	

Army Form C. 2118.

WAR DIARY
or
INTELLIGENCE SUMMARY.

(Erase heading not required.)

Instructions regarding War Diaries and Intelligence Summaries are contained in F. S. Regs., Part II. and the Staff Manual respectively. Title pages will be prepared in manuscript.

Place	Date	Hour	Summary of Events and Information	Remarks and references to Appendices
Lt ClYTTE	12.6	9.30	Went to see D.A.D.M.S. with application for J.P. Court Martial of Pte MacKinlay.	AN/1
La ClYTTE	13.6	9.30	Fine - h. wind - received warning from D.A.D.M.S. that wind would probably move tomorrow.	AN/2
Lt ClYTTE / HILHOEK	14.6	9.30	Fine - h. wind - Given orders at 8 am from 42nd Bept B. to follow average rate from 16 to turn 44th J.A. and move to billets in Sheet 27 Sq L 21 C. Please inform O.C. 44 J.A. 10 - 5 p.m. At 8.45 J.A. and arrived saying unit should have been at 8.15 - issued orders - called in detachment from Diep Bosch - Kruitfurst N cases 4 Battelul carried 45 rest camp Cates - Left Lieut Barton to check route Pt. 4 J.H. Who had not arrived. Marched off 10.30 to HILHOEK in Sq Q.21 C. - before departure St-Duff & NSuds arrived late, & told me event should have heard 8.15 explained no orders.	

WAR DIARY
or
INTELLIGENCE SUMMARY.
(Erase heading not required.)

Army Form C. 2118.

Place	Date	Hour	Summary of Events and Information	Remarks and references to Appendices
MILHO	12/14/6	9.30	Asked that operation orders be repeated by wire to F.A. Bde they told be in writing that he had not sent an orders as F.A. was not in Bde area. On arrival at MILMER reported to OC 41 C.C.S. Warned me of probable move to morrow. Saw DAD MS - Excellent billets - bivouaced in field pitched 12 tents & Offrs tents - for sick etc to augment 35 rest camp cases to MONT DES CATS C.C.S.	14.
SCHOUDE	15/6	9.40	Received orders from Ned 14 CA div to move to SCHOUDE to prepare to receive wounded York over Brick factory - consists of sheds filled with dried bricks - had place for 8 wounded - no lorry place fouled - Sheds had been used as stables - some as latrines etc. Spent whole day cleaning the place & preparing sheds by making walls of dried brick. Received orders from DADMS to send 6 motor ambulances to 42 ed F. Amb. at VLAMERTINGE	

Army Form C. 2118.

WAR DIARY
or
INTELLIGENCE SUMMARY.
(Erase heading not required.)

Place	Date	Hour	Summary of Events and Information	Remarks and references to Appendices
SCHOUDE	15/6		Sg H.Q.L. who send 50 blankets. to bears SCHOUDE at 11 pm. gave orders to Sergt COLES of M.T. at 8.30 rec'd message from 4 & Bde to send ambulance to Sq POTERINGE at 9.30 to reconnay sch...m to bring bridge. Feel very anxious about forward site for collecting station. This field with large manure and covered with long lush green. The sun dried bricks - infields by temans portable. all ground round filled by horses ect. & cultivated (and by liquid manure. Mens made cubicles of bricks under sheds & lined them with straw.	H
SCHOUDE	16/6	10 pm	Sent all Ambulances and 42 bearers to assist 4 and 7 & at VLAMERTINGHE returned at 7 am. Advance not regained. carried two registration sub - posts. Return constantly shelled up to bridfield as far as possible and made shelter for about 750 wounded.	AS
SCHOUDE	17/6	9 pm	Fine but cloudy - wind N. 2 officers 40 bearers & 6 ambulances sent last night to 42nd F.a.g	H

1577 Wt.W10791/1773 500,000 1/15 D. D. & L. A.D.S.S./Forms/C. 2118.

WAR DIARY
or
INTELLIGENCE SUMMARY

(Erase heading not required.)

Army Form C. 2118.

Place	Date	Hour	Summary of Events and Information	Remarks and references to Appendices
SCHOUVOL	17.6.		Party returned at 7.30 am. Sent fatigue party of 40 men again to 42nd F.A. to help clear up after dealing with heavy casualties - went in lorry with stns. to HAMERTINGHE and saw arrangements made there. Recvd verbal orders from HQ MS to move ambulance back to HILHOEK and there form Divisional rest station	AP
HILHOEK	18/6 7pm		Moved to HILHOEK at 10 am. to same camp as on 14th Fine. East wind. Discharged 12 men back to duty. Remaining 20. Have pitched 10 bell tents & 3 operating tents - detachment to billeted in barn and adjoin field adjacent to camp - inspected site of H.Q. camp with a view to taking over when HQ move - good site - water supply scanty	AP
	19/6	9.20	Camp too small. Recvd orders from A.D.M.S. to form Divisional rest camp - Camp too small - found a suitable site in farm near by - interviewed S.A.D.M.S who authorized move	AP

1577 Wt.W10791/1773 500,000 1/15 D. D. & L.   A.D.S.S./Forms/C. 2118.

WAR DIARY or INTELLIGENCE SUMMARY

Army Form C. 2118.

Place	Date	Hour	Summary of Events and Information	Remarks and references to Appendices
HILHOEK	20/8	9.15 p.m.	Moved to new farm - good site - two good fords - good slope drained with boilpipes - area left in very insanitary state by previous occupants - detailed large fatiguing party forward 6 tents from 43rd F.A. & 8 bell & 2 operating from 43rd F.A. Set up 6 cars & 40 bearers to assist 63rd F.A.	K
"	21/8	9.45 p.m.	Pitched bell tents & operating tents - secured two wooden huts & loose timber from left behind by H.Q. 16 the Division from C.A.D.M.S. - 25 patients remaining - effects have punctured good supply of tubs & three trolleys for baths - visited by Col Nichol D.M.S. 5th Corps who inspected sites - transferred two cases of scarlet to BAILLEUL	J
"	22/8	10 am	Fortunes prisoners camp - sent 6 cars to 4.30 F.A. & 8.30 A.M.S. Aug 82 - transferred on opp to BAILLEUL - two to C.C.S.	M
"	23/8	7 pm	MONT DES CATS - Transferred 6 to C.C.S. BAILLEUL - 9 returned to duty - detailed on Red cross for various stores - visited by R. men	R

WAR DIARY
or
INTELLIGENCE SUMMARY

Army Form C. 2118.

Place	Date	Hour	Summary of Events and Information	Remarks and references to Appendices
ALNOEK	23/6	7 pm	representative who took away indiv[iduals] - made claim for laundry area new farm house by sinking pipes 1'6" under soil. Bath charges returned from Div. H.Q. - C.R.E. returned some of loose timber collected. He has promised a party to attempt to erect huts. Made plan for laundry & wash house required by C.R.E.	AS
HILHOEK	24/6	7 pm	Cloudy. 2nd Found. Troops.) 7 to BAILLEUL 23 to duty. Remaining - 102 + 1 Offr. Spent day in carrying out various improvements to site. Arranged for new wash house by introducing with steel pipes and sinking trough for wash house & farm cookhouse water finished.	AS
"	25/6	7 pm	Warm Fair - 2nd Found. Troops & BAILLEUL 20 to duty. Remaining 139 + 1 Offr. camp inspected by D.A.D.S. 2nd Army who gave instructions that tents should be returned by particular form now being issued to Ordnance. Also by G.O.C. 4th Division. Asked for assistance from O.A.R. Doctor A.D.M.S. visited camp with Ordnance Offr.	AS

1577 Wt.W10791/1773 500,000 1/15 D. D. & L. A.D.S.S./Forms/C. 2118.

WAR DIARY
or
INTELLIGENCE SUMMARY.

Army Form C. 2118.

Place	Date	Hour	Summary of Events and Information	Remarks and references to Appendices
HLKOEKE	25		who promised three Sopra Shows and that he would work for 30 tents.	KA
"	26.	7.15	West wind - dreary - received 10 pr. Sloan Corp C to have R.E. escort to End buildings - went in to see My Gilett & OC. St Cops to arrange placed work still - amassing. Arrangements for tents.	KA
"	27.	7.	Fair. N.W. wind. New distribution of patients dispatched to help by means of refilling freely arranged no beds in use but thick disinfectal to kats & to keep from interference with others. C.R.E. came to camp. Promised lumber for new buildings arranged for transport to be supplied by such who are to draw it from ABELE	KA
"	28	6.30	West wind - Some Showers - received one case from 27th Divs to Place 43rd F.A. at VLAMERTINGHE on 30th with - admitted 55 discharged 44 to duty.	KA

121/6753

14th Division

44th Field Ambulance
Vols: III and IV
Jly & Aug 15

July & August 1915.

CONFIDENTIAL

War Diary

of

44th Field Ambulance

from July 31st 1915 to Aug. 31st 1916

(Volumns 2.)

3 and 4

Army Form C. 2118.

WAR DIARY
or
INTELLIGENCE SUMMARY.
(Erase heading not required.)

Instructions regarding War Diaries and Intelligence Summaries are contained in F.S. Regs., Part II. and the Staff Manual respectively. Title pages will be prepared in manuscript.

Place	Date	Hour	Summary of Events and Information	Remarks and references to Appendices
MILHOEK	July 1.	9.45	Fine but cloudy - continued building in Rest camp - great difficulty getting timber - collected material myself for making concrete floor for wash house - found two masons in the camp who are doing excellent work. Admitted 31. Discharged to C.C.S. 9. 16 bdl. Sick 28.	HS
	2.	7.	Received line. Wounded. Ad. 39. Sick. Adj 20. CCS. 3. Off. Received circular re rest stations from HQ 2nd Army. Huts to be supplemented from other 7 divisions. Total to be limited to 200. No case to be kept for more than 7 days. Further treatment up to 10 days at MONT DES CATS. Accord's ttees 50 for each division	HS
	3.	7.30.	Fine w. wind. ad. 43 July 37 Off. CCS. 8 Saw demonstration of smoke helmets of size H.Q - helmets to be sprayed with hypo + glycerin when dry.	HS

WAR DIARY
or
INTELLIGENCE SUMMARY.
(Erase heading not required.)

Army Form C. 2118.

Instructions regarding War Diaries and Intelligence Summaries are contained in F. S. Regs., Part II. and the Staff Manual respectively. Title pages will be prepared in manuscript.

Place	Date	Hour	Summary of Events and Information	Remarks and references to Appendices
HILHOEK	4.7	7pm	Fine - very hot. South wind. Ad. 47. Sick to July 23. CCS. 13.	#8
"	5.7.		Fine warm. West wind. Ad. 56. July 28. CCS 7. M.d. cats. 12.	#7
"	6.7.		Fine warm. West wind. Ad. 53 & 3 off. July 24. CCS. 20 & 3 offrs. M.d. cats 10. Went round to Napier, Mesken, Fransp. Units to collect oil drums for latrines. Have now accommodation for 222 reported true that well at ARELG is getting dry. Each unit tries round neighbourhood to find another supply - all forces bent in all forces in neighbourhood to becoming daily worse. Rtn H. STURROCK 7.R.B. sent from 43rd F.H. with severe G.S.W. of thumb - sent him to CCS. Message from A.D.M.S. to fetch him back for court of enquiry.	
"	7.7	7pm	Cloudy. West wind later changing to South. Adn. CCS R. des O	#8

1577 Wt. W10791/1773 500,000 1/15 D. D. & L. A.D.S.S./Forms/C. 2118.

WAR DIARY
or
INTELLIGENCE SUMMARY.
(Erase heading not required.)

Army Form C. 2118.

Place	Date	Hour	Summary of Events and Information	Remarks and references to Appendices
HLHoEK	8.7.	9pm	Some rain - S.W. wind. Adm. duty. C.C.S. R.d. Cots. Water failed at ABEELE - searched for likely spot for water - selected site about ½ mile W of the camp - and starting sinking well - good supply of water obtained near surface	
"	9.7	7pm	Rain Cloudy. Some rain in night and during day. Wind East. occurred 6 messages 10.46 p.m. 6th M.T.B 1. Are you collecting casualties from 41st Bde this evening Sgd: 14th Div. Reply No. 2. failed that L.J. BROWN to take over med charge 7th KRR's Reported same to A.D.M.S. duty. Adm. duty. C.C.S. R.d. Cats.	
"	10.7.	9pm	Cloudy. W wind. Adm. duty. C.C.S. R.d. Cats.	

WAR DIARY
or
INTELLIGENCE SUMMARY.
(Erase heading not required.)

Army Form C. 2118.

Place	Date	Hour	Summary of Events and Information	Remarks and references to Appendices
HILHOEK	11.7.	7pm	Cloudy. Some rain - South wind. Adm. to duty. Started better system of disposal of refuse. CCS improved with oil drums and wooden tops & rest of stools in equipment	To dir C.G.
"	12.7	9pm	Cloudy - South wind. Adm to duty. Conference of O.C.'s F.A's at H.Q re arrangements for evacuation of wounded. C.C.S.	To dir Cats.
"	13.7.	7pm	Cloudy - dry wind. Adm. to duty. Court of enquiry on Pte Stalbolt. adm. with accidental gun shot wound of foot. Sub F ADMS report on relative wastage of troops from different Brigades. C.C.S	To dir Cats
"	14.7.	7pm	Cloudy. Steady rain in afternoon. Water supply at #BEC again failed. Will send by unit unsatisfactory - wrote to CCS to arrange & with dentist for treatment of cases. Adm. duty. C.C.S.	To dir C.G.

WAR DIARY
or
INTELLIGENCE SUMMARY.
(Erase heading not required.)

Army Form C. 2118.

Place	Date	Hour	Summary of Events and Information	Remarks and references to Appendices
HILHOEK	15.7	6 pm	Cloudy. W. wind. Adm. duty. O.C.S. h.a.Cols. Received orders from A.D.M.S. 75 hours. 44th F.A. to take over dressing station at POPERINGE - from us at YPRES. Tengut Cottage HAMERTINGHE = from 43rd F.A. Rest Station not complete KD Latrine & wash house complete Exc for weather boarding.	
"	16.7.	7 pm	Heavy rain - S.W. wind - went to school at POPERINGHE to see O.C. 43rd F.A. re move. Sent Lieuts BROWN & FLOOD in morning to collect from aid posts KD	
	17.7.	7 pm	W. wind - showery. Handed over dio & Rest Station to O.C. 42nd F.A. Sent part of equipment to POP. in the morning - proceeded at 2 pm with rest of unit and took over dressing station in school at POP. & prepared to receive wounded - 2 guards had an 16 stretcher placed in asylum at YPRES & School HAMERTINGHE each consisting of 1 N.CO & 3 men - took over Adv. Dr. Staff at Prison YPRES with Lieut FLOOD & 1 Serg. 1 cook & 16 bearers - 2 teams of 4 men always at two reg. Aid posts. At 9.30 pm four additional bearers to proceed to aid posts to help evacuate wounded. 10 stretchers & 10	KD

1577 Wt.W10791/1773 500,000 1/15 D. D. & L.   A.D.S.S./Forms/C. 2118.

WAR DIARY
or
INTELLIGENCE SUMMARY.
(Erase heading not required.)

Army Form C. 2118.

Place	Date	Hour	Summary of Events and Information	Remarks and references to Appendices
P.o.P.	17/7	7 p.m	lins of spraying solution to be kept at A.D.S. also gassing equipment. Motor Ambulance car to remain at A.D.S. Three others kept at Ham D.S. to carry relief at 11 p.m to R.D.S. and evacuate wounded. Offrs of A.D.S to be relieved daily at 12 midday by car taking rations to the three detachments.	JS
Po-P.	18/7	6.30	Took over trenchfields at SCHOODMONT HOEK for transport of sick. Fine. W wind. Adm. 19 to C.C.S 11 to R.S. Inspected School at VLAM. Asylum YPRES. Prison YPRES. Satisfactory. Sisters called in afternoon - arranged to reconnoitre Meen Crouch Scotts of YPRES for different approach to Aid post.	JS
Po-P.	19/7	6.50	Fine. S.W. wind. Ad. 46 to C.C.S. 6 to R.S. Held D.H.Q.s at 10.30 H.Q. proceeded with Lieut Brown R.A.M.C to Asylum YPRES. Left car near asylum and thoroughly reconnoitred ground. S- SE of YPRES suitably E+W. Immediately S of YPRES - no road traversing Only alternative route by sewer proceeding to Front just west	KP

1577 Wt.W10791/1773 500,000 1/15 D. D. & L. A.D.S.S./Forms/C. 2118.

Army Form C. 2118.

WAR DIARY
or
INTELLIGENCE SUMMARY.
(Erase heading not required.)

Place	Date	Hour	Summary of Events and Information	Remarks and references to Appendices
POP	19.7.	6.30	of ETANG de ZILLEBEKE across canal by bridge in I.19.d and evacuating via KRUISSTRAETHOEK - DEN GROENEN - VLAMERTINGHE road. Would suggest chessnut tr in branch W of ETANG de ZILLEBEKE for collecting station	AD
"	20.7	9.30	June W tried Adm 135. to CCS 67. b RS 66. Sent additional bearers to front - formed there now 1 Offr 1 Sergt I took 2 drivers 1 Wag. Oldr + 23 Bearers - 2 bearers are stationed at each aid post - 4 others reinforce each at night to assist in evacuation. Inst Lieut Brown in turning with collecting officer 8 F.A. + See arrangements in area taken over evacuated by O.7. A but to be taken over by 14th division.	AD
	21.7	6 pm	June to road met Adm. 102 to CC8. 29. to RS 66. Met St/fers + W O's 41st Bde at Baths to arrange about new area - told them any arrangements for evacuation - saw A.O.C 41st Bde at 12.45 pm and explained same to him. He expressed wish that there should be no lack of Mos at A.D.S. I explained	AD

Army Form C. 2118.

WAR DIARY
or
INTELLIGENCE SUMMARY.
(Erase heading not required.)

Instructions regarding War Diaries and Intelligence Summaries are contained in F. S. Regs., Part II. and the Staff Manual respectively. Title pages will be prepared in manuscript.

Place	Date	Hour	Summary of Events and Information	Remarks and references to Appendices
POP.	21.7		to him that there would be two M.O's there every night, but that as a rule there would only be work for one. Detailed Lieut Flood to proceed to with 8th F.A. again.	fd
"	22.7	7pm	Showing S.W. wind. Adm. 55 R.C. 48. CCS. 8. Detailed Lieut Athew to collect with 8th F.A. to find out whereabouts of wheeled stretchers made following arrangements for evacuation after arranging briefly personally with O.C. 8th F.A.	fc

Place	Date	Hour	Summary of Events and Information	Remarks and references to Appendices
POP.	23.7.	7.7pm	Fine. N.W. wind. adm. 1 Off. 5g others rank 6 CCS. 17. R.S. 48. Last night Lieuts Atkins & Roberts went round to hid posts with collecting officers of 9th F.A. four bearers ordered to accompany them to take over aidposts D & E. Near E Hay 38502 Pte TOMLIN J.H. RAMC killed, Lieut Roberts ROBERTS C.A. RAMC wounded & Lieut ATKINS bruised down by high explosive shell. Lieut ROBERTS' wound slight - not evacuated. These are first casualties in unit. Reported to A.D.M.S. - H.Q. 14 "Div" D.A.g. 3rd Echelon. H.Q. 2nd army. Pte TOMLIN's identity disc. pay book & valuables sent to D.A.S. 3rd Echelon by registered post. Received following messages from A.D.M.S. 1. Evacuation of sick. From 24th inclusive - following arrangements. Motorcyclist will call at 7 am. to ascertain numbers for evacuation. O.C. No 4 M.A.C. will arrange to evacuate sick and wounded about 9.30 today except in cases of emergency, when a message should be sent direct to No 4 M.A.C at F22a 7-9 (Sheet 27) O.C. 7.F.A. will not call on services of M.A.C. after evac.² Telegrams for O.C. No 4 M.A.C. should be addressed to 6th Corps H.Q.	

WAR DIARY or INTELLIGENCE SUMMARY

Army Form C. 2118.

Place	Date	Hour	Summary of Events and Information	Remarks and references to Appendices
POP.	23.7.	7 pm	2/14 Division to come under 6th Corps from 12 noon today. 3/ Had weekly meeting of O.C.S. F.A. at Corps H.Q. at CHATEAU COOT F. 21 A (sheet 27) at 2.30 – a Saturdays – Sent Scheme for evacuation from Adv posts – A.B.C.D.E to D.A.D.M.S.	JS
"	24.7.	7 pm	Two sons Rwk. Wrst. Adm. Off. 3 Other ranks 84 – C.C.S. 3 Off. 39. O.R. J.R.S. 41. Attended conference at F.A. 14th Corps at 2.30 pm. J.S had read extracts from A.D.M.S. for treatment of wounded.	KS
"	25.7	7 pm	Cloudy and showery – Adm 1 Off. 25. OR. to C.C.S.53. J.R.1. 30. Sent the morning inspecting posts at VLAM. – ASYLUM + Prison YPRES. Made second reconnaisance of area S.E. of YPRES with a view to alternative route for evacuation. reconnoitred ZILLEBEKE road South of ETANG. Met Maj. Marse R.E. + consulted re dugouts at ZILLEBEKE – Selected site not exposed to evac. by road running South and round ETANG away to Styren. Kinches across road – any movement on road in day time	KR

Place	Date	Hour	Summary of Events and Information	Remarks and references to Appendices
Pop	26.7	7pm	near ZILLEBEKE attack, shrap shell fire - while at there this morning 2 killed & 15 wounded of a working party returned to LILLE gate YPRES by path north of ETANG. This car to used as for wheeled stretchers POPERINGHE shelled this afternoon too after return.	AD
"	27.7	7pm	to wind fine - went to YPRES again this morning - left car at LILLE GATE and proceeded via military & communication trench to C did pos-1- Frs.b.36 there dug outs which would do lot about 12 cases - some shelling on return - too. C.C.S. proceeded along PROVEN road in evening to find new billet for transport - unsuccessful - received orders from ADMS that Evacuation to R.S. should be at 9 & 5. Fine. S wind - ADMS & DDMS VI Corps visited dressing Station at POP at 3.30. I was at billet. searched new area for transport billet with Lt Roberts A.D.M.S. O.R C.C.S R S	AS AS

Army Form C. 2118.

WAR DIARY
or
INTELLIGENCE SUMMARY.
(Erase heading not required.)

Instructions regarding War Diaries and Intelligence Summaries are contained in F. S. Regs., Part II. and the Staff Manual respectively. Title pages will be prepared in manuscript.

Place	Date	Hour	Summary of Events and Information	Remarks and references to Appendices
POP.	20/7	7 pm	N.W. wned fine adm. to CCS. to X.R.S.	kf

Army Form C. 2118.

WAR DIARY
or
INTELLIGENCE SUMMARY.
(Erase heading not required.)

Place	Date	Hour	Summary of Events and Information	Remarks and references to Appendices
POP.	30/7	9 p.m.	ada. Offs. O.R. Evac. ORs. Offrs. O.R. Sick — 93 3 42 tops W.B. 52 60 1 died	

Received full account of 1 a.m. 1) HOOGE captured by enemy last night by enemy. Heavy casualties. Make all preparations. H.A.A. 43rd DA. Take over ASYLUM and HAMERTINGE. HH. Report #.7.O. " Receive messages during morning from 7 KRR & RB asking for assistance — m a P 12.16 decisor from H.Q. md 8. over 400 Cas. up to date — more anticipated. French division of 6/ w D.A. will be required — reports to Adv. HQ I.B.D. 3.0. from 2 P.m ar 12.3t. message from Lt. Inf. Bde. that In.O. 8 KRR was bad hit — Offr to take his place at once — to act H.Q. 8 KRR b SANCTUARY WOOD — Sent message to Lieut. SHEAR. to proceed there with papers TRACERS — 2nd BRISTER sent in relief.
message from 6, 1 St. B.M. asking for every the remit to dumping ground wired reply that all cases would be evacuated at night.

WAR DIARY
or
INTELLIGENCE SUMMARY.
(Erase heading not required.)

Army Form C. 2118.

Place	Date	Hour	Summary of Events and Information	Remarks and references to Appendices
POP.	30.7.		Lt SMIDTH had anticipated orders that left prison with 12 bearers for SANCTUARY WOOD. His party came under shell fire & one was wounded. He kept to bearers & C porry to render assistance. Proceeded to SANCTUARY WOOD, when he received orders not to screen off 31st battalion. I sent Lt BROWN with 6 bearers to MD corner of ZILLEBEKE LAKE to assist walking cases system of POP at 9 pm. Sent all cars afloat & 3 of the 7th F.A.S.C.W.M. at VOORA Cases came in steadily all day and even evening in as large numbers.	
POP.	31.7. 7.pm		Adm Sist Off 1. O.R. 66. Wounded Off 16 O.R. 514 Evac. C.C.S. 16 Off O.R. 406 S.O.S. O.R. 26 died of wounds sight. Four compltenens & other may: oprators all cases entered in A.D.P book bee 20 Sent on to CCS direct	HS

1577 Wt.W10791/1773 500,000 1/15 D.D.&L. A.D.S.S./Forms/C. 2118.

Army Form C. 2118.

WAR DIARY
or
INTELLIGENCE SUMMARY.
(Erase heading not required.)

Place	Date	Hour	Summary of Events and Information	Remarks and references to Appendices
Pop.	31.7		all cases given Anti tet. Serum — completed evacuation at 9.30 am this morning. Received message from A.D.M.S. that casualties had been left in SANCTUARY WOOD from previous night — told to prepare for 500 tonight.	
	1.8.		adm. Sick off 1. O.R. 10 all off 6 O.R. 242 evac to CCS & DRS. all cases sent to A.S.C.O.M. last night. Most of cases stretcher cases. — Two cases tinged by gas about face hands & clothing — handed to H.D.S. Boot message from A D.M.S. that 5000 wounded left lying fully in SANCTUARY WOOD. To post ed M.C.O. to hon apteke as before — Message from A D.M.S. at 1.30 that responsibility to evac. rests with O.C. 432nd F.A. 10 pm. acs from A.D.M.S. to that 432nd F.A. was relieving	fs fs

Place	Date	Hour	Summary of Events and Information	Remarks and references to Appendices
Pop	2.8	2pm	To Rest camp. O.O. LE to Jerome re: collection of wounded. Rech off 1 OR 30 g. 124	
	2.8	7pm	Recd 0.0. bad news. Some had been lying under a culvert in MENIN ROAD for three days. Stretcher bearers all killed or wounded. Two Amb "C" though 1 Col. Saw 8 T.R.S. in Jeremy. Arranged for evacuation to right. Reported for M. Bearers to remain at ASYLUM PRISON. Sent all cars to collect at 7.30. 30 bearers with Col Offr & 1 Off + 40 bearers of A2 T.A. turned out to hold one section in readiness — Col Offr proceed to forward Dressing Stn. Enemy Shel. No report received. Adm. Not Off. 3 OR 30. Wounds Off. 2 OR 80. I was too 7 T.R.S. went to ASYLUM & PRISON at YPRES. & Report arranged for 3 cars + 20 bearers from 4am 3A tuesday to 10pm 291.	
	3.8			

Army Form C. 2118.

WAR DIARY
or
INTELLIGENCE SUMMARY.
(Erase heading not required.)

Instructions regarding War Diaries and Intelligence Summaries are contained in F. S. Regs., Part II. and the Staff Manual respectively. Title pages will be prepared in manuscript.

Place	Date	Hour	Summary of Events and Information	Remarks and references to Appendices
Pop.	3.8.	2pm	A.D.M.S. & S.A.D.M.S. came to have D.S. in afternoon. Reflained scheme of evacuation & arranged to take two officers & 4 collecting Off'rs their journey — Off. O.R. Adm Sick — 41 C.C.S. F4. W — 1 69 R.S. 32.	A1
	4.8.	9.15p	Three officers of 11th Div. accompanied Collecting Off'r last night. O. i/c Sec. 11th Division called at I.D.m. and informed he at Evacuation of Southern Sector of this of area to collect from at present would be taken over on 6th ins. by 12 F.A. On Sun. 14th Div. came at 4.30 and gave orders to same officer there was verbal — Sub Lieut Flood with our cars to be collected from A13 & Lieut BROWN with 6 cars of 11th Div. & 3 of their Off'rs to collect from D + E. Off. O.R. Sick CCS Off. 1 OR 54 Adm Sick 2 — trch — MS 2 43 W. 1 — 65	A8
	5.8.	10.45a	O.C. 10th F.A. came at 1.30 — arranged with him that F4 F.A. would	A9

1577 Wt.W10791/1773 500,000 1/15 D. D. & L. A.D.S.S./Forms/C. 2118.

Army Form C. 2118.

WAR DIARY
or
INTELLIGENCE SUMMARY.
(Erase heading not required.)

Instructions regarding War Diaries and Intelligence Summaries are contained in F. S. Regs., Part II. and the Staff Manual respectively. Title pages will be prepared in manuscript.

Place	Date	Hour	Summary of Events and Information	Remarks and references to Appendices
POP.	5/8	10.45	Collect corning of 5/6. 1 Off. & 4 cars of 16 tent to attack that on 5th he would be responsible for collection from C.D. Sent Lieuts BROSTER & FLOOD to collect tonight with 6 cars. POPERINGHE heavily shelled in morning and twice in afternoon considerable number of casualties from troops in billets in POP. O.C. 4th M.A.C. called at 10.30 to clear & promised cyclist at 11.30 to call to A.C.C if he could help evacuation.	M
	6/8.	6.30	Adm. Sick Off. 3 O.R. 38 Wounded — 2 O.R. 75 Evac to C.C.S & A.R.S At 7 am it was reported to me that a shell had burst into cellar at PRISON occupied by bearers of 4th FA and that 1 man had been killed and fourteen wounded. Proceeded at 7. am to Prison and found cellar a shell had burst through through at only accessible spot and that the cellar was a broken mass of brickwork & arranged for all men at Prison to the rd. hospital. On return I called at Adv dsg line	

WAR DIARY
or
INTELLIGENCE SUMMARY.
(Erase heading not required.)

Army Form C. 2118.

Place	Date	Hour	Summary of Events and Information	Remarks and references to Appendices
			and withdrew 10 of Transport from Tiers	
			Names of casualties.	
			203445 Pte Peterson W. — killed — to CCS	
			32630 Pte Moulton S. — wounded — to CCS	
			84070 Pte Jinto J. " " to CCS	
			31185 Pte Austin W.H. " " to CCS	
			35430 Pte Roberts A. " " to CCS	
			37110 Pte Pearson J. " " to DRS	
			32984 Pte Southern G. " " to DRS	
			32971 Pte Rees W. " " to DRS	
			93156 Pte Lachlan J. " " to DRS	
			37791 Pte O'Hara J.R. " " to DRS	
			45804 Pte Anderson J. " " to DRS	
			32449 " Story S. " " to DRS	
			31257 " Rhodes T. " " to DRS	
			31862 " Martin G. " " to MRS	
			32495 " Sarjeant A. " " to DRS	

Army Form C. 2118.

WAR DIARY
or
INTELLIGENCE SUMMARY.
(Erase heading not required.)

Instructions regarding War Diaries and Intelligence Summaries are contained in F. S. Regs., Part II. and the Staff Manual respectively. Title pages will be prepared in manuscript.

Place	Date	Hour	Summary of Events and Information	Remarks and references to Appendices
			In addition to these the following casualties have occurred in this unit during recent operations:-	
			30702 Pte Tomlins T.H. Killed 22.7.15	
			34969 " Jones E.M. Wounded 30.7. C.C.S	
			39762 " Audley T.W. Shock 31.7. P.C.S	
			31804 " Wykes W. Wounded 30.7. C.C.S	
			31439 " Edwards J Wounded 31.7. C.C.S	
			32032 " Pearce T. Wounded 30.7. C.C.S	
			Lieut C.S. Potato Wounded 22.7. F.A.	
POP	7/8	9.10pm	Adm. Wounded Off OR C.C.S Off 3 OR 87	
			Sick 3 89 Evac. SPS 1 42	
			1 40	
			Attended conf. of H.Q. 4th Corps. Lt.Col. Clarke RAMC. S. Insp. Reserves gave information re drafts & wastage:- No recent information Staff Lt. Major P. re Med. Operations	
left Atto			+ BROWN - Sergt EASTHAM & Pte. DICKINSON - Ptes. JONES D. O'HARA & FREE Mentioned Lt. SMELL	

WAR DIARY
or
INTELLIGENCE SUMMARY.
(Erase heading not required.)

Army Form C. 2118.

Place	Date	Hour	Summary of Events and Information	Remarks and references to Appendices
P.O.T.	8/8	9.45	Abri Leeb. Off O R wounded 4 49 1 40 Evac. CCS Off 3 OR 35 SRS 1 - 55. Went to Div of Q and saw offration order. Made out 4 Y.A. operation order. Sent Flood to take charge of Adv. D. Staff at Prison YPRES. Told Lt. BROSTER to proceed there to furthr orders — 6 bearers to report at food aid post. Sent extra dressings & splinters to each aid post. Sent 12 extra Bearers — 10 to be at ASYLUM — 10 at Prison & 12 in aid posts.	W
	9/8	11.30	Adv. Lob. Off OR wounded — 78 20 Evac. CCS Off OR SRS 1 27 1 56 11 am.—approx — 4230 RB report 6 heavy casualties 9 to RB at Y wood ADMS. Informed O.C. A.D.S.— get into touch with A&B supports ascertain approx. casualties — whether no. of bearers required transit take any steps you consider necessary.	

WAR DIARY or INTELLIGENCE SUMMARY

Army Form C. 2118.

Place	Date	Hour	Summary of Events and Information	Remarks and references to Appendices
POP	9/8	2 p.m.	O.C. A.D.S. St. Nats. – Am sending 10 more bearers – 9w's Every possible assistance to 9th R.B. & Shrops. in bringing down lying down cases back to aid post from front. What reports have you from M.O's of these Regts. Am 6 earl suff. to keep you clear 18 bearers with Serjt. Eastham went over to R.B aid post.	
		At 2.30 p.m.	received messages from M.O's at H.P. help re Shrops. S.) reported 8 stretcher cases at H.P more in trenches how many he could say.	
		Up to 3 p.m. 6 Shrops Buchs reported 2 stretcher cases at front. By H 3 p.m. 13 stretcher cases and about 100 sitting had been been cleared to main dress. Stat	
		At 4.30 p.m.	message to O.C. A.D.S. How many cats will you require to evacuate tonight? Am sending up all stret cases at 7.30 p.m. Will you organize M.A.C. cars in addition. H all wounded of 9th R.B. & D.L.I. have been cleared by then notify me before 7.50.	

WAR DIARY
or
INTELLIGENCE SUMMARY.
(Erase heading not required.)

Army Form C. 2118.

Place	Date	Hour	Summary of Events and Information	Remarks and references to Appendices
			Return M.A.C. cars not required - 15 cars at A.D.S at 7.30 sent up collecting off[t] with 16 stretchers & 20 bearers of 4.3rd F.A.	
		7.	Message to O.C. A.D.S. wire immediately to O.C.'s of 5th S.L.? & 9th R.B. asking for no of cases which still require clearing as the O.C's appear to be unable to give information we ask regard to their aid posts	
		8.30	Message from 13 no Inf Bde. to A/b/c adv dressing Station Please Can you please arrange to send up a large number of stretcher bearers to 5th Sh. L. Inf's tonight who are in RAILWAY WOOD and trenches in vicinity there are about 100 wounded up there the evacuated. This message was endored with foll necr from OC ADS. 15 of our bearers at B post since 1 pm. helping bring down these cases there from 9 to R.13 & no has reported but cases brought down.	

WAR DIARY or INTELLIGENCE SUMMARY

Army Form C. 2118.

Place	Date	Hour	Summary of Events and Information	Remarks and references to Appendices
		2.45	Sent following message to O.C. 4 D.S. "Send bearers & stretcher to RAILWAY WOOD. Get notification in writing from O.C. 5th S.L.I. that all cases have been cleared before bearers leave trenches - so additional bearers are being sent up to you - Send enclosed copy of message from 4.D.S.Hqrs Bde to info to 5th St L.I. for his information. Collecting Officer got in touch with N.O's of R.B. & 5th Sh.D.I. in evening who told him their casualties were being evacuated. Officer casualties ever to HQ 5th S. L.I. who informed him that all wounded were cleared. At 2.36 he received message from Stretcher bearer W.B. of Sh. Stewart to await stretcher bearers to be sent along HENIN road to clear wounded from Relay. New DUGEON street." Proceeded with 15 bearers & 2 Subaltern - We were now light and party were covered heavily shelled all the way. They had to take refuge and Sergt DUDGEON was wounded	

Army Form C. 2118.

WAR DIARY
or
INTELLIGENCE SUMMARY.
(Erase heading not required.)

Instructions regarding War Diaries and Intelligence Summaries are contained in F. S. Regs., Part II. and the Staff Manual respectively. Title pages will be prepared in manuscript.

Place	Date	Hour	Summary of Events and Information	Remarks and references to Appendices
PoP	9/8		As it was impossible to keep clear in daylight with cars – he met a bearers of 40th Divn with wheeled stretcher showing that 11th Div. were clearing with these cases.	#5
"	10/8	7 pm	Adm. Sick Off. 1 O.R. 31 Evac. CCS #7 O.R. 130 #5T 60 wound. 6 144 Removed old picture of collecting – org 2 bearers at each aid post reinforced by 4 men each at night 1 off + 10 men at forum. 1 RSO + 10 men at Asylum	#5
"	11.8	9.p.m	Adm. Sick Off. 4 O.R. 70 Evac. CCS Off 1 O.R. 34 wound. 5 18 SAS. 6 50 Visited YPRES. Prison + Asylum went to Camp of 43rd F.A. – Saw arrangements there	#5
"	12.8	9.30 pm	Adm. Sick Off. 2 O.R. 24 Evac. CCS Off 2 O.R. 23 W. 3 34 SAS. 3 1 22	#5

1577 Wt.W10791/1773 500,000 1/15 D. D. & L. A.D.S.S./Forms/C. 2118.

Army Form C. 2118.

WAR DIARY
or
INTELLIGENCE SUMMARY.
(Erase heading not required.)

Place	Date	Hour	Summary of Events and Information	Remarks and references to Appendices

POP.	12.8	9.30	Received Message from O.C. A.D.S. Prior asking for cars - stating that #5 C.C.S had been shelled in sight of cathedral by heavy shells. Large number buried - cars sent. Later reported that rescue party including 6 bearers of this ambulance had been caught by heavy shell & two bearers had been killed and two missing.
			
			Name 32035 Pte McCALLUM. C. 44 7 A killed
			        33592 " Vine 7 " " killed
			        34286 " WILLIAMS. A. " " " missing
			        31376 " McINTYRE. J. " " " wounded
			
			I sent up 10 bearers from POP. with orders that all orderlies at Prior should be relieved. Number of wounded admitted from YPRES during day including Major BESANT W.I. Sun major & Rev. HARRIS. Chap. 6 7 Welshes. Both wounded while leading rescue parties. Received a message from POP. in afternoon that roads	

WAR DIARY
or
INTELLIGENCE SUMMARY.

Army Form C. 2118.

Place	Date	Hour	Summary of Events and Information	Remarks and references to Appendices
P.o.P.	13.8		Though ROADS were impassable - and giving alternative route North of Town - Cars & collecting officer proceeded by new route.	
			Adm. Sick Off. 1 OR 45 Evac CCS Off 5 OR 42	
			W. 2 46 S/RS - - 51	
"	13.8	9 p.m.	Proceeded to A.D.M.S. 8th D.A. at HAMERTING N°2 & arranged with Capt DENYER for one of my officers to go with his collecting Offr to CHATEAU POTIJZE where are the aid posts of Sector to be taken over by 14th Division —	
			Attended funeral of Pte McCullum. View of this unit Lieut ROBERTS proceeded to new aid posts & posted 2 bearers there.	
"	16.8	7.30	Adm. Sick Off. 1 OR 48 Evac CCS Off 12 OR	
			W - - 19 S/RS 2 51	

WAR DIARY
or
INTELLIGENCE SUMMARY.
(Erase heading not required.)

Army Form C. 2118.

Instructions regarding War Diaries and Intelligence Summaries are contained in F.S. Regs., Part II. and the Staff Manual respectively. Title pages will be prepared in manuscript.

Place	Date	Hour	Summary of Events and Information	Remarks and references to Appendices
PoP.	15/8	7 p.m.	Adm. Off. OR sick - C.C.S. off. OR sick. 1 32 5 W. 2 26 F.R.S. 1 84	
St JAN DER BIEZEN	16/8	8 p.m.	From PoP. shelled - Adm. post taken over by 45th FA. Adm. Off. OR Off. OR Sick. 1 17 sick. CCS 3 30 W. 1 17 F.R.S. 1 22 Party at ASYLUM & that at Prison relieved by 62nd FA is formn left to W. Sketches. to this French sold. to this Arthur Sold. at Prisn also 25 Stretchers. Blankets & large quantity of dressings. In afternoon handed over gear. Dressing station at PoP. to 62 & 2nd left all stretchers. conservancy equipment & about 100 blankets. Proceeded at 2.30 to Rest camp in Sh 27. L 3 a. 5. 9. near college of St JAN-DER-BIEZEN. taking over 5 patients from 43rd FA. Notified A.D.of W. of move.	
			Adm. 4. Stch. nil. Sanitary arrangement of camp any thing	

WAR DIARY
or
INTELLIGENCE SUMMARY.

(Erase heading not required.)

Army Form C. 2118.

Place	Date	Hour	Summary of Events and Information	Remarks and references to Appendices
ST JAN DER BIEZEN	17.8		hot satisfactory - + Sullage + bath water drawn into a ditch which has no fall. a sump + pump is required. Lieut BROWN detailed to take charge of divisional baths POP.	A1
	19.8	7.30	Capt DENYER. reported his arrival for duty Lieut SMEALL detailed to attend at 16 + 5W Amm Park WATOU daily to see sick. Lt Col SIMSON proceeded on 7 days leave. Capt JENNER. C.H. took over charge of unit.	A2

WAR DIARY
or
INTELLIGENCE SUMMARY.
(Erase heading not required.)

Army Form C. 2118.

Place	Date	Hour	Summary of Events and Information	Remarks and references to Appendices
ST JAN DER BIEZEN	20/8/15	7 a.m.	Lt. Col. Barton R.A.M.C. proceeded for duty note. to 6 Cav. Fd. Ambulance. Lt. Atkinson at Hd. qrs. Attending sick & wounded - 17 Jos. the day. 8.a.m. 1st R.F.A. action - 32/20 Sgt. Pearson R.A.M.C. Rejoined	
	21/8/15	9.30 a.m.	Attended Conference (fortnightly) at 6 Corps Head Quarters. Points raised (1) Storage of Water at Regimental Aid Posts Station (2) 3 Ricksha lorries every Tu. Fr. to ensure bug hommes ... of hommage of 45. 20 men's daily engagements (Upper School Regiments mown into R & F Area. 10 Brabham Ld. - B.R.C.M.	
	22/8/15 -	7.30 h.	Nothing of importance to note	
	23/8/15	7 a.m.	Instructions from A.D.M.S. to Shift Camp S/ a light nature to Roads, 14 horses Sanitary Control of Camps in Rest Areas. Sump Pits for the Mens Washing Places.	
	24/8/15	8.15 p.	Inspection of Camp by D.D.M.S. 5th Corps. Mr. Suggested more R.L. accumulation of Fresh Horses ...	
	25/8/15	7.15 a.m.	Lt. Barton R.A.M.C. detached to 11 No.16 Cav. Field Ambulance during absence on leave Lt. Buckley. Leave granted - B Lt. Andigier R.A.M.C. from 28/8/15 to 11/9/15. Forty 17 and 3/4 Pt. Brown 15/14xx removed from killed to 10x10 Ambulance for Pot Mortem Examination which was envies mad by Lt. Roberts. Temperature Station of Lt. Branker taken over by Lt. Roberts.	
	26/8/15	7 a.m.	Lt.Col A. Cameron returned from leave to England. Col. Guthrie Moore visited Camp. Lt. McFarland over the deaths of A.D.M.S. from Aldershot.	

Army Form C. 2118.

WAR DIARY
or
INTELLIGENCE SUMMARY.
(Erase heading not required.)

Instructions regarding War Diaries and Intelligence Summaries are contained in F. S. Regs., Part II. and the Staff Manual respectively. Title pages will be prepared in manuscript.

Place	Date	Hour	Summary of Events and Information	Remarks and references to Appendices
STN	27/8	7pm	Returned from leave	H
			adm. 10 to C.C.S. & to R.S. 3	
	28/8	6.30	adm. 1 Off. to C.C.S. 9 M. deCats 1 Off. D.R.S. 2	HJ
			Lieut DUDGEON. Proceeded to England on 6 days leave	
			Capt ATKINS proceeded on Temp duty as A.D.M.S. 7 to R.B.	
	29/8	6.30	adm. 9. to C.C.S. nil to D.R.S. 1	HJ
	30/8	6.30	adm. 3 to C.C.S. nil to D.R.S. 2.	HJ
			Sanitation of camp is being steadily improved - new grease pits have been made and wash house for scabies is being floored with concrete - two sumps have been sunk and water is being removed to fields.	
	31/8	6.30	adm. 3. 6 C.C.S. nil to D.R.S. nil duty	HJ
			Lieut SMEAL proceeded yesterday to W.A.H. to take over med. charge of 5th Dr. L.J.	
			Capt DENNY R.A.M.C. reported his arrival for duty.	

Confidential.

WAR DIARY
—OF—
44th FIELD AMBULANCE.

From Sept 1st to Oct 31st 15

(VOLUMES 3.)

14th Division

121/7594

WAR DIARY
or
INTELLIGENCE SUMMARY.
(Erase heading not required.)

Army Form C. 2118

Place	Date	Hour	Summary of Events and Information	Remarks and references to Appendices
St Van	Sept 1.	7.30.	Adm. 7. — CCS nil — duty 2. — Inspection of all three ambulances left DVS. by DDS. IInd army brought message from G.O.C. II army congratulating amb. of 14 Divn for way in which wounded had been collected during recent operations — also expressed pleasure at the way wounded were treated & their condition on arrival at CCS stated that they had never been better dealt with since commencement of war. Inspected Camp of 14 Div. Sign. Sec. Mortuis antan[?] also Cavalry lines — Latrines insatisfactory no incinerators	#1
	2/9.	7.30	Adm. 14 — CCS 4 to DVS 4 to duty 10. Inspected camps of 9 R.B. & 9 KRR both insanitary attempt at trench disposal most insanitary. Indatisfactory no proper incinerators. Lieut DUDGEON returned from leave.	#3
	3/9.	7.	Adm. 12. — to CCS. 2 to duty 5. Inspected ASC camps No 3 Co & No 1 satisfactory arranged for collection of reach in area — horse ambce	#5

Army Form C. 2118.

WAR DIARY
or
INTELLIGENCE SUMMARY.
(Erase heading not required.)

Instructions regarding War Diaries and Intelligence Summaries are contained in F. S. Regs., Part II. and the Staff Manual respectively. Title pages will be prepared in manuscript.

Place	Date	Hour	Summary of Events and Information	Remarks and references to Appendices
St PAN			to proceed to M.T.O.W. at 9 am. collect sick was back at refilling point and motor ambulance. and other units near ambulance to at St PAN ser B12 26 N. other units near ambulance to head when necessary. Rain	
			Inspected schools at St PAN with view of taking over for winter billets numbers in regt area. Rain	Ky
	4.9.	7pm	adm S. to CCS 1 to DRS 3. to DSty 3. attended conference at HQ 6th Corps - saw various types of stretchers for trench work. Rain	
	5.9.	7pm	adm 8. & CCS. and to DRS. 4. & Duty. 4. Sergt Cole A.S.C. M.T. departed on 6 days leave. Rain	Ky
	6.9.	7pm	adm. 14. to CCS 2. to DRS 1. to Duty 7. Rain ceased - sunshine during most of day. N. wind Lieut Atkin returned to unit. Ssgt Cox left this day for duty with No 4 Coy ASC. Cpl BROAD. Ch RSC reported this day for duty. ADMS inspected camp	

1577 Wt. W10791/1773 500,000 1/15 D. D. & L. A.D.S.S./Forms/C. 2118.

WAR DIARY
or
INTELLIGENCE SUMMARY.
(Erase heading not required.)

Army Form C. 2118

Instructions regarding War Diaries and Intelligence Summaries are contained in F. S. Regs., Part II. and the Staff Manual respectively. Title pages will be prepared in manuscript.

Place	Date	Hour	Summary of Events and Information	Remarks and references to Appendices
ST TRN des BIEZEN	7.9.	7 p	N. wind. fine - adm. 15. 6 C.C.S. 2 J.R.S. 4 duty 10. Capt ATKINS reported his return from short ten day with 7 R.B.	
"	8.9.	7 p	N. wind fine.	
"	9.9.	9 a.m.	N. wind fine. adm 11 to Aug 5. 10. Capt FLOOD reported return from duty with 9. R.B. 10 reinforcements arrived from base - good physique - trained at Colchester. all new army.	
			E. wind fine adm 2 J.R.S. 6 duty 14. Capt PENNY + T/28098 Dr Lloyd in A.S.C. departed on short leave to England.	
	10.9.			
	5.		Surg Genl R. Porter A.D.S. S Ind II army inspected camps. Received notification from A.D.M.S. of case of para typhoid in civilian in ST TRN des BIEZEN C.C.S.	
	11.9		E. wind fine. adm. J.R.S. duty. visited case of paratyphoid - took all precautions necessary detailed Lieut MORRISON to look after case - made report to A.D.M.S. one reinforcement reported.	

Army Form C. 21

WAR DIARY
or
INTELLIGENCE SUMMARY.
(Erase heading not required.)

Instructions regarding War Diaries and Intelligence Summaries are contained in F. S. Regs., Part II and the Staff Manual respectively. Title pages will be prepared in manuscript.

Place	Date	Hour	Summary of Events and Information	Remarks and references to Appendices
SPAN	12.9	7 pm	Held Court of Enquiry on No 34286 Pte Q WILLIAMS, enquiry believed killed in action — Court was of opinion he had been killed in action. Lieut BARTON R.A.M.C reported his arrival as relief to the unit — Lieut CB ROBERTS reported his departure to join No 2 F. A.	
	13.9	7 pm	Adm 2 to CCS nil to DRS 1 to duty 1	
	14.9	7 pm	Adm 10 to CCS nil to DRS 1 to duty 4. Proceeded with unit at 1.30 pm to take over Divisional Rest Station. Found camp divided into Ambulance + Rest Station units. Separate returns forsooth. Some improvement had been carried out notably a shelter for men's dinner — Machine gun mullahs of camp found good	
AILADEW	15.9	7 pm	Amb. Adm 13. to CCS. 1. Au des cotés 2 Aug. 7	
			D.R.S. " 26 " 2 " " " 13	
			S. Major MARTIN proceeded to-day on 5 days leave to England. Unit found to be in and sorted out Rest Camp cases from Australian cases.	

1577 Wt.W10791/1773 500,000 1/15 D. D. & L.   A.D.S.S./Forms/C. 2118.

Army Form C. 2118

WAR DIARY
or
INTELLIGENCE SUMMARY.
(Erase heading not required.)

Place	Date	Hour	Summary of Events and Information	Remarks and references to Appendices
AlLHOSPL	16.9.	9.30 p.m.	Amb adm. 13 to CCS 4 to Duty 5 " Off. 1 " Off. 2 " 9 STRS OR. 31 OR 2 T/2 58930 Dr Lloyd RAMC reported arrived from leave	
	17.9	7 pm	Amb adm. 6 to CCS 5 to Duty 9 to ORS. 9 " Off 2 " 2 " 22 STRS " OR 36 Laundry & Surgery still not of completed owing to bank of timber Issued to Army troops. To RE at ABEELE and secured much wood to complete building. Attended conference at office of ADMS. Received instructions for action in case of an advance – and French map. 1. Div R.S. to be closed immediately 2. Stores etc laid down in W.E. only to be taken 3. NCO & 2 men to be left with supplies stores etc 4. These to make an inventory & hand in to Div billets POR	

Army Form C. 2118

WAR DIARY
or
INTELLIGENCE SUMMARY.
(Erase heading not required.)

Instructions regarding War Diaries and Intelligence Summaries are contained in F. S. Regs., Part II. and the Staff Manual respectively. Title pages will be prepared in manuscript.

Place	Date	Hour	Summary of Events and Information	Remarks and references to Appendices
HILLHOEK	18.9.	7 p.m.	Adm. Amb. 11 Sims COS 1 SRS. 4 Sects 3	
			SRS. 19 off 2 " 17 42ⁿᵈ FA. 5	
			GR 9	
			Capt Penny reported arrival from leave.	
"	19.9.	6.30	Adm. Amb. 4 Sims COS. O SRS. 14 duty 4	
			SRS 14 " 9	
"	20.9.	7 p.m.	Drew up orders to be posted in Baths & Laundry. Ssrjt Kennedy Place in charge.	
			Lieut BROSTER departed on 5 days leave to England.	
			Lieut DUDGEON reported departure for duty with 10 Div. F. A.	
"	20.9.	7 p.m.	Adm. Amb. 4 off 1 6 COS. nil SRS 14 Sec no C.I duty 4	
			SRS OR. 25. " 9	
"	21.9.	7 p.m.	Adm. Amb. 8 COS nil SRS 9 duty 3	
			SRS. 35. COS 1 off 1 duty 55.	
			OR. 3.	
"	22.9.	7 p.m.	Adm. Amb. 17. SRS. 7 2 dsts C.2. duty 4	
			SRS. 26. CS. 1 42. FA. 1. " 12	
			G.O.C. Sixth corps inspected Camp at 4 p.m.— Expressed	

WAR DIARY
or
INTELLIGENCE SUMMARY.

(Erase heading not required.)

Army Form C. 2118

Place	Date	Hour	Summary of Events and Information	Remarks and references to Appendices
HILROEK	23.9	7.pm	Fine S.E wind. Later Amb 15. CCS 1. JRS 9. Aty 3 JRS 29. " 5 2 des 12 " 20 Amb 9 ccs 4 JRS 6 Inf 9 JRS 0ffr 2 ccs 1 2 des 0 3 Aty 12 Himself as pleased with all he saw, advised cmn of Amb CO & ASC. Said we had first claim on new hutts erected by division.	
"	24.9	7.pm	Showery SE wind. Adm Received operation orders from ADMS. Opers orders of Amb 6 CE Capt Flood & ATKINS with Jr bearer will proceed to ASYLUM an evening of 25th inst leaving camp at 6.30 pm. They will take 3 Horse Amb 6 cr & will carry 1 days rations & Iron rations & 18 stretchers. To report to O.C. 42 F.A. at ASYLUM. The Horse Amb will be at disposal of OC & report required by him will return at once to HQ. Wheeled stu will be used in evacuating cases from aid posts	

WAR DIARY or INTELLIGENCE SUMMARY

Army Form C. 2118

Place	Date	Hour	Summary of Events and Information	Remarks and references to Appendices
WHOEK			2 O.S. kept at Prison YPRES. remainder stand to S.S. at Will when all wounded have been evacuated. Bearer division of 46 F.A. will rejoin H.Q. pending orders from O.C. 42 F.A. All Sunbeam Motor Amb available will rendezvous road at 10.2.30 at 7. a.m. Sept 25th. They will be under direct O.C. 42 F.A. They will take 2 days rations & drawing petrol.	
"	25.9.	6.30.	~~Sent~~ S.E and Rush in Adm Club 13 O.S. 1 S.R.S.P. 10 O & 1 L.R.S. 5P. 4 20 O. 1. 4 20 3 Stretchers left H.Q. at 6.30 (1 at H.Q. 1 under repair) 30 R.C. & men selected for O.C. details in case of horse. Received 10th message at 7.30. Casualties heavy and arrange for bearer subdivision & move at A.W.V.O.M. at 8 pm Friday. 4 DAYS. Complied with.	
"	26.9.	6.30	Adm Amb. 7. O.S. & G.S. + O..(39. hr des. C. to 3rd x R.S. 17. du 5. 15. Lieut BROSTER reported his arrival this day from leave.	

WAR DIARY
or
INTELLIGENCE SUMMARY

Place	Date	Hour	Summary of Events and Information	Remarks and references to Appendices
			Reinforcements returned during the day. Left flood reported to locoms	
			as Evacuated to O.C.8. wounded	
			33046 Pte EDKINS. T. Sent by "	
			31870 " COX. H " "	
			32929 " TURTON. W. V. " "	
			Two men admitted I.R.S suffering from shock	
			32659 Pte ROBERTSON. D.	
			32120 Pte PEARSON. J.	
			Received message from O.C. 4⅓rd F.A. that Bearers had done splendidly	
MILFOLD 17.9		6-30	Amb. C.W. Amb. 6. I.R.S 3. Int. A.	
			I.R.S. I.R.S 15. O.C.S. D. had C. to step 78.	
			Many of these returned to duty. only fit for light duty. duty	
			St own the D.O. were remaining	
			5 men i return from leave to A.P.M. 8 Corps for road controls	
			Returned on 28th	

WAR DIARY
or
INTELLIGENCE SUMMARY.
(Erase heading not required.)

Army Form C. 2118

Instructions regarding War Diaries and Intelligence Summaries are contained in F. S. Regs, Part II. and the Staff Manual respectively. Title pages will be prepared in manuscript.

Place	Date	Hour	Summary of Events and Information	Remarks and references to Appendices
HILHOEK	27.9		ADMS inspected men of DTC in afternoon - enquired about rifles - informed them that order of 177 admitted on 26th 21 brand ft their rifles with them. 2 LCOs sent to 4th Road control. 2 men to Armourer's Shop. POP. Pte McCANN reported as time from leave. Sent 3 wagons to MONT des CATS for road metal.	
"	28.9 8.30 pm		Some showers - Adm. T.A. 5 & EMS duty 4. DRS. 26 ACS 2 duty 10 ff 44 men O.C. 61st I.O.RE called to morning re men for loading road metal bastant them to POP. Informed him they should be attached to some unit at POP. Lieut. BROWN returned from DeS Batk.	
"	29.9 6 p.m.		A third showery. Amm. T.A. = 6 I. DRS = 3 duty = 5 DRS = 39 " ACS = 2 " = 35	

1577 Wt.W10791/1773 500,000 1/15 D. D. & L. A.D.S.S./Forms/C. 2118.

No. 44 T. O.

Gotras

Army Form C. 2118

WAR DIARY
or
INTELLIGENCE SUMMARY.
(Erase heading not required.)

No 44 2.0.

Instructions regarding War Diaries and Intelligence Summaries are contained in F. S. Regs., Part II. and the Staff Manual respectively. Title pages will be prepared in manuscript.

Place	Date	Hour	Summary of Events and Information	Remarks and references to Appendices
Nikosia	30/9/15	6 pm	Adm. OR. 6 In AMS 0 Duty 4 DPS 9 CCS 3 " 0	OPO
"	1/10/15	6.30pm	Capt E. G. Hunt returned from departure on 7 days leave to Ireland. Sgt Cuthbert proceeded 7 days furlough to Scotland Sept 30 - 6 Oct. Adm. OR 6 In AMS 5 Duty 2 DMS 29 " CCS 1 " 22	OPO
"	2/10/15	6.30 am	Adm. OR 8 In AMS 7 Duty 5 DMS 36 " CCS 4 " 13	OPO
"			Divisional Routine Orders No 819 d/1/10/15 re Identity Discs & be worn & mask N.C.K. in Class parade.	OPO
"	3/10/15	6.30pm	Adm. OR 14 In AMS 1 Duty 1 DPS 27 " CCS 2 " 9	AO
			Lt Knolles W.F. returned this evening from duty interview in charge of 17 Barton W23 the cases to take over Supply Unit on mount of 1 KRR.	
"	4/10/15	7 pm	Adm. OR 20 In AMS 3 Duty 2 DPS 8 " CCS 3 " 19	AO

Army Form C. 2118.

WAR DIARY
or
INTELLIGENCE SUMMARY.
(Erase heading not required.)

Place	Date	Hour	Summary of Events and Information	Remarks and references to Appendices
Hulluch	Sept. 5	3 pm	Adm. BA 10 To DRS 2 Ont 5 —	
			DRS 17 " CCS 6 " 13	
			Sgt Harvey A.S.C graded 6 days through Rest S - 10.	
"	Sept 6	7pm	Adm. BA 11 To DRS 4 Rest 5 3	to W. W. Sam on
			DRS 26 " CCS 3 " 12	
"	Sept 7	8pm	Adm BA 27 1 Off 21 OR To DRS 2 To Convalescent Camp 10	
			DRS 12 " CCS 3 " 12 " on Leave	
			Capt Shaw + Sgt Cuthbert reported returned from leave	
"	Sept 8	7pm	Adm. BA — 11 2 DRS 8 Rest 3 Lt Col Stanton admitted to Field Ambulance to	
			DRS — 24 " CCS 1 " 32 N.Y.D (Pyrexia)	to S&C Squad
"	Sept 9	6pm	Adm. BA 1 Off 40 OR To DRS 6 Ont 5 3 Lt. Col. Stanton transferred to 10 to CCS	
			DRS 29 " CCS 4 " 8 " Hazebrouck	
			9 men details from MDS transport to Camp Convalescent at — DS Hope	
			173 Pte Cox + Beerman Rfm Barratt + Bergen	
			17 men details from DRS to Cooks K.W. Horsemand Bombing School +	
			two to Orderlies. Cooks — Pte Chas Cook, Evans, Malcolm — Pte Taylor, + Downing	

WAR DIARY or INTELLIGENCE SUMMARY

Army Form C. 2118

Place	Date	Hour	Summary of Events and Information	Remarks and references to Appendices
Aylesbury	10/10/15	5.30p	Adm. JA 9 L. APS 5 - L. Amb 4 EWms One. APS 19 " CCS 4 " 13 Lt. Brown deleted as M.O.C. Divisional Engineers (Temporary duty) Nº 31328 Sgt. Paton R.A.M.C.) Proceeded to England on 5 days furlough T/S 6802 A/Cpl. Warren Claws A.S.C.) Lt. Paton reported for return from Tenby Amb. into 9th K.R.R.	(APP)
"	11/10/15	5.45pm	Adm. JA 10 M 18 OR. L. APS 12 Amb. 2 APS 23 CCS 2 M 3 OR. " 13 Adm. from 14th Div. Hqrs. — In advance being ordered from Sailly-Laurette to Heilly 43 Bde. CHASTEL to report to Hqrs. 43 Bde. Que S.E. Wms	
"	12/10/15	5.30p	Trinity S.E. Wms Adm. JA 16 L. APS 16 Amb. 0 APS 23 CCS 2 OM 3 OR. " 13 Recommendations for Commissions 324440 Sgt. Robertson A.A. Edwards Cambridge 34284 Pte Webb S.A. " Clifton College.	(APP)

Lt. Capt. Allan 123/3/15 dated 12/10/15 — Council Inquiry in mission re slight wound caused to 50 CCS for future Sent to 10 or 17 CCS

WAR DIARY
or
INTELLIGENCE SUMMARY.
(Erase heading not required.)

Army Form C. 2118.

Place	Date	Hour	Summary of Events and Information	Remarks and references to Appendices
Hilah	12/9/15	8.30pm	Skinny. S.E. Wins. 4 men from DRS transfd to OE. Adm. 9A 11 to DRS 6 Duty 1 ... in 1 Section Portable Force Details DRS 38 ... CES 5 ... 15 ... (14.10.15) Reinforcements arrived from RonE. 6 Sm. Sent to 42" Inst Ambee & Sm. Taken with Stong K W3 Serg. Pte Stockley 30361 the RaE	AM
"	14/9/15	4pm	3 N.C.o. 1 3 men transferred to Sy. Majs. Richardson of Camp Guards. Lt Tamperley RE visited camp to estimate hutting requirements for the Field Ambulance, Divisional Rest Station & Personnel of the Ambulance also branching in of Dining Shed, Laundry & Latrines etc. Adm 9A to DRS 11 Duty 4 ... DRS 44 ... CES 3 ... 22 Numb. the Cat. 5.	AM
			New S.E. Will.	
"	15/9/15	4.31pm	New S.E. Misty. Adm 9A 8 to DRS 9 Duty 10AR 2 or Eve Hosp at ARQUES reopened. DRS 36 ... CES 10AR 7or 11AR 21 or ... Lt. Col. Emerson & refreshmts proceeded to Bros. Cook House erected next to Kitchen.	

Army Form C. 2118.

WAR DIARY
or
INTELLIGENCE SUMMARY.
(Erase heading not required.)

Instructions regarding War Diaries and Intelligence Summaries are contained in F. S. Regs., Part II. and the Staff Manual respectively. Title pages will be prepared in manuscript.

Place	Date	Hour	Summary of Events and Information	Remarks and references to Appendices
Arlowste	16/10/15	4 p.m.	War Office. Arrived GuOfs CurPce. Eye Hosps at ARQUES closed. Adm. SA In Ans 9 Duty 1 " ARS 62 " CCS 3 " 1 offr 20 O.R. New General Labour made up for personnel.	CMD
"	17/10/15	5.30 p.m.	War Sp. Ch=37 Adm. SA. In Ans 6 Ank 8 " ARS 32 " CCS 6 " 63 Lt Brown reported for annual Fr duty with Barnwell Division. Under O/C Hants Factory Meath hvy going & seen to be shown Trenches to H Heurts for Aurcoud & Rail Station. Birth Ambulance Bearer Rooms & Battalion R.A.M.S. Infantry Comp. Supp of Agmts & Instruction.	CMD
"	18/10/15	5 p.m.	War E Ave Adm. SA 24 In Ans 15 Duty 2 " ARS 58 " CCS 6 " 18	

WAR DIARY
or
INTELLIGENCE SUMMARY.
(Erase heading not required.)

Army Form C. 2118.

Place	Date	Hour	Summary of Events and Information	Remarks and references to Appendices
Arques	18/10/15	5 p.m.	Lt Col. Turner (M.A.M.C.) Inspected Camp accompanied by Capt Amyes Medical Officer.	
			Lt Jackson O/C Anti Post Area approved Site for Hosp. for K.O.S. & D.A.S Reception Room. Aux Hosp. ARQUES to house No Ophthalmic & Dental Cases.	
"	19/10/15	6 p.m.	Nos F. Sick Adm. 29 to DRS Dicks	OMP
			DRS CCS "	
"	20/10/15	10:30 p.m.	Staff in hospital RE Removed Construction of Huts for DRS. 1420 for Revd Control No DRS	
			Adm. DA 11 J. DRS 9 Duty 2 1 Offr 52 OR	
			DRS 8 1 Offr 31 OR CCS 4 2015 4	
			10 Non Absentees for Chevyul Meeting of Officers of Union & L Mere Club for Troops	
			General & 10-15 ; Lt Boulton proceeded on 5 days leave to England.	
"	21/10/15	7:30 p.m.	Nos S.E. Sick J. DRS 15 Duty 0 J. 42 DA 1	OMP
			Adm. DA 15 DRS 27 CCS 1 " 33	
			Sgt Warren & Pte Chaffey (both France) reported their return from England.	

WAR DIARY
or
INTELLIGENCE SUMMARY
(Erase heading not required.)

Army Form C. 2118

Instructions regarding War Diaries and Intelligence Summaries are contained in F. S. Regs., Part II. and the Staff Manual respectively. Title Pages will be prepared in manuscript.

Place	Date	Hour	Summary of Events and Information	Remarks and references to Appendices
Millwock	22/10/15	7 am	Wnd NE. Fine. Adm. LA 9 In ARS 9 Body 0 DRS 27 " CCS 5 " 18	
"	23/10/15	6.30 a	In village of ABEELE shews end of trees SS from Town AS. Wnd SE. Fine Adm. LA 12 In ARS 10 Wnts 1 DRS 41 " CCS 4 " 27	(MR
"	24/10/15	7 am	No 4193 Pte Ollerton Rowe E Surrendered to CCS. Wnd E. No Rain Adm. LA 18 In ARS 12 Wnts 5 DRS 26 " CCS 30A 3 OR. " 40 Monthly report to be studied & further preparations of ADS. Lt Wallis returned his appointment with 48 Bde RFA & for R now exchange Dt WMS from Lt Foster.	
"	25/10/15	10 am	Wnd E. Rain Adm. LA 6 In ARS 3 Wnts 0 " CCS 16 " 21 1 Aberdeen hut (36x15ft) complete ready for shifting to nxt 9 windows in ready had latter made temporarily of wood. Boards & Roof not fitting accurate but same in hut. New ARRO.S. & opened. Said clothes (Box 30 pkg) to camp hut without an inventory Satisfactorily receipt for length. Want of Store similar at present to must present	(MR

1875 W.t. W593/826 1,000,000 4/15 J.B.C. & A. A.D.S.S./Forms/C. 2118.

WAR DIARY
or
INTELLIGENCE SUMMARY

(Erase heading not required.)

Army Form C. 2118

Place	Date	Hour	Summary of Events and Information	Remarks and references to Appendices
Hellebek	25/9/15	10 am	Wrote OC No 4 Aux Section to MR Trinder but was informed that other men at present Weekly Report - mentions to A.D.M.S. re efficiency of Driving Room E. Sgt Storey proceeds on 6 days furlough 4716 Pte Potuto appointed Acting Inspector L/C Corporal.	App/
"	26/9/15	10 am	N.W. Rain. Adm ... S.A. 11 J.S. B.P.E. 6 Duty 6 D.R.S. Officer 1 O.R. ... C.E's 2 Lt Burton Ran C leave expired - now reporting sick - States reporting first to his Office. 1 NCO (Sgt Burton) 1 Sick man detailed to attend inspection by Corps Commander under Major Roberts Ranc OC 142 Field Ambulance	App
"	27/9/15	7 am	N.W. Rain. Adm. S.A. 21 J.S.Nos 9 Duty 4 D.R.S. O.R.s 3 " 13 1 Horse Hit to Patient of Field Ambulance Amplifier. Latter moved to him Tents	
"	28/9/15	7:15	N.W. Rain. Adm. S.A. 8 J.N.O.S 1 Duty 5 D.R.S 1 Offr 23 O.R. O.R.s 4 " 10 Officer Conference A.D.M.S Record issued on Subject for protoned - Amplifier Receipt for fitting 9/9/15 .	Authority Glasgow orders No 1 a/25/8/15 40400 A/Sgt Barlow) Asst made Pay 35752 Cpl Freeburn) 34490 L/cpl to married Rd/Cpl 32683 . Corporals rates pay

WAR DIARY
or
INTELLIGENCE SUMMARY
(Erase heading not required.)

Army Form C. 2118

Place	Date	Hour	Summary of Events and Information	Remarks and references to Appendices
Hillhust	19/10/15	6.30pm	Nos SE Fine. Adm. OPs 26 In AVs 18 Duty 7 DRs 27 CCS 6 31	
"	20/10/15	8.45h	ADMS (Col Guinness DMS) Inspected Camps.	(A)
			Adm to Bull Adm. OPs 21 Jr AVs 1 Duty 2 DRs 10pm 18 OR CCS 10pm 4 OR " 1 9pm 23 OR	
			Instruction received from ADMS I have the "Brit" Aurilla to Pitersungh in Ubps by whom told new main Actim Dressing Station from 4.30-5A	
"	21/10/15	7h	Nos E Bull Adm OPs 21 Jr AVs 12 Duty 11 DRs 41 CCS 10pm 7 OR " 12	
			Orders to Brown 1 NCO +6 men to take over Dest from 4/3 AA at Mam Dressing Station Pitersungh on 1/11/15. Lt Prosser to take over Dresser chart Lines. In rest-church of town.	(A)

44 k. 7. a.
vols 7

121/7656

140 Kurowin

Nov 15

Nov 1915

Confidential

War Diary
of
44th Field Ambulance.

from November 1st to Novbr 30th 1915

Volume 4.

WAR DIARY or INTELLIGENCE SUMMARY

Army Form C. 2118

Place	Date	Hour	Summary of Events and Information	Remarks and references to Appendices
Peterborough	1/11/15	9 am	Wind F. Dull. Aneroid at Peterboro' Y. 30.8 Lincoln 3 Lincoln L. W/b to 12 noon Pres 12 Pres 5 1 hr W.S.R. The 44th Fd. Ambulance handed over the Divisional Rest Station of the College Peterborough which was opened out at 2:15 pm marching to the College Peterborough taken over as a Main Dressing Station from the 4 3rd Fd. Ambulance (Commanded by Lieut. Vaughan-Rowe). Reported to A.D.M.S. never complied by 3:45 pm. A certain amount of Medical Equipment was taken over from the 43rd Fd. Amb. Weekly Report as to sys in Room forwarded to A.A.Q.M.G. 14th Divisional Signals notified Change of address	(W)
2/11/15	6 am	Wind F. Raining. Adm. 39. 10 Pr 37. O.R. To CCS 1 Pres O Ndrs 10 Pr 13 OR 1/3 OR NTRS 10 Pr 13 OR The Hosp. Lorries taken over from 43rd Fd. Amb require roofing & standing completed. Signal Station now used S. Cnr. S.S. at Peterborough To 34 2 84 Patients examined & found fit for Temporary Commission. 2 Col. Sencester, 69 Ony RE. accidentally knocked down by G.S. Wagon in Peterborough. Brought into Dressing Station & a few minutes later. His O.C. notified. Injuries traumatic, recent reductions by attending Officer on duty.	(W)
3/11/15	6:45 pm	Wind SE. Fine Adm 30. 23 To CCS 5 To DRS 15- Pres 1 Pres 72 Lt. Booster Asheles Temporary Duty with 7 R.B.	

WAR DIARY or INTELLIGENCE SUMMARY

Army Form C. 2118

Instructions regarding War Diaries and Intelligence Summaries are contained in F.S. Regs., Part II and the Staff Manual respectively. Title Pages will be prepared in manuscript.

(Erase heading not required.)

Place	Date	Hour	Summary of Events and Information	Remarks and references to Appendices
Peronne	3/11/15	6.15	Following detailed for Duty this morning Lieut. (68 & 24) Sheet 28 Instructions ADMS. Lt. J.H.J. NOEL. Attached to RAMC. Work following syringe prints & Sheffields Trocho work. " 31252 Pt. SOMERSDEN " " 33030 " CRAWLEY " Medical Report on death of Cpl Lancaster Sg Cay RE handed over to ADS OC Pt. (Dr Crawford)	
"	"	7pm	Lieut N. JINX Athn JA " O. OR. Or. C.O.S. 5 - L Bgt tpi 1308 Lt 43 RA. Z Bn.y 8. Reinforcement - L.J. Pt Gault RAMC from No 10 Genl Hosp L. Choices to which at No 23628 Pt Ellett RAMC arrived this evening Taken on Strength & one Supply. No 65/5 32 Pt Geo Smith " " " " " " No 106 121 " " Pickmer } Taken on Strength & duplies kupdn Cpl E Rose NSK (Cav Path Amb Transfer to Dieu Accounts Assessed Refueled	
"	5/11/15 - 7.45pm		Lieut J.N. Remming to OOS w TH3E 6 TN33A 1 TH25 1 attrwerd Orders from O Capt RSV DEVENISH proceeded to leave & England Central O Capt BROWN & Capt CORNISH CC Solsbury Held Pishburg & Two others went to Capt CORNISH CC Solsbury Held Pishburg & Lt WALLIS admitted to hosp per change thoushort sim	
"	6/11/15	7pm	Lieut J. Simi Adjn 21 TOCS " " " KR25 " " " Attended NCo's Conference of C Coy Inspection duty & mr to Gunner WAFF.	

WAR DIARY
or
INTELLIGENCE SUMMARY

Army Form C. 2118

Place	Date	Hour	Summary of Events and Information	Remarks and references to Appendices
Poperinghe	7/10/15	7.30 pm	Wnd SE fine Admn. 19 To CCS 4 To DRS 6 Duty 5. ADMS inspected the Dressing Station Rue de Poperinghe. M out 653 - Pte Healey ASC MT. Admitted for duty on 6/10/15 stated on driving M.T.	MB
"	8/10/15	7 pm	Wind SE fine Admn. 12. To CCS 2 To DRS 6 Duty 6 Third Pte. 62 Co. R.E. unfortunately arranged to make a double inclined plane apparatus to attach to stretchers for abdominal wounds.	
"	9/10/15	7.37 pm	Rain NE fine Admn. 17 To CCS 3 To DRS 5 Duty 5 LRes 1 Pte Pit 7 Units Regt brought in dead to Dressing Station. Neck and Arm fractured Skull, result of Motor lorry accident. OC notified. Lt. BROSTER reported his arrival from Tenby. Units with 7th Inf. Bde.	AB
"	10/10/15	7 pm	Wind N.E. Admn 10 To CCS 2 To DRS 5 To Duty 5 CAPT WALLIS proceeded on 14 days leave to England. Sgt Hodgkinson MT AC on 5 days furlo. Had a double inclined plane apparatus attached to a stretcher for abdominal wounds, excellently made by Sgt Fee 7 Unit. Rank. Pte Fox 7 Units Regt buried in 6th Municipal Cemetery Poperinghe (near Chateau Elizabeth) on Poperinghe Kinning Furnished	AP

Army Form C. 2118

WAR DIARY
or
INTELLIGENCE SUMMARY

(Erase heading not required.)

Instructions regarding War Diaries and Intelligence Summaries are contained in F.S. Regs, Part II. and the Staff Manual respectively. Title Pages will be prepared in manuscript.

Place	Date	Hour	Summary of Events and Information	Remarks and references to Appendices
Pop.	11/11/15	8 p.m.	Xmas W.F. Xmi. Adms 7 to CCS 1 to DRS 4 Nrty 5. Attended Conference of ADMS. Lt-BROWN & Pte COLE due from leave today, absent.	
"	12/11/15	7.30 p.m.	Xmas W.W. Rain. Adms 17 To CCS 7 To DRS 3 Nrty 4. Lt. BROWN, QMS DEVEREUX reported return from leave also Pte COLE, delay due to non-sailing of Steamer. Replies were ADMS to a letter dated (31.10.15. G.M.G.) from the Adjutant General re the possibility of restriction of the personnel of the Inds Ambulance, ie., ADMS suggested that OBS stores transport be replaced by M.T. ASC (with the exception of 2 Battens) to attempt to hire one 1 m.a.c. + 1 m.a. for each Section Commander. (3) The processing officer at the Carnaul by Motor Transport, the harstval Equipment + Baggage it by currently Motor Lorries, obstructing the OSC, (J.S.F.) would reduce to Personnel by about 'half' ie from 40 to 20 per Fld Ambulance & was of the opinion that any return of the Pack Officer n.c.o's or men would diminish the efficiency of the unit.	CWP
"	13/11/15	7 p.m.	Xmas NW. Rain. Adms 1 Mr. CCS 2 To D.S. 14 Nrty. O Q.R CAPT DEVENISH C.F. reported return from leave.	CWP

1875 Wt. W593/826 1,000,000 4/15 J.B.C. & A. A.D.S.S./Forms/C. 2118.

WAR DIARY
or
INTELLIGENCE SUMMARY

Army Form C. 2118

(Erase heading not required.)

Place	Date	Hour	Summary of Events and Information	Remarks and references to Appendices
Poperinghe	14/11/15	7am	Wind S.E. Fine. Above 10th 24 grs. To CCS 3 To ADS 10hr 10 or 10hr 5. All leave cancelled. Lt/Qmtr Boyles + Sgt Richardson now proceeding	
"	15/11/15	7.3 am	Wind S.E. Fine. Above 8 To CCS 4 To ADS 0 Duty 6 To 43 29 3 No 82/1 Fd Amb Range. Proceeded the day to duty with V Corps (corr) cutting party. Motor Machine from ADMS Wdrawn.	
"	16/11/15	7am	Wind S.W. Rain. Above 15 To CCS 1 To ADS 13 To Duty 2 Attended at Office ADMS. Received instructions to reconnaissance & Reg Aid Posts attended by No 3 Fd Ambulance. Left Poperinghe 1.7.a.m. with Lt Pearce Boyton. Left— High Ambulance Dressing Station at 8 h.m. C26 c.60. (1 Aid Post. Cottage) Sheet 28 Thus. The Aid Posts were at La Brique C26 c.60 (1 Aid Post. Cottage) Sheet 28 St Jean C27 d.a.3 (2 Cellars) Scale 1/40,000 Essex Farm. (C25 a 3.8. Sheet 28) Advanced Dressing Station next Dressing Sta sq/Known, collected wounded from La Belle Alliance Station (Bryant at C30 d.9.7. I am arranged to have a Collecting Post at Reigersburg Chateau (H6 b3.4. Sheet 28 Scale 20,000 by the 1 Motor Ambulance with 2 Drivers, 1 NCO & 2 RAMC Pte Advanced Dressing Station from the Prison Ypres I 7.7.10. Sheet 28 to no 2 Main Dressing Station Poperinghe The College Sheet 16.100 CAPT ATKINS RAMC Transferred to No 12 CCS HAZEBROUCK N.Y.D (Pyrexia.)	

WAR DIARY
or
INTELLIGENCE SUMMARY

(Erase heading not required.)

Army Form C. 2118

Instructions regarding War Diaries and Intelligence Summaries are contained in F.S. Regs., Part II. and the Staff Manual respectively. Title Pages will be prepared in manuscript.

Place	Date	Hour	Summary of Events and Information	Remarks and references to Appendices
Poperinghe	17/11/15	5 pm	Adms SO to CCS 3 To RRS 10/11 Pnen to Duty O Nos 3019 Rg Bomber Renue operated out of Knee with fractured Leg. (Right Tibia Shipk.) W/CPL Denison returned from Sick leave & took over the Ambulance.	Attempt Optime
POP.	18/11 10 pm		Fine - Frost - attended Adms office and reported arrival. Made arrangements with O.C.'s of 17th & 18th F.A. aus with regard to taking over aid posts. Following arrangements were carried over: 1.) Capt Flood with 1 nco & 10 men took over PRISON YPRES at 10 am with equipment left there previously by 1/2 F. Dgn. 1.) 1 A.Co. & 3 men with rations proceeded at 8 pm to aid post at POTIJZE and reported to M.O. - took 2 wh. stretcher 2.) 1 A. Co. & 3 men with rations & 2 wh. stretchers proceeded via ESSEX FARM and Bridge 4 to aid post at LA BELLE ALLIANCE at 8 pm and reported to Lieut O'LOUGHLIN 2/c 9th KRR 3.) 1 A.co. & 3 men with rations & 2 wh. stretcher proceeded to aid post at ST JEAN reporting to M.O. Adm sick 1 off 13 or to CCS 6 to DRS 15 or 1 off to duty 12 or wounded	H

Army Form C. 21

WAR DIARY
or
INTELLIGENCE SUMMARY
(Erase heading not required.)

Place	Date	Hour	Summary of Events and Information	Remarks and references to Appendices
POP	19/11	10 pm	Fine - Frost - N. Wind. —	

1. Capt. FLOOD with 1 NCO & 10 men & 1 Mot. Amb. & 1 mot. Bicycle took over from YPRES & from 10 to 7 A.M. with mid equipt. left behind by 14 to 7. F.A. previously.

2. 1 N.C.O. 2 men 1 Mot Amb. & 2 drivers proceeded to REIGERSBURG CHATEAU collecting Mot patients over from 17th F.A. Orders to collect from Canal bank at road junction I.16.d.9. at 9 pm to 6 at 9 pm at 3 pm & 9 pm. daily —
Car to remain at CHATEAU. & one to collect from ESSEX FARM (C.15.a.3.9).
& once twice daily to men drawing stores.
Expected transport lines in afternoon — shelters in horse lines in unfinished state — some falling down — men trench digging found no huts for present — viz RSC & 30 drivers made arrangements for collecting as follows tonight

1. 2 cars £1.44.45 to leave POP at 8pm & evacuate POTIJZE to take rations & water for 4 men

2. 2 cars as above to leave POP at 4 a.m. 20 to most to men to POP.

WAR DIARY or INTELLIGENCE SUMMARY

Army Form C. 2118

(Erase heading not required.)

Instructions regarding War Diaries and Intelligence Summaries are contained in F.S. Regs., Part II. and the Staff Manual respectively. Title Pages will be prepared in manuscript.

Place	Date	Hour	Summary of Events and Information	Remarks and references to Appendices
POP.			2. 1 car 44 tr } 1 " 43 " } to leave POP at 8 pm & travel to aid post at ST JEAN 1 car 17 tr } to take rations & water up to same	
			1 car 44 tr } 1 " 43 " } to leave POP at 4 am 20th & travel as above	
			3. 1 car 44 tr } 1 " 43 " } to leave POP at 8 pm. Track aid post at LA BRIQUE 1 car 17 tr }	
			1 car 44 tr } 1 " 43 " } to leave POP at 4 am 20th & travel as above	
			Lieut. O'LOUGHLEN called at main dressing station about 9.30 pm and said that it would be very difficult to take their G.R. way this aid post from LA BRIQUE - he promised to arrange to take them himself.	
	20/1		Adm. Sch. 22 # CCS 1 6385 14 7463 741 48 Lieut BROSTER & transferred to Scots CCS with keys /type Conference at 7th Corps H.Q. Proceeded at 9 pm with 2 Buses 17th Corps & aid posts at ST JEAN & LA BRIQUE - these are 2 to widposts at ST JEAN & are at LA BRIQUE - late inspected P.R.I.S.N. YPRES - all quiet.	

1875   Wt. W593/826   1,000,000   4/15   J.B.C. & A.   A.D.S.S./Forms/C. 2118.

Place	Date	Hour	Summary of Events and Information	Remarks and references to Appendices
Pop R	20/h		Adm. Sick 3) to CCS. 29 to 8725 wounded officers 2 - to CCS. 29 to 8725 29	
	21/11		Proceeded to G.H.Q's advt post at LA BELLE ALLIANCE on the way up visited Collecting Post at REIGERSBERG CHATEAU - here there is good accommodation for cases & personnel - also adv. D. S. at ESSEX FARM. belonging to 1st Riding Ambulance of 49th Division. they allow us to evacuate through here & one orders of H.Q. F.A. is posted here. Motor Cars can only go as far as ESSEX FARM - from there to LA BRIQUE ABUTTRECE is a good track for 1½ miles suitable for wheeled stretchers - also a light railway with stretcher trolley. The aid post is a good hut and one + two men in a dug out - and had very little accommodation - I went to Res. S.A.O. dugout & saw Lieut Col GREEN Comdg 8th K.R.R. He told me trenches were very bad - communicator trenches fallen in & impassable and that he could not get through f front trenches except at night - He agreed that it would not be possible to evacuate cases etc. except at night & then in the open. I inspected some trenches verified this	f/s

Army Form C. 2118

WAR DIARY
or
INTELLIGENCE SUMMARY
(Erase heading not required.)

Instructions regarding War Diaries and Intelligence Summaries are contained in F.S. Regs., Part II. and the Staff Manual respectively. Title Pages will be prepared in manuscript.

Place	Date	Hour	Summary of Events and Information	Remarks and references to Appendices
POP	22/11	7 pm	Adm. [?] sick 1 Off 50 OR to CCS 2 Off to [?] 8.30 wounded 1 Off 13 OR 29 OR	
			Col GERRARD S. reported himself to HQ. I was fetched up in Lieuth. B.S. to assist adm of division went to come out I showed him over Adm. & shelters & explained work of collecting & various orders & circulars	
	23/11 12pm mid night	Adm. sick 2 Off 65 OR to CCS 1 Off 23 on TRS 1 Off wounded 1 - 21 45 OR	
	24/11 12pm mid night	Adm sick 2 - 72 to CCS 1 41 to an 2 Off wounded 1 - 29 22 OR visited outposts afoot. Found [?] entering into Adm Area & Col GERRARD. A.M.S. restricted from on return.	
	25/11 11.30 pm	Adm. sick 2 Off 66 OR to CCS 1 Off to QS 2 Off & Sgt & Off wounded 4 OR 43 OR 36. 8 or 9 trench feet are being admitted daily all were in trenches when they boots and O.C's of Reg[?] were issued circulars with regard to prevention. 2 officers & 3 of 7th accompanied collecting officer Steeple preparatory to taking over St JEAN & LA BRIQUE and Lieut BROSIER returned to duty	

1875 Wt. W593/826 1,000,000 4/15 J.B.C. & A. A.D.S.S./Forms/C. 2118.

WAR DIARY
or
INTELLIGENCE SUMMARY
(Erase heading not required.)

Army Form C. 2118

Instructions regarding War Diaries and Intelligence Summaries are contained in F.S. Regs., Part II. and the Staff Manual respectively. Title Pages will be prepared in manuscript.

Place	Date	Hour	Summary of Events and Information	Remarks and references to Appendices
P.o.P.	26/11	11.30 p.m.	Adm. Sick opp. 49 to CCS. 32 to duty 1 off 1 BR. TRS. 36. W. ORs. 1 off 30 OR. 2 BR. Aid posts at ST BEAN & LA BRIQUE taken over by L.S.C. F.A. who collect from taught inclusive all bearers at different aid posts relieved tonight and prison then morning. Infected horse lines during day took tea on stables progressing — still no timber for huts. 34.784 Pte Corbett F.A. departed to attend course at Cadet School London	(b)
	27/11	7.30 p.m.	Adm. Sick 10 off 29 OR to CCS. 8 to TRS. 20. to Duty 20. ORs. 1 Si. 4	(H)
	28/11	7 p.m.	Adm. { Si. 26 6 to CCS. 8 u 16 u 1	H)
	29/11	7 p.m.	Adm. { Si. 24 to CCS. 9. TRS. 1 off 43 70. 4 W. 1 off 10 OR 15 OR	H8
			No. 17273 2.nd Lt. W.H. Jones R.A.M.C. reported arrival for duty. Capt. Clt Drysen departed on leave to England. Under instructions to sup. T.7th Corps. following American Med. Offr attached for work in aid posts at POTIJZE - Phillips. S. CHANCELLOR & J.H. NEFF from 23 General (amer.) Hosp. at PRISON YPRES.	

1875 Wt. W593/826 1,000,000 4/15 J.B.C. & A. A.D.S.S./Forms/C.2118.

WAR DIARY or INTELLIGENCE SUMMARY

Place	Date	Hour	Summary of Events and Information	Remarks and references to Appendices
POP.	30/11	7.30	Allen { Sick 2 - 44 OR 6 } { Wounded 6 OCS 7 6 d= P.O. 30 63 P.a. 1 went to H.Q.M.S Office - inured him - left letter requesting that 2.M.S. to H. JONES NMC night be posted to another unit - pointed out that there are no Regulars in this unit, that as R.C.O has been doing duty as 2.M.S for 9 mo most satisfactorily - also other N.C.O's further that it would not be to the advantage of the Service to put in regular N.C.O. over heads of R.C.O's of unit Surgt Gen. Porter S[?] II Army inspected main dressing station - American doctors visit with Collecting Coyˢ to and fros at LA BELLE ALLIANCE	AP

44 F.A.
Vol. 8

D/7909

Confidential.

11th Division

F/1144

Dec 1915

War Diary

of

44th Field Ambulance R.A.M.C.

from December 1st to December 31st 1915

Volume — 5/8

WAR DIARY
or
INTELLIGENCE SUMMARY

(Erase heading not required.)

Army Form C. 2118

Place	Date	Hour	Summary of Events and Information	Remarks and references to Appendices
POPERINGHE	1/1/17	7.30 p.m.	Adm. Wound Off 1 OR 31. ECCS 33 Sick 1 duty 6 4+7A 29 Sick 61	AP
			Nos 2.2n. Lt. FOSTER reported return from leave	
	2/1/17	7 pm	Adm. W. Off 2. OR 9 to CCS Off 2. 6+7A 30. 43rd A S duty 8 S. 43 Pme OR 13	AP
			Capt W.E. WALLIS. joined 9th RA for duty.	
	3/1/17	10 pm	Adm. W Off 1 OR. 14 CCS Off 1 87RS. 28 43rd 7A 2. duty S. 36 OR 14	AP
			Lieut S.F. MARSHALL RAMC reported arrival for duty with ambulance #14 taken on strength.	
	4/1/17	7 pm	Adm. { W. Off 1 OR 3 to CCS { 1 Off. to 13 43rd { 2 duty 5. S. 18 { 6 OR. ZRS }	AP
			Capt F. FLOOD reported departure for duty with 10th D.K.7.	
			Conference at Tk Ck Corps H.Q. — Reminded SSTNS Y Fd Ams re 2-In. S. Trues RAmc	

WAR DIARY
or
INTELLIGENCE SUMMARY

(Erase heading not required.)

Army Form C. 2118

Place	Date	Hour	Summary of Events and Information	Remarks and references to Appendices
Pop.	5/12	6pm	Adm. W. 6 S. 24 CCS. } 6 42 FA. 16. Other } 8 duty 2 2 A. Conference at ADMS office – instructions given regarding a move in connection with transport. Lieut BROSTER rejoined transport Offr. proceeded in afternoon to H.Q. to see O.C. No train arf to annuals. Inspected wagon lines – arranged for drying clothes at cottages near lines. Officer prisoner Boyd wh. into main dressing station.	FS
"	6/12	7pm	Adm. W. 5 } to CCS. 42 FA other 24 to duty	FS
	7/12	7pm	Rain. went round to Adm. W. 8 } to CCS. 42 FA other FA. duty	FS
	8/12		Rain. went round to Adm. W. 5 } to CCS. 6to FA SRS duty	FS

Rain throughout

1875 Wt. W593/826 1,000,000 4/15 J.B.C. & A. A.D.S.S./Forms/C. 2118.

WAR DIARY
or
INTELLIGENCE SUMMARY

(Erase heading not required.)

Army Form C. 2118

Instructions regarding War Diaries and Intelligence Summaries are contained in F.S. Regs., Part II. and the Staff Manual respectively. Title Pages will be prepared in manuscript.

Place	Date	Hour	Summary of Events and Information	Remarks and references to Appendices
Pop.	8/11	?	aid post at ESSEX FARM were all day to heavy shelling — collecting offr arranged with 10 Rifled Bde to share their dug out. Notified A.D.M.S. — Capt. DENYER returned from leave	H
Pop.	9/k	7.30	left wound saw. Adm. S. D.R.I. other 7A duty. 6 CCS	H
			last night Capt PPRN went to 3rd Bde H.Q. Had been detailed to take him to new dug out to used as collecting post. He reported as sick on and was difficult to get at 2 B.S. Trans proceeded to Corps F.A. for duty.	
Pop	10/11	7pm.	left wound saw. 6 CCS. Adm. S. E.T.P.S. Other 2H duty. W. Submitted names of those for mention to A.D.M.S. Lieut C R. DUDGEON No. 3166? Sergt. Richard EASTHAM No. 32143 Pte HENRY AYRE No. 32,791 Pte. JOHN ARTHUR O'HARA.	H

Army Form C. 2118

WAR DIARY
or
INTELLIGENCE SUMMARY
(Erase heading not required.)

Instructions regarding War Diaries and Intelligence Summaries are contained in F.S. Regs., Part II. and the Staff Manual respectively. Title Pages will be prepared in manuscript.

Place	Date	Hour	Summary of Events and Information	Remarks and references to Appendices
POP	10/12		Lieut A. HEARTY R.A.M.C. & A.R.GRAY R.A.M.C. reported arrival — Lieut GRAY R.A.M.C. held to report to OC 63rd FA. Lieut HEARTY taken on strength & sent for temp'y duty to 29th Bde R.F.A. Capt KEEGAN R.A.M.C. reported & taken on strength	A
do	11/12 7pm		Adm. 51 OCS. 14 duty 10 off SRS. 21 b.a.R.	B
do	12/12 9pm		Adm. 35 OCS 6 SRS 14 duty 2. 13 men of ASC reported arrival	C

WAR DIARY
or
INTELLIGENCE SUMMARY

Army Form C. 2118

Place	Date	Hour	Summary of Events and Information	Remarks and references to Appendices
Poperinghe	13/2/15	7pm	Wms. N. sine Adm 8.19.4.5 men OCS 14.31 men ORS 19 Inf.ty 7 To 17 FA & To 7 FA / To 29.34. It Col. H. Simpson proceeds this day & takes over the duties of A.D.M.S. during the temporary absence on leave of Col. Grice-Hure. Capt.-Chr Flanigan took over the duties of O.C. 4th 3rd Fd Amb.ce (N.Z.C.H. Simpson) during his absence. Capt. Rev. J.H. Harden CF., Sgt. Hegarty, OC the Reinf. proceeded on 8 days leave. The following statement was made by Capt. O.H. Barr MO 147 Bde R.F.A. to No 32352 Sgt Harney H.H.R.A.M.C. (Soldier who was on duty at the Reports being Chateau Collecting Post. (H.8.3.4. Belgium Sheet 28) During the shelling of this place yesterday (Should like to say how great assistance the help of Sgt Warner Rand was afterwards). He showed great presence & coolness under very heavy shell fire.	Cks.
	14/2/15	7.30pm	Vlamertin. Ops Adm 2 off OCS 2 off ORS 13 Inf.ty 16 36 OR 18 OR	
	15/2/15	7pm	Vlamertin. Ops Adm 8 off OCS 7 off ARS 20 Inf.ty 1 off 53 OR 21 OR 11 OR Four of the above officers admitted belonged to 2 Notts & Derbys V.T.R.H. They were caught by a shell. 1 severely wounded 3 immediately slightly No ½ 5898 Mallard & No ½ 13957 Lt Oxford A.S.C. remanded by Court ASC martial on account of their Supmen. Officer (NCO, Capt. Oft.) marched.	Cks.

Army Form C. 2118

WAR DIARY
or
INTELLIGENCE SUMMARY
(Erase heading not required.)

Place	Date	Hour	Summary of Events and Information	Remarks and references to Appendices
Poperinghe	16/12/15	7 am	Heavy Rain. Adm. 3 Offr. CCS. 3 Offr. ATT & SOR Duty 72, 33 OR	
			Under instructions from ADMS Got collected from A.P.B. Hosp. 18 Camp (A 30) & treated. Superior Herd Parkhurst 2 motor Amb-s leave Pop. Siding & taken to am. S. Reilly's from AMB Camp by 2 Horse Ambulances leaving 11 am from Pop. Siding Station. Detachment of Brig. out N'Coist Jaan Yser Canal Bank relieved by buntz of H Division. Half la buntz at R.A. Posts at P.O. 1735 & 6A Belle Alliance Farm also relieved. ADMS notified. Hand over 1 light Ambce to 42nd FA Ambce to No 1 Coy ASC	AD/
"	17/12/15	7.30 R	Rain. Adm. 4 Offr. CCS. 3 Offr. Duty 3, 36 OR 4 OR	
			Detachment withdrawn from Ppm Ypres & Relieved by 18 FA VI Division Regensbury Chateau (H66 3 u. Belgium Sheet 28) " at R.A. Post La Belle Alliance relieved by bntz of VI Division. Essex Farm Yser Canal (C29.a.2.8. Belgium Sheet 28) (G6.a.7.4.) Capt Brace Pte Griffin, Shuttle with Pte Brunson & Canterbury Rau. Medical Selection Unit. relieves by L/Col McDonald	AD/

Army Form C. 2118

WAR DIARY
or
INTELLIGENCE SUMMARY
(Erase heading not required.)

Instructions regarding War Diaries and Intelligence Summaries are contained in F.S. Regs., Part II. and the Staff Manual respectively. Title Pages will be prepared in manuscript.

Place	Date	Hour	Summary of Events and Information	Remarks and references to Appendices
Pop'ghe	18/4/15	7 pm	Weather dull. Attn. 2/YR 1/YR Oct 1/YR Bty. 13 to 17 YA. Lt Marshall Rowe Turk'd over the duties of Medal of Rt. Ceme of the 3rd Ambulance which also for the time being as Divisional Rest Station. (Rtl College Pop'ghe.)	AD
Do.	19/4/15	7.30 pm	Weather — Attn. 1/YR West part 3 offrs. Attn. 39 R H.O. GR. Oct 3 offrs 160R. Weather. 8. Remaining to Wytles A/p at 5.45 am by Shells opening over the Enemy gunfire & heard a cone bombardment of Kemy gunfire approaching in front. 16, 17, 18, 19 of Yorks. German Reserve Gunners were Kop. In morning Kotaaysed Brought Result of Bomb attack — Brought in Emergency Station. Chaplain HR Bate AcD Wound of Rt Leg, & amp. T. Tibia. La Rue. 2 Belgian boys wounded Transport to Carl Hosp'ls. Worn. 1 Belgian Boy Killed. Result of Shell fire. 6893 Pte Kersite 1/E Yorks Gen P. Sunt Lttles R. Ambel 1651 N. Smith Gun Wech & LR Dor't. 70654 Sp. HarJag. (dead). Bootd 10th High Machine Platen. Copy Signal M 016842 Cpt Chadwick (dead) D.D.S. Rouck.	AD · HP

WAR DIARY or INTELLIGENCE SUMMARY

Army Form C. 2118

Place	Date	Hour	Summary of Events and Information	Remarks and references to Appendices
Poperinghe	19/7/15	7.30 pm	There was apparently a German Offensive on Ypres. Continuous rumble of heavy gunfire this morning from 5.45 am. Continuous movement of the morning about to State German gunfire on P.B. [?] were put into different Batts by the train to [?] rendered into "The Place" [?] during the afternoon whilst Lt John G. FOSTER R.A.M.C. was & [?] entering the Training of hospital equipment under the performing the College. A shell came over Khonried [?] him in the leg. Pres. a slip. [?] from Capt. D.S. Wright R.A.M.C. to Lt Forster R.A.M.C. will [?] also be [?] States. The 2 Letter were forwarded to C.O.s.	seen "The Place" (formerly Croton) A.P.O.
Pop.	20/7/15	7 pm	Weather - Dull, Raining. Offrs 1 Offr Ces. 38 OR Rnng. #9 51 OR Offr 1 Offr Dnty 1 Offr Rnmng #9 33 OR. The two Moth Ambulances detailed to assist 18th D.A. VI Dvr. or were [?] [?] to St Jean was quite outside Ypres. No changes have wounded. Drvrs how to wear their Smoke helmets on entering Ypres as Gas was still drifting about in places. Sgt Pady Handy was in charge of the Care. [?] to the 18th D.A. at Wanrweltgle Lt. Col. SIMPSON R.A.M.C. returns from Temporary Duty as A.D.M.S.	O.R.S.

Army Form C. 2118

WAR DIARY
or
INTELLIGENCE SUMMARY
(Erase heading not required.)

Instructions regarding War Diaries and Intelligence Summaries are contained in F. S. Regs., Part II. and the Staff Manual respectively. Title Pages will be prepared in manuscript.

Place	Date	Hour	Summary of Events and Information	Remarks and references to Appendices
POP	21/1/16	7 P	Adm. 29 to CCS 13 to July 7. ORS 13	
POP	22/1/16	7.30	Adm. 33 to CCS. 14 to July. 28 Westbound — ran. Rev. T. H MARTIN returned from leave. IRS. closed	
do	23/1/16	7.30	Lieut GRANT detailed for temp duty @ 5th Div. A. } Lieut MARSHALL " " " @ 9 KRR Adm. 40 to CCS 13 to July 11	
	24/1/16	6 pm	Adm. 10 CCS 15 to July 11 Off 1 Went to office of home who gave instructions re move — promulgated Court-martial on Pte Ashford ASC & Pte Floyd ASC. 90 days F.P. No 1	

WAR DIARY
or
INTELLIGENCE SUMMARY
(Erase heading not required.)

Army Form C. 2118

Place	Date	Hour	Summary of Events and Information	Remarks and references to Appendices
Pop.	25/12	7pm	Adm. 33 6CS 10 duty 17 50CCS 4 Tuft Bde. Received detailed instructions to move from C.C.S — Tuft Bde. Motor ambulances left 4 cars & the R.C. reported for duty & cars & the R.E. reported for duty for collection from all these Brigades & morrow morning. At 6.30 received following average. "All orders regarding move are held in abeyance" Similar average from 4.50 13 cle Medical 14 to Siv.	f.O
do	26/12	7pm	Adm 2 Off 17 OR CCS 26 duty 27 Received full average. Cancel all orders relating to move A.A.A. normal condition resumed today A.A.A. Send cars belonging to 4 M.A.C. back to them at .... on return of our cars — our cars returned about 1pm Lieut BARTON sent to divisional train for temp duty	f.O

Place	Date	Hour	Summary of Events and Information	Remarks and references to Appendices
# POP	29/12	a.m.	& CCS & duty	
			An Proceeded at 1 pm to 3rd West Riding F.A. saw O.C. and learnt details of evacuation of sick & wounded by 49 Div: - At 6 pm went to dug outs in canal bank at C.19.c.4.0. Belgian & France Sheet 20 - with 6 bearers & Capt DENVER. Found him with 2 bearers to aid post at C.13.13.4.3. called GLIMSE LANE - SKIPTON ROAD. Went myself with 2 bearers to # aid post at LANCASHIRE FARM - C.13.d.9.4. Other two bearers sent with guide to aid post C.20.B.1.9 - BOAR LANE. Communication trenches very bad through temporary running from aid posts to canal bank broken up in places by shell fire. Stretcher trolleys are supplied to each line. Two cars taken with two horses to each. Returned # to POP by new road (cotton crop) leading direct from BRIELEN to HAMERTINGHE. good road - Sent Capt DENNY to FROOMORTH road leading to aid post on canal bank at H.23.c.0.9.	M

Place	Date	Hour	Summary of Events and Information	Remarks and references to Appendices
POP	28/11	6.30.	He returned saying that O.C. 2nd W.R. & Auber had told him he would have him taken round in the morning – as he could get their by daylight. reached POP at 1 a.m. found orders to send 2 stretcher over from 49 th Div. a. ## Sent Capt PENNY there yesterday he submitted report – good tramway from Canal bank to X roads at B 23.a.9.9. – cellar just north of [illeg.] where bearers can be accommodated – Res. aid post in canal & bank is in telephone communication with no 2. W.R. D.R. Went to A.D.M.S. Office at N. an m. He informed me that from 10 a.m. 30th inst I was to be responsible for collection. bearers at Div halted to be relieved by 50 Div. Sent four bearers to each aid post A.B.C & D in relief of 49th Div F.A's – also Capt DENYER Sergt EASTHAM and three men to aid post add dressg	[init] [init]

WAR DIARY
or
INTELLIGENCE SUMMARY
(Erase heading not required.)

Army Form C. 2118

Place	Date	Hour	Summary of Events and Information	Remarks and references to Appendices
			Station at C.19.c.b.o. — told bearers who were going to A.23.c.o.a. that two bearers (bearers of Regt aid post and two at KILL FARM north of tramway	
P o P.	29/12	10.30 pm	Actn. 49 Gees Q to APS 8 [btrly 8 Runaway OR 93 left to POP shelled in afternoon — received message. Gas alert, about 7½ hours. Collecting post at C.19.c.4.0 in evening at 8 pm. sent there cars & adv. staff two O.R. cyclinders & 6 boys to o/lc Adv. Coll. Post for distribution to Regt aid posts of 4/81 Bde.	
	30/12	10 pm	Adv. S.b. off. } 6 CCS. { 2 off 6 STRS. } off ? Actv 5.14 6's OR. 32 on 2 OR 96 took over collecting from 10 am this morning — wrote all rest camp cases to the 12 CCS. HAZEBROUCK — now roll call to a.D. b. & up ZH. Saw A.D.M.S. in afternoon and suggested that another ambulance collect from left sector, as the evacuation	

1875 Wt. W593/826 1,000,000 4/15 J.B.C. & A. A.D.S.S./Forms/C. 2118.

WAR DIARY
or
INTELLIGENCE SUMMARY

Army Form C. 2118

Place	Date	Hour	Summary of Events and Information	Remarks and references to Appendices
Pop.	31/12	10 pm	continuously divides dugouts two sectors the evening sent two cars with 8 bearers & Lieut BROSTER to X roads B.23.a.9.9. at 8 pm with instructions to take to aid posts in left sector and find out about accommodation for bearers — all bearers to return by cars making second collection at 4.30. Lieut BROSTER reported no room at Regl aid post O.C. 5th OP Bucks said he could find room for bearers at SARAGOSSA farm. Lieut BROWN returned from Leave. Pop shelled at noon and again heavy in evening. Attn { OH 3 on 82 } to CCS OH 3 OR 15 to STS 6 & duty 10 Collection same as on previous nights 8 bearers & 1 NCO taken up from 43rd F.A.	#1 #2

1875 Wt. W593/826 1,000,000 4/15 J.B.C. & A. A.D.S.S./Forms/C. 2118.

Nominal Roll of Officers of
44th Field Ambulance N.Z.
19th Dec. 19–

Rank	Name
Lt Col.	H. Simson
Capt.	C.H. Dwyer
Capt. Adj	C.H.G. Pinay
Capt	F.G. Flood
Capt	W.L. Scott
Lieut.	B.H. Barton
Lieut	L.R. Broster
Lieut	L.G. Brown
Lieut	S.E. Marshall
Lieut	A. Hegarty
Lieut	G.M. Grant
Lieut QM	G. Foster

C.H. Dwyer
Capt. R.A.M.C.
for O.C. 44 Fd Ambce

Nominal Roll of NCOs & men
44th Field Amb RAMC
19th Dec/15

No	Rank	Name	No	Rk	Name
34525	Sgt Major	Martin CH	31158	Pte	Bradbury L
40015	Sgt	Cattrall JE	57328	"	Brown WJ
32552	"	Warner HH	31198	"	Butler GH
31318	"	Watson WD	33611	"	Braithwaite HE
32440	"	Richardson AS	32721	"	Brickell H
32150	"	Cook JJ	32000	"	Britton W
31848	"	Hegarty M	31868	"	Broomhead E
31416	"	Tapping G	31867	"	Bruce E
31978	"	Bailey E	31202	"	Brunsdon WH
31658	"	Corbishly J	33011	"	Bullock J
31667	"	Eastham R	31776	"	Burkhardt GA
32551	"	Sutton J	31147	"	Bury JA
23821	"	Keegan W	31148	"	C.. M. C
40440	"	Barlow A	33030	"	Carbury J
35852	Cpl	Freeborn WJ	31787	"	Chaffey H
31515	"	Davies HS	31212	"	Chalke JY
31539	"	Breeze J	31179	"	Churchland AD
33045	"	Edwards GA	30537	"	Clest M
32307	"	Elliott R	53693	"	Cole W
31084	"	Lusty C	57380	"	Collup J
31951	wagr wounded	Wright PH	31576	"	Cooney E
32076	"	Dougherty W	31930	"	Cox H
32563	A/Cpl	Garrett J	33668	"	Goss C
31529	Pte	Adams J	57400	"	Cummings S
47628	"	Adams JW	31883	"	Curtis WH
45804	"	Anderson J	57358	"	Douglas A
6300	"	Arthur A	32302	"	Duggan WG
32050	"	Aspland B	32003	"	Dunham J
32142	"	Atkinson JG	57252	"	Dye H
32143	"	Ayres H	31886	"	Dyson CJ
32056	"	Bailey LW	31606	"	Earley OB
40410	"	Barratt EW	33047	"	Easton W
46797	"	Bartlett A	31888	"	Eaton H
47066	"	Blake H	31872	"	Edwards G
30833	"	Bowick G	31873	"	Eke PJ

46233	Pte	Emery H A	31497	"	McDonnell W H
31228	"	Fletcher A W	44951	"	Lees J
31841	"	Fox W	31759	"	Lister C H
32087	"	French A	31488	"	Levett H
55143	"	Freeborn J C	32206	"	Lill C
37922	"	Fildes F	32261	"	Linton H J
31525	"	Gawman H	53699	"	Lound J
32206	"	Gilmore J B	43626	"	Lovell F
31581	"	Gordon A	31449	"	Macdonald J
31673	"	Gore S	31371	"	McIvney J
31559	"	Gorringe A	31699	"	Manuel M
32019	"	Green J	32634	"	Marshall A
57317	"	Greenwood S	40352	"	Mathieson E
37094	"	Griffin A J	31696	"	McDade F
32088	"	Griffin S	31397	"	McGregor C
33056	"	Groves C H	31376	"	McIntyre J
32209	"	Guthrie H	31042	"	McKenzie A
31465	"	Hadden D	31063	"	McKillen C
31508	"	Harbard G	32034	"	Moore L
31615	"	Harmer D	32189	"	Mossman J
31509	"	Harris J	31497	"	Newsham E
34981	"	Harrison R	31791	"	O'Hara J A
31510	"	Haslam A	31648	"	Parker G
34994	"	Hector A M	31033	"	Passman H
37099	"	Hillyer W W	31772	"	Paul G
57357	"	Hindmarch J M	37170	"	Pearson N
27680	"	Hilliard A R	32120	"	Pearson J
57403	"	Holden W	31474	"	Perry C W
31253	"	Isaac R	50202	"	Philips J B
32337	"	Johnstone J J	32649	"	Philip J C
31428	"	Jones G A	31863	"	Preston E
31614	"	Jones H H	32972	"	Raines W
39797	"	Keen A H	31449	"	Randall E J
31425	"	King W	39685	"	Ratcliff R J
31257	"	Knowles J	32971	"	Ress W
31712	"	Kynaston A H	30818	"	Rimmer J
60067	"	Kennedy J H	39675	"	Roberts E H
32156	"	Lackin J	32659	"	Robertson D
45149	Pte	Larke L B	33327	"	Robinson J H

30361	"	Rose J.J.N				
31172	"	Rose W				
32974	"	Rumball P				
31925	"	Ryfter H				
32879	"	Shenis P				
32136	"	Sherwood A.J				
32187	"	Shuttleworth H				
32475	"	Slade H.P.				
44466	"	Smirfitt F				
32984	"	Southern G				
53906	"	Southwell F				
31302	"	Speel H				
32449	"	Storey L.				
5209	"	Stockley E				
31495	"	Townend A				
32988	"	Traill W				
31305	"	Tree E.J				
57442	"	Trow C				
31809	"	Ward A				
40175	"	Ward E				
31371	"	Watkins H				
30692	"	Weatherhead S.E.W.				
31517	"	White W				
33197	"	Whyte J				
4007	"	Whitrow W.H				
40262	"	Wilson W				
34285	"	Wright F.H				

No. 44 FIELD AMBULANCE
ROYAL ARMY MEDICAL CORPS

Capt RAMC
pro OC 44 Fd Amb

Nominal Roll of N.C.O.'s and men
A.S.C. M.T. att'd 44 Fd Amb'ce
19th Dec 1915

No	Rk	Name
M2/3975	Sgt	Cole A
M2/104907	A/Sgt	Houghton A
M2/055169	Cpl	Bruce G H
M2/106121	Pte	Church G W
M2/055505	"	Hinton W H
M2/08634	"	Lingett A S
M2/055213	"	Nicholls D H R
M2/055129	"	Padleigh P
M2/055215	"	Pipkin J
M2/018532	"	Smith J E
M2/20805	"	Smith J P
M2/054567	"	Spencer G W
M2/080593	"	Todd J
M2/046655	"	Vesey G
M2/054570	"	Wright G H
M2/053850	"	Wright J W

Capt RAMC
for OC 44 Fd Amb

Nominal Roll of the ASC attached to
44th Field Ambulance RAMC 19 Dec /15

No.	Rk	— Name —	No	Rk	— Name —
T/987	S/Mjr	Corps J W	T/11309	Dr.	Smith J
T/1018	Sgt	Harvey A	T/272	"	Snell C H
T/016446	"	Bowmar C L	T/128800	"	Stewart F
T/2150	"	Broad C H	T/10475	"	Stuart A J
S/4605	Shoeing Smth	Moxon A E	T/36015	"	Taylor A A
S/6442	"	Clevenshaw J	T/16013	"	Taylor J
T/027029	Cpl	Shackleton J	T/091755	"	Tommey J
T/02309	L Cpl	Wood C H	T/064388	"	Turley W
T/12394	Dr	Ackland J	T/4451	"	Virgo G S
	"	Ashford E	WT/069862	"	Warron W
	"	Aston W	T/SR567	"	Waterhouse A V
	"	Boyes R E	T/27575	"	Wilmott C E
	"	Belton E	T/628	"	Whitaker J
	"	Capon W	T/17559	"	Wicks A J
	"	Carroll J	SR929	"	Wray X
	"	Carter C E			
	"	Cattrell A			
	"	Cooley E			
	"	Dolphin A			
	"	Griffith D			
	"	Hayden P			
	"	Hopkins A			
	"	Hutchinson W			
	"	King J			
	"	Lewin F G			
	"	Lloyd W			
	"	Louden W			
	"	Lowe V			
	"	Miller H			
	"	Owen P			
T/016774	"	Raeburn A			
T/480	"	Ricketts F			
T/017307	"	Schofield W D			
T/1742	"	Shuttleworth S H			
T/271	"	Simson J			

No. 44 FIELD AMBULANCE
ROYAL ARMY MEDICAL CORPS

Capt RAMC
OC 44 Fd Amb

44th F.A.
Vol. 9

14th Division

F / 144 / 2

44 F A

S January 1916

"Confidential"

War Diary
— of —
44th Field Ambulance

From Jan 1st to Jan 31st/16.
(Volume 6.)

WAR DIARY or INTELLIGENCE SUMMARY

Army Form C. 2118

Place	Date	Hour	Summary of Events and Information	Remarks and references to Appendices
POPERINGHE	1/1/16	10pm	Adm. 5 { off / 120 on. to CCS 21. H.O.P.S 9 to batty 11 duty 21. 91. SRS cases transferred to 10 CCS. H.O. E.D ROVER. Attended Corps Conference at 8.30 - discussion re gas Regt MO's 11th Div. Gas gun experiences - helmets satisfactory if put on quick. Some cases recorded of men being asphyxiated during day of gas attack and collapsing in convoys to No 8. The army state that French had found antidote of little use unless given at once. Retreat bearers of 2nd dorsets to night.	
do	2/1/16	9pm	S. to wound Down - Adm. 2 off. CCS off L. duty 15. 56 OR. OR 22. 43rd F.A. medical instructions from A.D.M.S. took over collection of Capt Spector Wright, cars only proceeded to dug out near ROBT FARM. 3 motor Amb: of 63rd FA. sent back.	

Place	Date	Hour	Summary of Events and Information	Remarks and references to Appendices
POP	3/1/16	10 p.m.	Adv 95. 1 O.S. 22 & BRS 5. duty 22. Large numbers of kyds pyrexia — with pains all over either influenza or paratyphoid B. Lieut FOSTER RAMC proceeded on leave temporarily with 9th KCR & MARSHALL returned from temp. duty with 9th KCR. Wrote up myself to collect tonight — found engineers were making new dug out next to adv. coll post. Saw G.O.C. 151st Inf. 13 DB arranged that up at crossways to K.K. & I.A. to sent through L.S. R.Q.O Signals to 432 I.A. in camp at A. 23. R & C. as well as through Div signals. also organised that when apply for sprayers, cole two weight be sent in Dec. with divis orders. Capt SCOTT. soon after returning Capt HOOD this evening fell on bridge & and fractured right tibia. Sent Lieut BROSTER in relief. Wind S.W. Stop fine. Capt F.G. FLOOD & Capt R.R. ATKINS officers of this unit mentioned in recent dispatches.	

WAR DIARY
or
INTELLIGENCE SUMMARY

(Erase heading not required.)

Army Form C. 2118

Instructions regarding War Diaries and Intelligence Summaries are contained in F. S. Regs., Part II. and the Staff Manual respectively. Title Pages will be prepared in manuscript.

Place	Date	Hour	Summary of Events and Information	Remarks and references to Appendices
P.P.	4/1/16	7pm	Adm. Off: 1 to C.C.S. Off: 1 St.S.5. Aug 17 O.R. 101. O.R. 21. Cold & showery. In afternoon sent 60 cases & 7 2nd P.A. who however returned to D.R.S Lieut GRANT reported return from duty with 6th Shr. L.Y.	
do	5/1/16	10pm	Adm. 50 to C.C.S. Off: 1 to St.S.107 to St.S.36. O.R. 33. O.R. 35. As daily two be helmet parade under Lieut MARSHALL all men to attend two parades a week. reliefs carried out at collecting post and and posts at present there is 1 Off. 1 Sergt 4 men at Adv. Coll. Post 4 bearers at GLIMPSE COTTAGE aid post. every 3 weeks. 4 bearers at LANCASHIRE FARM " " " 4 bearers at BOAR LANE " " "	
do	6/1/16	7pm	Adm. 51 Off. to C.C.S. 32 Sent 1 duty 13. O.R. 53. Motor Lorry Helden taken in charge - Lieutenant they reported for duty.	

1875 Wt. W593/826 1,000,000 4/15 J.B.C. & A. A.D.S.S./Forms/C. 2118.

WAR DIARY or INTELLIGENCE SUMMARY

Army Form C. 2118

Place	Date	Hour	Summary of Events and Information	Remarks and references to Appendices
POPERINGHE	7/1/16	7pm	Adm. { Off. 4 OR. 85 } to CCS 11. BTRS. 5 duty 2. Remaining { Off. 6 OR. 102 }	
do	8/1/16		Capt DENVER reported his departure to take over command of 17th to Amb. 17th division. 7 reinforcements arrived and taken on strength.	
			Adm { Off. 3 OR. 99 } to CCS { Off. 1 OR. 17 } BTRS 50 & duty 8 Rem. 111	
			Ordered to march for tracers there times a week. Received operation order No 11 from 17th Div. 44 to FA to take over 6 to 8 siv a day out in canal bank and post traces at aid post at LA BELLE ALLIANCE as there is no room for bearers posted to ROAR LANE. Motor bearers ordered to LA BELLE ALLIANCE. All Tracers are relieved every 4th day. Was obtained authority for issue of 15 gum boots thigh	
do	9/1/16	10pm	Adm. { Off. 1 OR. 52 } to CCS. 22 BTRS. 86 & duty 24 Rem. 24	
			Lieut BROST & R proceeded to canal bank this morning to take over medical of 8 KRR.	

WAR DIARY
or
INTELLIGENCE SUMMARY

Army Form C. 2118

(Erase heading not required.)

Place	Date	Hour	Summary of Events and Information	Remarks and references to Appendices
Pop.	9/11/16		Extract from D.R.O. 1687 of 8.16. a Card for gallant & meritorious service has been awarded to — 3,667 Sergt R. EASTHAM. R.A.M.C.	
do	10/11/16	7pm	Adm. 57 & ces. off & 642 Y.A.6 duty off OR. 16. OR. 11. BRIELEN forward collecting post been relieved by 1 h. Amb. 1 h.c.o and 2 men (2 drivers & 1 orderly in addn. on car) Lieut MARSHALL returns Lieut BROWN in charge of adm. collecting posts. One car sent to base today with two drivers M/2 070 Pte SMITH JP & M/2 0/5/322 Pte SMITH J.F. struck off strength. Rec C.M. NEERS (CF) Wesleyan . reported arrival in relief to Rev. MARTIN	
do	11/11/16	10.30	Adm. off & 2 & ces. 54 & 642 Y.A 5. duty 4 Res. 118. OR. eq. 94. Spent day at H.Q of div. enquiring for A.D.M.S. sent to C.R.E.'s office & reported bad state of BRIELEN road used by our cars — record requisition note for 100 trench boards for improving co.	

Army Form C. 2118

WAR DIARY
or
INTELLIGENCE SUMMARY
(Erase heading not required.)

Place	Date	Hour	Summary of Events and Information	Remarks and references to Appendices
Pop.	12/1/16	7 pm	Adm. ST2. OR to CCS { Off 2, OR 2 } Off. 34 to DRS. 50 L. wd 7A Q. duty {off 2, OR 11}. O.C. L2 wd 7A called and we arranged for transfer of cases to DRS. - cyclist to call every evening at 6 pm to report on accommodation. Rev Martin J.A.H. (CF) reported his departure ex-struck off the strength. (Boulogne)	
"	13/1/16	6 —	Adm {SB. OR, Nil Off} to CCS {15 OR, Nil Off} to DRS (42nd 4A) 47 duty {15 OR, Died 1 OR}. Lieut. Knott relieves Lieut. Marshall at Adv. Coll. Post (Essex Farm). 30692 Pte. S.E.W. Heathhead R.A.M.C. departed this date to England to be commissioned + struck off the strength from this date. Reliefs, carried out at 8 pm. Collecting post (Essex Farm) - Ptes. Eaton, Stockley, Bucknell, + Chalke. B " - (Glimpse Cottage) - Hannon, Parker, Chaffey, + Aspland. C " - (Lancashire Farm) - Holden, Preston, Green, + Linton. D " - (La Belle Alliance) - Phillips JB, Guthrie, Low, + Gilmore. Collecting post relief carried out Sgt. Richardson, Pte. Emery, Pte. Lowell, Pte. Bruckin adv. coll. post.	

WAR DIARY
or
INTELLIGENCE SUMMARY

(Erase heading not required.)

Army Form C. 2118

Instructions regarding War Diaries and Intelligence Summaries are contained in F.S. Regs., Part II. and the Staff Manual respectively. Title Pages will be prepared in manuscript.

Place	Date	Hour	Summary of Events and Information	Remarks and references to Appendices
Pop.	13/1/16		Arrival. T/4605, Wheelwright Moxon A.E., A.S.C. reported his arrival from 8 days furlough to England (3rd – 10th inclusive) 12.1.16.	
"	14/1/16	7 p.m	Adm. { 66 O.R / 2 Off } to CCS { 13 O.R / 2 Off } to D.R.S. 19 O.R. to 42nd F.Amb 10 O.R. to duty { 29 O.R / 1 Off }. Arrival. Temp: Capt. H. Monro. R.A.M.C. reported his arrival for duty, taken on the strength 7.1.14.	
"	15/1/16	5 p.m	Adm { 66 O.R / 1 Off } to CCS 14 O.R. to D.R.S. 31 O.R. to 42nd F.A. 19 O.R. to duty 2 O.R. Relief. S/Sgt Warner proceeded to Essex Farm dugout at 8 pm relieves Sgt Corbishley.	
"	16/1/16	6 p.m	Adm { 74 O.R / 3 Off } to CCS { 20 O.R / 1 Off } to D.R.S. 20 O.R. to 42nd F.A. 10 O.R. to duty { 24 O.R / 1 Off }. Relief. Capt Monro relieved Lieut Grant at advanced collecting post. The following relief were carried out at 10 A.M. Bridge Alt. Coll. Post. Sgt Robinson & Fothergill Knipe. Arrival. M/2 074914 Pte Killinger H. A.S.C. reported for duty, taken on the strength from this date. Promotion. C.S.Majr Corps. W. A.S.C. is promoted to acting Staff Sgt Majr with A.A.S.A. from 13/28/15	
"	17/1/16	6 p.m	Adm { 77 O.R } to CCS 29 O.R. to D.R.S. 10 O.R. to 42nd F.A. 16 O.R. to duty { 111 O.R / 2 Off }. Departure. Lieut Col H. Simson reported his departure on 8 days leave to Eng. (17th – 24th incl.) 17/1/16	

WAR DIARY
or
INTELLIGENCE SUMMARY

(Erase heading not required.)

Army Form C. 2118

Instructions regarding War Diaries and Intelligence Summaries are contained in F.S. Regs., Part II. and the Staff Manual respectively. Title Pages will be prepared in manuscript.

Place	Date	Hour	Summary of Events and Information	Remarks and references to Appendices
Toph.	17/1/16	6 p	Departure 32551 Sgt Sutton J. RAME. 31428 Pte Jones G.A. RAME., 32679 Pte Robertson D. RAME. 32772 Pte Rainer W. RAME. + T/24451 Dr Virgo G.S. ASC. Granted 8 days furlough Eng (17-24th incl.) 17.1.16.	
	18/1/16	5 pm	Adm. { 99 O.R. to CCS 19 O.R. to DRS. 10.O.R. to 5th Yorks. 27. O.R. totals { 1 off. 2 o/r	
			Relief. Lieut Barton relieves Capt Monro at 1.45 P.M. Capt Monro will take over DR Service from Lt. Marshall	
	19/1/16	6 -	Duties Lieut Marshall takes over charge of DRS crews from Lieut Barton.	
			Relief. The following reliefs carried out at 8 p.m. D/WM Parke (Evans Farm) Pte Bannockm, Williams, Griffiths, Kerr, Rainie, Johnston, Innis, + Steel (B) hut (Shrapnel Cnr) O/C Apps, Hannam, Levett, + Southern. C hut (Somerville F.) Pte Broomhoot, Jennings, Jeavon, Roberts R.W. D hut (Le Bell All.) Pte { Jennings, Bradshaw, O'Hara.	
			Adm. { 86 O.R. to CCS 21. O.R. to 42. Y.A. 80. O.R. to 17th Y.A. 1.O.R. totals { 4 off. 1 o/r	
		5 pm	Arrival. Lieut. J.G. Shoahan. RAMC. reported his arrival this date. Taken on the strength 19th	
			Relief. The following relief carried out 10 pm. Bombdr Air Post Sgt Macdonald, O/C { Eke, Stenio, Sgt Cook. relieves Bof Warner at Evans Farm. Dugout at 8 pm.	
	20/1/16	6.30 pm	Adm. 76 O.R. to CCS { 26 O.R. to DRS 7 O.R. to 42nd 4 O.R. to Bucks. hp. 1 O.R. totals { 3 O.R. 2 o/r 3 o/r	
			Departure. 55143 Pte Jackson J.B. evacuated sick out of area, 19th. Lieut Marshall name was submitted to ADMS as requested, for instruction in "Gas".	

Army Form C. 2118

WAR DIARY
or
INTELLIGENCE SUMMARY
(Erase heading not required.)

Instructions regarding War Diaries and Intelligence Summaries are contained in F.S. Regs., Part II. and the Staff Manual respectively. Title Pages will be prepared in manuscript.

Place	Date	Hour	Summary of Events and Information	Remarks and references to Appendices
Poperinghe	21/6/16	6 pm	Adm { 63 OR. to CCS {11 OR to 42" FA Amb 3 OR. To duty 4. 8. R. { 1 off. } { 1 off. }	
			Arrival M/2/080593 Pte Todd 4/E. ASC. MT. reported his arrival from 8 days furlough to England (10-17th)	
			Estaminet Blanke Linde (about 27) F.7, c 2.5. just out of bounds for troops until further orders. from 19 inst.	
			Relieved. Advanced Coll. Post. Capt Hood relieved Lieut Baxter.	
			The following reliefs took place at 8 pm.	
			Adv. Coll. Post. (Essex Farm) Pte Haslam, Elliot, Earley, Knowles, Greenwood, Hall, Storey, r. Henderson.	
			B Post (Glimpse Cottage) Ptes Cooney, Page, Southwell, + Palmer	
			C. Post (Lancashire Farm) Ptes Lollop, Upton, Philip, SC, + Cox.	
			D Post (La Belle Alliance) Pte Rimmer, Thomas, Pearson, H. Gordon.	
			Departure. Rev C.S. Drewnah (CF) C.F.E. reported his departure to proceed to War Office, London on mobilisation this date.	
			Adm { 64 OR to CCS { 13 OR to DRS 20. OR. to 43rd FA Amb 1 OR. t17th FA 2 OR. { 2 off. } { 2 off. }	
22/6/16			Arrival 2/021211 Pte Ross E.C. ASC. reported his arrival for duty, more taken on the strength on 21/6/16	
		11.30 pm.	Bright moonlight. Enemy aeroplane circled town when defect 7 bombs, killing 1 Belgium + 1 Eng. soldier.	
			Adm { 81 OR. tr CCS { 40 OR to DRS. { 68 OR. tr 43rd FA. 7 OR. To duty { 20 OR { 2 off. } { 2 off. } { 1 off. }	
			Brown took over charge of Divisional Baths.	

1875 W.J.W 901/326 1,070,000 4/15 J.B.C. & A. A.D.S.S./Forms/C. 2118.

WAR DIARY
or
INTELLIGENCE SUMMARY
(Erase heading not required.)

Army Form C. 2118

Place	Date	Hour	Summary of Events and Information	Remarks and references to Appendices
Poperinghe	24/1/16	6 PM	Adm { 62 OR. to CCS { 26 OR. {1. Off to DRS 20. OR. to 42nd F.A. 20 OR. died 1 OR. to duty { 11 OR {1. Off	
			Relief. Lieut Marshall returned Capt. Floret at advanced collecting post at 8 pm	
	25/1/16	5 PM	Adm { 91 OR to CCS { 10 OR 1st DRS 1. OR. to 43rd F.A. 11. OR. to duty 4 OR. {3. Off {1 Off	
			Reliefs. The following ratify list places at 10 am. Brielen. Sgt Richardson. Ptes { Bullock, McIntyre	
			The following ratify list place at 8 PM	
			Auto Coll Post (Essex Farm) Ptes Allum (cook) Moorsman (runner) orderly Gunners J.A. Fox, Johnson, McKinley, Harrison & Lovett	
			B four (Hospital Battery) Ptes Hannen, Parker, Philip, B, Keen	
			C post (Chemical Twos) Ptes Chalk, Green, Prector, Cumming	
			D post (La Belle Alliance) Ptes Emery, Grover, Anderson, Phillips A.J.	
	26/1/16	9 PM	Adm { 62. OR. to CCS 15. OR. to DRS. 30. to 42nd F.A. 17 OR. to 43rd F.A. 20 OR. to duty 10	
			Divisional T/2 - 4451 Dr. Vingo G.S. ASC arrived back from furlough to England 8 days (17-24)"	
			Officer 19113 Pte Lamont J. Coy 4. 1st Lincolns attached to 42nd F.A. arrived 7 Jan. 26th	
			He proceeded to No 2. Advanced from duty without leave 7.15 am — 8.30 p.m. 1.15 P.M.	
	27/1/16		Adm { 91. OR. to CCS { 0. OR. to DRS 30. OR. to 43rd F.A. 29. OR. to duty { 8. OR. {1. Off {1. Off	
			Relief Lt Lamont returned Lt Marshall at Adv Coll. Post at 8 pm. Sgt Cookrill	
			Sgt Cockrell at Essex Farm Auto Coll: Post.	

WAR DIARY
or
INTELLIGENCE SUMMARY

Army Form C. 2118

Place	Date	Hour	Summary of Events and Information	Remarks and references to Appendices
Poperinghe	28/1/16	8 pm	Adm. {107 OR, 1 Off.} to CCS {13 OR, 1 Off.} to DRS 30 OR, to 42nd FA 10 OR, to 42nd FA 17 OR, duty 5 OR.	
			Relief. Sgt Sutton & Pte Ravenhead & Southwell relieve Pte Newman at Brielen at P.O.	10 A.M. 28.1.16
	29/1/16	7 pm	Adm: 73 OR. to CCS 18 OR. to DRS 44 OR. to 3rd FA 15 OR. to 42nd FA 17 OR. duty 21 OR.	
			Relief.	
			Arrival. Lt. & 2nd Lieut. Yoxall.G reported his arrival from three weeks leave to England (3rd – 28th incl.)	
	30/1/16	8 pm	Adm. {100 OR, 1 Off.} to CCS {14 OR, 1 Off.} to DRS 31 OR. to 42nd FA 5 OR. to 43rd FA 17 OR. duty 7 OR.	
			Relief. Lieut Shanahan relieves Lieut Grant at 8 pm.	
	31/1/16	6 pm	Adm {72 OR, 2 Off.} to CCS {17 OR, 1 Off.} to DRS 40 OR. to 42nd 10 OR. to 43rd 6 OR. duty 4 OR.	
			Relief. Sgt Brown relieves Sgt Sutton at Brielen. Sgt Southern relieves Sgt Watson at Evan Farm	

Confidential.

War Diary
of
414 Field Ambulance

from 1st February to 29th February, 1916.

Volume 10.

Army Form C. 2118

WAR DIARY
or
INTELLIGENCE SUMMARY
(Erase heading not required.)

Instructions regarding War Diaries and Intelligence Summaries are contained in F. S. Regs., Part II. and the Staff Manual respectively. Title Pages will be prepared in manuscript.

Place	Date	Hour	Summary of Events and Information	Remarks and references to Appendices
Poperinghe	1/2/16	7pm	Adm. 88.OR. to CCS.12.OR. to DRS 10.OR. to 43"4A.B.OR. total 7	
			Relief. Capt Yeo relieves Lieut Strachan at Essex Farm. 1/2/16	
			Evacuation. Ptes Blake & Macphype evacuated sick 1/2/16	
	2/2/16	8.pm	Adm. {72.OR {2.Off} to CCS {17.OR {1.Off} to DRS. 40.OR. to 42"4 4A.10.OR. to 43"4A.B.OR. total 40.OR.	
			Relief. The following reliefs were carried out. The bearers at Essex Farm & the Reg Aid Posts	
	3/2/16	9 pm	Adm {100.OR {1.Off} to CCS {14.OR {2.Off} to DRS.31.OR. to 42nd 4A.5.OR. to 43"4 17.OR total 70.OR	
			Relief. Sgt Cough relieves Sgt Brannon at 10am at Brielen and pm.	
	4/2/16	8pm	Adm. 70.OR. to CCS 17.OR. to DRS.14.OR. to 43"4A.13.OR. to 17 4A. 3.OR. total 11.OR.	
	6/2/16	4.pm	Adm. 63.OR. to CCS. 18.OR to DRS 20.OR. to 42"4A. 1.OR. to 43"4A B.OR total 12.OR	
			Relief Capt. Owen R.O.w.c. relieved Capt. Perry R.O.w.c. by O.C 4th F.A. Capt Yeo	
			relieves Capt Munro as observers approved. Pte Williams 5.9692 - Pte Williams 48513	
			Pte Ridley 43663. reported for duty. G - Ungstveini has proceeded to Hazebrouck to MT Column	
			Corps. MS.13945. Sgt Cole M.T. & SC. 45749. Pte Lache R.a.w.c. 33611. Pte Bull ret.	
	7/2/16	6.pm	R.O.w.c	
			Adm- 51.OR. to CCS.16.OR. to DRS 10.OR. to 43"4A 1.OR. to 43 FA 11.OR. total 9.OR. 1.Officer	
			Relief. Sgt Richardson awa D.O.R. relieves Sgt Cool. awa 2.O.R. at Brielen A Post.	
	4/2/16	7.Pm	Adm. 1Officer. 43.O.R. to CCS.20.O.R. to DRS. 23.OR. to 42"FA.1.OR. to 43"4A.14. W.duty. 20.OR.	
	8/2/16	4.pm	Adm. Major Davies reports for duty awa M.O. Pates awa 4th Diving.	
	9/2/16	4.pm	Adm. 2 officer 75.O.R. to CCS 4 Officer 25.O.R. to D.R.C. 22.O.R. to 43 FA 13.O.R total 2offices 2OR	
			Adm. 60.OR. to CCS. 23.OR. to DRS.21. & 43 FA 13. total 4	

1875 Wt. W593/826 1,000,000 4/15 J.B.C. & A. A.D.S.S./Forms/C. 2118.

WAR DIARY
or
INTELLIGENCE SUMMARY
(Erase heading not required.)

Army Form C. 2118

Place	Date	Hour	Summary of Events and Information	Remarks and references to Appendices
Poperinghe	10/2/16	5:P.M.	Adm 3 officers 39 O.R. to CCS. 1 officer 23 O.R. to 43 F.A. 10 R. to 42 F.A. 11 O.R. to Spec Hosp Boulogne 1 O.R. 16 July 1 O.R.	
	11/2/16	6.P.M.	Adm. 2 officers 35 O.R. to CCS. 1 officer 40 R. to O.R.S. 12 O.R. to 43 F.A. 9 O.R. to 17 F.A. 1 O.R. to duty 2. Captain Moore - Rawe. and Lt Boat. Rawe 42nd F.A. evacuated to 12 CCS	
	12/2/16	7.P.M.	Adm 4 officers 68 O.R. to CCS. 2 officers 31 O.R. to duty. 1 O.R. Lieut Hopkins reported for Trench duty. German Aeroplane dropped bombs on Pop below 5 & 6-7. 20 mi Shelling Moo Station.	
Mun gehe	13/2/16	9.P.M.	Adm. 4 officers 101 O.R. to CCS. 2 officers 25 O.R. to O.R.S. 2 officers 14 O.R. to 66 F.A. 3 officers 52 O.R. Relieves by 60th F.A. handover dressing station at Creep Popm(?) to d 9-30 pm 3 P.M. marched to Yarn 3 incl. N.W. Vian Zel counties at 4-45. Now billets in 3 Farms Onterleth.	
	14/2/16	8.P.M.	Adm. 3. O.R.	
	15/2/16	6.P.M.	Adm. 10.R. 15 CCS. 3. including 1 case of scales 15 CCS. Visit from A.D.M.S.	
	16/2/16	7.P.M.	Adm. 3 O.R. Br.Gl.Brown went over 14 Hosp. Loure	
	17/2/16	6 P.M.	Adm 1. O.R. Lieut 1.O.R.	
	18/2/16	6 P.M.	Adm 3 O.R. including 1 transfer from 42 F.A. to CCS. S.O.R.	
	19/2/16	5 O.M.	4 am S.O.R. to CCS 4 O.R. to duty 1 O.R.	
	20/2/16	7 P.M.	Adm 3.O.R. to CCS 2.O.R. to duty 5. Lieut Hyr purrier with motor Ambulance.	
	21/2/16	12-30 P.M.	Adm 5.O.R. to CCS. S.O.R.	
Vanniller	22/2/16	8.P.M.	Marched from billet at Farm 3 north by J. Meanings at 12 noon. Parker up B. Section of horse drawn cut 1.18 pm. arrived ...	

Army Form C. 2118.

WAR DIARY
or
INTELLIGENCE SUMMARY.
(Erase heading not required.)

Instructions regarding War Diaries and Intelligence Summaries are contained in F. S. Regs., Part II. and the Staff Manual respectively. Title pages will be prepared in manuscript.

Place	Date	Hour	Summary of Events and Information	Remarks and references to Appendices
Alouette	23/2/16	5 pm	Adm. 1 officer. 3 O.R. L.o.O.S. 1 officer. in billets in town —	
	24/2/16	9 pm	Adm. 9 O.R. tcos 11 O.R.	
	25/2/16	9 pm	Adm. 3 officer. 26 O.R. to 19 C.C.S. heavy fall of snow - march to Doullens - roads very bad. 3 officer 10 O.R. left Doullens at 11 A.M. in heavy snow storm - roads very bad — arrive at OPPY. 10 P.M. - No Particulars - or to J train on march. telesto for rig to OPPY	
Sombrin	26/2/16	6 P.M.	Adm. 3 O.R. L.o.C.S. 28 O.R. marched from OPPY 10. A.m. arrive SOMBRIN. 12.15. P.m. went into billets	
	27/2/16	7 P.m.	Adm. 11 O.R. L.o.C.S. 10.O.R. - Conference. at A.D.M.S. Sus Saint Leger -	
	28/2/16	11 PM.	Adm. 11 O.R. L.o.C.S. 9 O.R.	
	29/2/16	5 PM.	Adm. 2 officer. 28. O.R. tcos. 2 officer. 21. O.R.	

March 1916.

14th Div   44 F. Amb
            Vol 11

Confidential.

War Diary

of

44 Field Ambulance.

from 1st March 1916 to 31st March 1916

Volume 11.

WAR DIARY
or
INTELLIGENCE SUMMARY.
(Erase heading not required.)

Army Form C. 2118.

Instructions regarding War Diaries and Intelligence Summaries are contained in F.S. Regs., Part II. and the Staff Manual respectively. Title pages will be prepared in manuscript.

Place	Date	Hour	Summary of Events and Information	Remarks and references to Appendices
Somitieu	1/3/16	1 PM	Adm. 2 officer 26.O.R. & ccs. 2 officer 22.O.R. & duty 3.	
Torreux	2/3/16	5 PM	Adm. nil	
			& ccs. 3 O.R. & 43"A.F.A. 6 O.R. & duty 10 R.	
	3/3/16	6 PM	Adm. 10 officer 2 O.R.	
		3 PM	Adm. nil	
	4/3/16	4 PM	Adm. 2 O.R. & duty 1 officer	
	5/3/16	4 PM	Adm. nil & ccs. 10 R. & 43 F.A. 10 R.	
	6/3/16	10 AM	Adm. nil	
	7/3/16	1 PM	Adm. 10 O.R. & ccs. 6. & 43 F.A. 2. Moved to Torreux Chalier from Torreux Rd. I.T. Bienn, intimes	
Torreux Chaleur	8/3/16	7 PM	for duty, with 44 field Ambut benet.	
	9/3/16	2 PM	Adm. 10 O.R. & ccs. 6 A.R.	
	10/3/16	1 PM	Adm. 19 6 R & ccs. 3 O.R. to D.R.S. 10 R. opened D.R.S. at Torreux Chaleur.	
	11/3/16	6 PM	D.R.S. Adm. 32 O.R. & duty 5 O.R. — 44 Y.A. Adm. 4 O.R. & ccs. 4 O.R. & D.R.S. 10 R.	
			Both injured — attached for Duty as Sorrison M.O. Garrison. 3 tems from it. I.T. on Champs.	
	12/3/16	7 PM	Adm. 1 officer 30 R. & ccs. 1 officer 10 R. & duty 1 O.R. & D.R.S. 15 O.R. & ccs. 6 O.R. & duty 2 O.R.	
	13/3/16	2 PM	Adm. 2 O.R. & duty 3 O.R. Adm. D.R.S. 17 O.R. & duty 2 O.R.	
	14/3/16	1 PM	Adm. 1 officer 8 O.R. & ccs. 1 O.R. & D.R.S. 1 O.R. & ccs. 1 O.R. & duty 1 O.R. Adm. D.R.S. 32 O.R. & ccs. 20 R. Echay 11 R.	

Army Form C. 2118.

WAR DIARY
or
INTELLIGENCE SUMMARY.
(Erase heading not required.)

Instructions regarding War Diaries and Intelligence Summaries are contained in F. S. Regs., Part II. and the Staff Manual respectively. Title pages will be prepared in manuscript.

Place	Date	Hour	Summary of Events and Information	Remarks and references to Appendices
Loroux Ottou	15/3/16	2 pm	Adm - 26.O.R. & duty. 3.O.R. Adm. D.R.S. 58.O.R. & CCS. 2.O.R. to duty. 4.O.R.	JB
	16/3/16	4 pm	Adm. 11.O.R. & CCS. 4.O.R. to duty. 3.O.R. Adm. D.R.S. 36.O.R. & CCS. 40.R. to duty. 14.O.R.	JB
	17/3/16	5 pm	Adm. 40.R. to duty. D. D.R.S. Adm. 10 pm 54.O.R. & CCS. 3 O.R. to duty. 40.O.R.	JB
	18/3/15	6 pm	Adm. 10 pm. 40.R. & CC 10 pm 4.O.R. D.R.S. Adm 44 O.R. & CCS 9.O.R. to duty. 5.O.R	JB
	19/3/16	5 pm	Adm. 30.R. & D.R.S 10.R. to duty 40.R. D.R.S. Adm 62.O.R. & CCS 5.O.R. to duty 30.O.R.	JB
	20/3/16	4 pm	Adm. 30.O.R & duty. 6:O.R. - D.R.S - Adm 56.O.R. & CCS 14 to duty 23.O.R. Lieut. Hart & Johnston to duty as were tu on the Strength.	JB
	21/3/16	6 pm	Adm 40.R. & CCS 40.R. to duty 30.R. - D.R.S. adm. 27.O.R. & CCS 10.R. & 43.FA. 2.O.R. & 56? D.R.S. 10.R. to duty. 20.O.R. Capt Baylin for Club. with 4.K.R.R.	JB
	22/3/16	7 pm	Adm - 5.O.R. & CCS. 10.R to duty. 1.O.R. - D.R.S. Adm 10.R & CCS 18.O.R to duty - 17.O.R.	JB
	23/3/16	5 pm	Adm 9.O.R. & CCS. 40.R & to duty 5.O.R. D.R.S. Adm. 10.R. & CCS 80.R & duty 4/? 8.O.R	JB
			Lieut Ludlow E.D. Reported to duty as to be on the Strength - Lieut Oldell? J Shaw Levis & 42 F.A.	
	24/3/16	2 pm	Adm. 4.O.R. & CCS. 10.R. D.R.S. 2.O.R. to duty 2.O.R. - D.R.S. Adm. 20.R & CCS. 10.O.R & duty. 24.O.R.	JB
	25/3/16	4 pm	Capt. Storch Proceed on Leave. England. Adm. 4.O.R. & 56. D.R.S. 10.R. to duty. 3.O.R. D.R.S. Adm nil & CCS 30.R. & duty. 21.S.R.	JB
	26/3/16	2 pm	Adm. 10.O.R. & CCS. 10.R. & duty. 2.O.R. D.R.S. Adm nil & CCS. 10.R. to duty. 22.O.R.	JB
	27/3/16	4 pm	Adm. 8.O.R. & CCS. 10.R. & duty. 3.O.R. D.R.S. Adm. 90.O.R. 15 duty. 18.O.R.	JB
	28/3/16	5 pm	Adm. 6.O.R. & CCS. 20.R. to duty. 3.O.R. D.R.S. Adm. 15.O.R. & CCS. 10.R. & duty. 9.O.R.	JB

T2134. Wt. W708—776. 500000. 4/15. Sir J. C. & S.

WAR DIARY
or
INTELLIGENCE SUMMARY.

(Erase heading not required.)

Army Form C. 2118.

Place	Date	Hour	Summary of Events and Information	Remarks and references to Appendices
Forres Station	29/3/16	6pm	D.R.S. Adm. 15.O.R. to C.C.S. 5.O.R. to duty 15.O.R. F.A. adm. 4.O.R. to C.C.S. 10.R. to duty 9.O.R. & Capt. B.H. Borloui R.A.M.C. proceeded to England on sick leave.	ff
	30/3/16	4.pm	Adm. F.A. 4.O.R. to C.C.S. 10.offi. 4.O.R. to 42.F.A. 10.R. to duty 5.O.R. D.R.S. adm. nil to C.C.P. 10.R. to 42 F.A. 11.O.R. to duty 16.O.R.	ff
	31/3/16	6pm	Adm. 4.O.R. to duty 30.R. D.R.S. adm. 20.O.R. to C.C.S. 10.R. to duty 14.O.R.	ff

[signature] Capt R.A.M.C.
COMMANDING No. 44 FIELD AMBULANCE

14th Div 44 F Amb Vol 12

Confidential

War Diary of

44 Field Ambulance

for Period

1st to 30th April, 1916.

Volume 12.

April 1916.

WAR DIARY
or
INTELLIGENCE SUMMARY.
(Erase heading not required.)

Army Form C. 2118.

Instructions regarding War Diaries and Intelligence Summaries are contained in F. S. Regs., Part II. and the Staff Manual respectively. Title pages will be prepared in manuscript.

Place	Date	Hour	Summary of Events and Information	Remarks and references to Appendices
Fosseux	1/4/16	3 P.M.	Adm. F.A. 5.O.R. to C.C.S. 1. - to 42° F.A. 20.R. to duty. 3. D.R.S. adm. 2.O.R. to C.C.S. 1.7.O.R. to 42 F.A. 1.	
	2/4/16	6 P.M.	Adm. 40.R. to duty 40.R. D.R.S. Adm. 5.O.R. to C.C.S. 2.O.R. to duty. 24.	
	3/4/16	6 P.M.	Adm. 5.O.R. to C.C.S. 2.O.R. D.R.S. Adm. 1 officer 26.O.R. to C.C.S. 9.O.R. to duty. 1.O.R.	
	4/4/16	4 P.M.	Adm. 6.O.R. to C.C.S. 1.O.R. to 42.F.A. 1.O.R. to Hynd Hosp. Off Pol. 1.O.R. to duty. 2.O.R. D.R.S. Adm. 39.O.R. to C.C.S. 3.O.R. to duty. 26.O.R.	
	5/4/16	6 P.M.	Adm. 1 officer 3.O.R. to C.C.S. 1 officer 1.O.R. to duty. 5.O.R. D.R.S. adm. 6.O.R. to C.C.S. 2.O.R. to 42.F.A. 1.O.R. to duty 13.O.R.	
	6/4/16	6 P.M.	Adm. 4.O.R. to C.C.S. 2.O.R. to duty. 4.O.R. D.R.S. adm. 24.O.R. to C.C.S. 6.O.R. to duty. 17.O.R.	
	7/4/16	6 P.M.	Adm. 2 officers 5.O.R. to C.C.S. 3.O.R. to duty. 2.O.R. D.R.S. adm. 39.O.R. to C.C.S. 5.O.R. to duty. 22.O.R.	
	8/4/16	6 P.M.	adm. 3.O.R. to C.C.S. 2.O.R. to 42 F.A. 2.O.R. to duty. 3.O.R. D.R.S. Adm. 36.O.R. to C.C.S. 4.O.R. to duty. 5.2.O.R.	
	9/4/16	4 P.M.	Adm. 3.O.R. to C.C.S. 1.O.R. D.R.S. adm. 25.O.R. to C.C.S. 3.O.R. to duty. 18.O.R.	
	10/4/16	6 P.M.	Adm. 4.O.R. D.R.S. adm. 15.O.R. to C.C.S. 2.O.R. to duty. 9.O.R. to pont. prowds. on line to duty on	
	11/4/16	4 P.M.	Adm. 6.O.R. to Hynd Hosp. off Pol. 1.O.R. to duty. 3.O.R. D.R.S. adm. 10 officers 10.O.R. to C.C.S. 2.O.R. to 42 F.A. 1.O.R. to duty. 17.O.R.	

Army Form C. 2118.

WAR DIARY
or
INTELLIGENCE SUMMARY.
(Erase heading not required.)

Instructions regarding War Diaries and Intelligence Summaries are contained in F.S. Regs., Part II. and the Staff Manual respectively. Title pages will be prepared in manuscript.

Place	Date	Hour	Summary of Events and Information	Remarks and references to Appendices
Lozeux	12/4/16	6 p.m.	adm. 1 Offer. 4.O.R. t. Gewel. Hosp. H.R.of. 1.O.R. t. 42 F.A. 1.O.R. † 42 F.A. 1.O.R. D.R.S. adm. 18.O.R. † 42 F.A 1.O.R.	
	13/4/16	2 p.m.	adm. 2 Offers. 1.O.R. t.c.c.s. 3.O.R. t duel. 1.O.R D.R.S. adm. 25.O.R. t.c.c. 3.O.R. t duel. 15.O.R.	
	14/4/15	6 p.m.	adm. 6.O.R. t.c.c. 1.O.R. Echel. 4.O.R. D.R.S. adm. 60.O.R. t.c.c.s. 30.R † 42 F.A. 10.R. t duel. 24.O.R.	
	15/4/15	1 p.m.	adm. 10.R. t.c.c.s. 1.O.R. t duel. 3.O.R. D.R.S. adm. 13.O.R. t duel. 51.O.R. H. Ray on R.O.W.C. aspec. lift duty.	
	16/4/16	6 p.m.	adm. 3 Offers. 10.R. t.c.s. 1.O.R. (+ D.M.S. t. Boulogne) - 3.O.R duel. D.R.S. adm 13.O.R. t.c.c.s. 3.O.R. t duel. 51.	
	17/4/16	9 p.m.	adm. 5 O.R. t duel. 3 offers. 5.O.R. D.R.S. adm. 19 offers. 19.O.R. t.c.c.s. 6.O.R. t duel. 14.O.R.	
	18/4/16	4 p.m.	adm. 3.O.R. t.c.c. 10.R. t duel. 1. A.R.S. adm. 20.O.R. t.c.c.s. 3.O.R. Levi. 11.O.R. Leid. Liudar E.D. Rowe R. Returned fr. Temporary duty.	
	19/4/16	5 p.m.	adm. 1 Off. 9.O.R. t.c.c. 10.R. t 42 F.A. 10.R. D.R.S. adm. 1 Off. 10.R. t.c.c. 30.R. 4 days 10.R.	
	20/4/16	6 p.m.	adm. 2 Off. 4.O.R. t duel. 6.O.R. D.R.S. adm. 1 Off. 15.O.R. t.c.c.s. 4.O.R. t duel. 17.O.R.	
	21/4/15	6 p.m.	adm. 1.O.R. t duel. 1 off. 1.O.R. D.R.S. adm 30.O.R. t.c.c.i. 30.R. 4 duel. 9.O.R. Y.R. infr. march to Km. on Pl......p.m.	

Army Form C. 2118.

WAR DIARY
or
INTELLIGENCE SUMMARY.
(Erase heading not required.)

Instructions regarding War Diaries and Intelligence Summaries are contained in F. S. Regs., Part II. and the Staff Manual respectively. Title pages will be prepared in manuscript.

Place	Date	Hour	Summary of Events and Information	Remarks and references to Appendices
Hosseux	22/4/16	1 PM	adm 6.O.R. to dut. 3.O.R. DRS adm 35.O.R. to CCS. 3.O.R. Reinft 1 Officer 19.O.R.	
	23/4/16	6 PM	occu 1 off 1.O.R. I deal 3.O.R WRS occu 20.O.R to CCS 70 O.R. to Rolor H. 18.R. Evac 38. O.R.	
	24/4/16	6 PM	adm 3.O.R. to CCS 60R to 42 FA 1.O.R. to dut. 1 off. 1.O.R. DRS adm 40.O.R. to CCS 6 O.R.	
			to 42 FA 1.O.R. to dut. 20.O.R	
	25/4/16	7 PM	adm 6.O.R. to CCS 1.O.R. to dut. 2.O.R. DRL adm 15.O.R. to dut. 15.O.R.	
	26/4/16	3 PM	adm 6.O.R. to CCS. 10.R. to 42.FA. 202. Relies 10R. DRS adm 30.O.R. to CCS 3.O.R.	
			to 42 FA. 1.O.R. to evac 12. O.R.	
	27/4/16	7 PM	adm — 1.O.R. to CCS. 20/5 1.O.R. to DRS 1 off. to dut. 26. P. O. RS adm 5 Officer	
			20.O.R. to CCS 4 O.R. to 42.F.A. 1 O.R. to eve 38.O.R.	
	28/4/16	6 PM	adm — 4 O.R. to CCS. nil to DRS 1.O.R. to dut 2.O.R. DRS adm 1 Officer 21.O.R	
			to CCS 2.O.R. to dut 1 Off. 4.O.R.	
	29/4/16	5 PM	adm 2.O.R. to CCS. 1.O.R. to DRS nil to dut 3.O.R. DRS adm 1 off. 35.O.R. to CCS	
			to 5 O.R. to dut 1 off 19.O.R.	
	30/4/16	6 PM	adm 9.O.R. to CCS. 1O.R. to O.R.S nil to dut 3.O.R. DRS adm 1 off. 15.O.R. to CCS 2 off. 4.O.R. to dut 2 off 23 O.R.	

44. F Amb
Vol. 13

Confidential.

14th Div

War Diary
of
44 Field Ambulance
for period
1st to 31st May 1916.

Volume 13.

May 1916

Army Form C. 2118.

Instructions regarding War Diaries and Intelligence Summaries are contained in F. S. Regs., Part II. and the Staff Manual respectively. Title pages will be prepared in manuscript.

WAR DIARY
or
INTELLIGENCE SUMMARY.
(Erase heading not required.)

Place	Date	Hour	Summary of Events and Information	Remarks and references to Appendices
Lessars	1/3/16	6.30p	Major J. Cram VC, D.S.O. proceeded on leave to England. Lieut. Jenkins transferred for duty in charge S.E. of. Farm 30.	
			Adm. O.R. 3. D.R.S. Adm. O/1, O.R. 15; L.C.C.S. O.R. 3, L. duty O/11.	
	2/3/16	6.45p	Adm. arrived to C.C.S. 1 O.R.; D.R.S. Adm. 20 or. to C.C.S. Y or. to duty 1 off. 16 O.R.	
			Lieut. Hart proceeded on temporary duty with No. 1 F.A.	
"	3/3/16	6.45p	Capt. Munro BARNETT injured his foot doing P.T. Sent to Hynn & Sanders No. 1 at 6.45p for duty	
			Adm. 3 O.R. D.R.S. Adm. 2 off. 9 or. Dis. 2 or. to duty 18	
"	4/3/16	1 pm	Ptes Binns Marshall, Eke Hill were 3 Philip J.R. were appointed batmen to public vice off. for	
			as from 2nd May authority A.D.M.S. 16th Division	
			Adm. 30 or. to C.C.S. 1 O.R. to duty 3 O.R. D.R.S. Adm. 1 off. 10 or. to C.C.S. 1 off. 3 or.	
			to duty 1 off. 21 or.	
"	5/3/16	6.25p	Adm. 5 O.R. to C.C.S. 1 O.R. L. duty 5 O.R. D.R.S. Adm. 1 off. 30 or. L. C.C.S. 25 or.	
			to duty 19 or.	
"	6/3/16	6.15p	Capt. Walker transferred for duty with 4.E. Bn. R.F.A. on arrival of Sect. Jenkins who	
			on arrival from Field Ambulance to take on strength of 42nd Fd Amb.	
			2nd Lieut. N. Hart from Field Ambulance and duty of duty to 3 Bn. R.F.A.	
			Reffer: Trans. Infantry to duty 2 O.R.	

T2134. Wt. W708—776. 500000. 4/15. Sir J. C. & S.

Army Form C. 2118.

WAR DIARY
or
INTELLIGENCE SUMMARY.
(Erase heading not required.)

Instructions regarding War Diaries and Intelligence Summaries are contained in F. S. Regs., Part II. and the Staff Manual respectively. Title pages will be prepared in manuscript.

Place	Date	Hour	Summary of Events and Information	Remarks and references to Appendices
Frévent	6/9/16	6.10pm	Capt the G.O. 5 officers & other ranks of 2/1st Wessex Field Ambulance SS Section arrived. Went to dispatch orders but got lost thro' ignorance of road. Adm. 5 O.R. to CCS 60 R, 42nd F.Amb 20 R. to duty 20 R, D.R.S. Adm 19 ff 30 O.R. to CCS 3 O.R. to 42nd F.Amb 4 O.R. to duty 27 O.R.	
Frévent	7/9/16	6.14pm	Lieut Boyd reported his arrival for duty today. Adm 19 ff 30 O.R. to CCS 1 O.R. to 42nd F.Amb 10 O.R. to duty 2 O.R. D.R.S. Adm 10 O.R. to CCS 4 O.R. to duty 10 ff 27 O.R.	
Frévent	8/9/16	7.0pm	Lieut Grant relieved Lieut Hart for temporary duty with the 4th R.B.R. Adm. 5 O.R. to duty 1 O.R. D.R.S. Adm 10 ff 20 O.R. to CCS 30 R. to duty 10 O.R. Capt Boyden proceeded on leave to England.	
Frévent	9/9/16	6.45pm	149 O.R. transferred from Frévent to Lievarest, 2nd R.B. Section of 800 Zn ambulances went to Lievarest. Adm 0 R 2 to CCS 0 R 2 to duty 19ff 10 R. D.R.S. Adm 15 O.R. to CCS 17 O.R. to 42 F.Amb 2 O.R. to duty 9 O.R.	
Lievarest	10/9/16	6.30pm	Frévent Château & grounds handed over to 2/1 Wessex Field Ambulance. All officers & patients transferred to them. Remainder of the Unit marched to Lievarest & took over the Camp & huts of 2/1 Hants Field Amb.	

WAR DIARY
or
INTELLIGENCE SUMMARY.
(Erase heading not required.)

Army Form C. 2118.

Place	Date	Hour	Summary of Events and Information	Remarks and references to Appendices
Lucheux	10/5/16	6.30 pm	Cont	
			Adm. 6 O.R. to CCS. 1 O.R. to 2/1 Western field Amb. 2 Offrs. D.R.S. Adm. 20 O.R. to CCS. 1 O.R. to 2/1 Western field amb. 6 off to duty 3 offs 2 O.R. Lieut Booth proceeded on temporary duty to G.H.Q H.S.	
Lucheux	11/5/16	6.30 pm	Lieut Hart proceeded to H.Q. 3rd Army for a 3 course. Adm. 2 O.R. to CCS. 1 O.R. to duty 2 O.R. D.R.S. Adm. 30 O.R. to CCS. 5 O.R. to duty 20 O.R.	
	12/5/16	6 P.M.	Adm. 4 O.R. & CCS. 1 O.R. & D.R.S. 6 O.R. & duty. 5 O.R. D.R.S. Adm. 6 O.R. & CCS. 3 O.R. to duty. 20 O.R. Major & Beau Rowe returned from leave in England.	
	13/5/16	5 Pm	Adm. 11 O.R. & CCS 10 R. to duty. 1 O.R. D.R.S. Adm. 24 O.R. & CCS. 3 O.R. & duty 14 O.R.	
	14/5/16	6 Pm	Adm. 6 O.R. & CCS. 2 O.R. & 42 F.A. 1 O.R. & duty. 2 O.R. D.R.S. Adm 9 O.R. & CCS 6 O.R. & duty – 6 O.R	
	15/5/16	6 Pm	Adm 14 O.R. & CCS. 1 O.R. & duty – 2 O.R. D.R.S. Adm 8 O.R. & CCS. 4 O.R. & duty. 8 O.R.	
	16/5/16	5 Pm	Adm. 11 O.R. & CCS. 1 O.R. & D.R.S. 6 O.R. & duty 4 O.R. D.R.S. Adm. 19 6.R. & CCS. 5 O.R. & 42" F.A. 2 O.R. & duty 9 O.R. Lieut Baul – Rawc reported to duty.	
	17/5/16	5 PM	Adm 18 O.R. & duty 2 O.R. D.R.S. Adm 22 O.R. & CCS 26 R. & duty 9 O.R.	
	18/5/16	6 Pm	Lieut Booth Rawc proceeded to England on leave on completion of tour service. Adm. 11 O.R. & duty 1 O.R. D.R.S. Adm 5 O.R. & CCS 1 O.R. & duty – 20 O.R. Capt Stona detailed for duty rank of 9 D.B.	

WAR DIARY
or
INTELLIGENCE SUMMARY.
(Erase heading not required.)

Army Form C. 2118.

Place	Date	Hour	Summary of Events and Information	Remarks and references to Appendices
Lillers	19/5/15	6pm	adm 8.O.R. & D.R.C. H.O.R. & Prevd. Hosp. 81. Pol. 1.O.R. & duly. 8.O.R.	
			D.R.S. adm. 11.O.R. & duly. Y.O.R.	
	20/5/16	5 P.m.	adm 1. officer. 10.O.R. & C.C.S. 1 officer. 30.R. & 42.F.A. 20.R. D.R.S. adm. 19. & C.C.S. 3 O.R.	
			& 42 F.A. 1 officer & duty. 9.6.R.	
	21/5/16	6 P.m.	adm 4 O.R. & C.C.S. 2 O.R. & 42 F.A. 2 O.R. & duty. 6. O.R. & C.C.S. 1 O.R. & duty. 116 R.	9/6.
	22/5/16	6 P.m.	adm 3. O.R. D.R.S. adm nil. & C.C.S. 1.O.R. & duly. 3.O.R.	
	23/5/16	6 P.m.	adm 12 O.R. & C.C.S. 1. O.R. D.R.S. 1 officer 14. O.R. adm — & C.C.S. 8.O.R. Cpl. Lequell returned to duty ac	
			& Hos. 2/1 Q.H. Wessex F.A. 1 officer & duly. 4.O.R. Cpl. Lequell returned to duty ac	
			inc ob/nes of Bomy throw in England —	
	24/5/16	3 P.m.	adm 2.O.R. & C.C.S. 2.O.R. & D.R.S. 11.O.R. & 42.F.A. 3.O.R. & duly. 2.O.R. D.R.S. adm 1 officer	4/4.
			19.O.R. & C.C.S. 1. O.R. & 2/1 Wessex F.A. 1 officer & duly 13.O.R. Cpl Penny Power reported sick §	
	25/5/16	6pm	adm. 10. O.R. & C.C.S. 20.R. & duty 4. O.R. D.R.S. adm 20.R. (1 summons). & duly. 11.O.R.	4/6.
			Captain Penny for temporary duty — at P.R.B. Capt Agnew. & "Royal" Leafpart to 10 D.H.	
	26/5/16	6 P.m.	adm. 20.R. & C.C.S. 1.O.R. & duty. 3O.R. D.R.S. & C.C.S. R.O.R. & duly. Y.O.R.	4/8.
			Captain Boston for Trench duty 9. K.R.R. Capt Floor to Y.R.B.	
	27/5/16	6 P.m.	adm 2 officer 18 O.R. & C.C.S. 1 officer 30.R. & D.R.S. 4/6.R. & 2/13 Hunts F.A. 10.R. & duty	4/4.
			20 R. & 2/1 1st S.M.M.F.A. 1 officer, D.R.S. adm 4/8. 6.R. & C.C.S. 2 O.R. & duty 8.O.R. Lieut Hart	
			War Jelos. 16. 37 C.C.S. from 6/8 D.H. D.H.S.	

WAR DIARY
or
INTELLIGENCE SUMMARY.

Army Form C. 2118.

Place	Date	Hour	Summary of Events and Information	Remarks and references to Appendices
Lou(bœuf)	28/7/16	2 PM	adm 3.O.R. & 42 F.A. 30.R. & 42 F.A. 10.R. D.R.S. & 42 F.A. 10 R. D.R.S. & duty 10 R. D.R.S. & duty 12 O R	Off.
"	29.5.16	3 PM	adm. 4.O.R. & ccs. 10.R. & duty. 10 R. D.R.S. adm 10 R. & duty. 11 O R	Off.
"	30/5/16	3 PM	adm. 1 Off. 10 R. & cs. 10 R. 2 / Gospard 11 Off. Envoy. 4 O R	Off.
			D.R.S. adm 2.O.R. & ccs. 2.O.R. & duty. Y.O.R.	
"	31.5.16	3 PM	adm - 19.O.R. & duty. 11. D.R.S. adm 23 O R & ccs 2 O R & duty 10 O R	Off.
			Captain Howard reported to hqrs from Tembroy duty with Rgt R.B.	

44 Field Amb
Vol 14
June

Confidential

War Diary
of
44. Field Ambulance.
for period
June 1st to 30th 1916.

WAR DIARY
or
INTELLIGENCE SUMMARY.
(Erase heading not required.)

Army Form C. 2118.

Place	Date	Hour	Summary of Events and Information	Remarks and references to Appendices
Lieuven	1/6/16	6pm	adm. 2 O.R. & CCS 10 R & check 6 O.R. D.R.S. adm 13. O.R. & CCS 8 O.R. & det 17 O.R. System Pusey. Capt Worth for duty from 9.R.B. - Capt Hyland from 6 Y & Y & Capt Barlow from 9 K.R.R. Capt Booth. R.A.W.C. returns from 6 mos of absence in England.	
	2/6/16	10am	adm 1/officer & 6a 1.O.R. Evac. R. 22. O.R. & H. 27 A 1. O.R. & Check 2. O.R. D.R.S. adm 22 O.R. CCS 2. O.R. & check 4 O.R.	
	3/6/16	6pm	adm 2 O.R. 1. CCS. Evac 8 dm 5. O.R. & check 3 O.R.	
	4/6/16	6pm	adm 4. O.R. 10 CCS. 42 F.A. 1.O.R. D.R.S. adm 1. O.R. & CCS. 5. O.R. & check 15 O.R. Lieut Bryant R.A.W.C. returns from 10 D.A.H. & Dresser on Louis Capt Booth R. relieves him & proceed.	
	5/6/16	8pm	Evac 5. O.R. D.R.S. & CCS 4 O.R. & check 19 O.R.	
	6/6/16	8pm	adm. 16. O.R. & CCS 10 R. & det 10 R. D.R.S. adm 50. O.R. Evac 9 O.R. Col Barlow proceeds to 6 Corps R.E. Park to duty. Capt Pearce in Lithian forming M.G. Washcluis.	
	7/6/16	6pm	adm 4. O.R. W.O. 2/Lieutenant Heisein 2 t 42 F.A. Evac 6 O.R. D.R.S. adm 18 6 R. & CCS. 4. O.R. & check 15. O.R.	
	8/6/16	4pm	adm. 8 O.R. & CCS 10 R. & D.R.S. 24 6 R. D.R.S. adm. 31. 6 R. & CCS 26 R & check 24 6 R.	

WAR DIARY
or
INTELLIGENCE SUMMARY.
(Erase heading not required.)

Army Form C. 2118.

Place	Date	Hour	Summary of Events and Information	Remarks and references to Appendices
Ben Bout	9/6/16	4 p.m.	adm. 1 O.R. & C.C.S. 1 O.R. & D.R.S. 8 O.R. D.R.S. adm 1 O.R. & C.C.S. 1 O.R. & disch. 3 O.R.	
"	10/6	4 p.m.	adm - 11 O.R. & D.R.S. 6 O.R. & disch. 1 O.R. D.R.S. adm 33 O.R. & C.C.S. 4 O.R. & disch. 13 O.R.	
	11/6/16	6.15 p.m.	adm. 2 O.R. & C.C.S. 1 O.R. & disch. 2 O.R. D.R.S. adm 6 O.R. & C.C.S. 3 O.R. & 42 F.A. 1 O.R.	
			& disch - 28 O.R. D.M.S. visited camps & D.R.S.	
	12/6/16	6 p.m.	adm. nil. & D.R.S. 8 O.R. D.R.S. adm 24 O.R. & C.C.S. 10 O.R. & disch. 11 O.R.	
	13/6/16	5 p.m.	adm - 1 O.R. & D.R.S. 8 O.R. D.R.S. adm 1 O.R. D.R.S. 2 O.R. & C.C.S. 2 O.R. & 42 F.A. 1 O.R.	
			& disch. 8 O.R. Capt Deeves returns for temp duty at Wakala Capt Gyger holding on QMO	S M O Wakala
	14/6/16	6 P.m.	adm 19 O.R. & C.C.S. 2 O.R. to Turah Hospital. St Pat. 1 O.R. & 42 F.A. 1 O.R.	
			& disch. 1 O.R. D.S.S. adm 29 O.R. & C.C.S. 6 O.R. & disch 18 O.R.	
			Capt Poole ill	
	15/6/16	3 P.m.	adm. 7 O.R. & C.C.S. 2 O.R. & D.R.S. 9 O.R. & disch 1 Offr. - D.R.S. adm 13 O.R.	
			& C.C.S. 10 O.R. & disch. 26 O.R. Col. Perry proceeds to L. on L. to England.	
	16/6/16	4 p.m.	adm. 10 O.R. & 42 F.A. 1 O.R. & disch. 2 O.R. D.R.S. adm 26 O.R. & disch. 1 O.R.	
			Capt Baker - returns from 6 Cav. R.E. Fd. Ambulance on one month	
			Booth relies Thim	

Army Form C. 2118.

WAR DIARY
or
INTELLIGENCE SUMMARY.
(Erase heading not required.)

Instructions regarding War Diaries and Intelligence Summaries are contained in F. S. Regs., Part II. and the Staff Manual respectively. Title pages will be prepared in manuscript.

Place	Date	Hour	Summary of Events and Information	Remarks and references to Appendices
Lemnos	17/6/15	5.30 p.m	Major J. Evan. U.S.S. evacuated to 19 CCS Jaundice. Lieut Shoret returned from leave.	
			Adm. 1 Off. 6 O.R. to C.C.S. 1 Off. to B.R.S. 6 O.R. to duty 3 O.R, 14 " B.R.S. adm. 1 Off. 73 O.R.	
			To 2/1 Lowland F.A. 1 Off. To duty 8 O.R	
	18/6/15	6 p.m	Capt Brown returns with from duty at 14 "Fiev Batte. Adm. 3 O.R. to CCS 1 O.R. to duty 1 O.R.	
			14" B.R.S. adm. 3 O.R. 2 CCS 4 O.R. to duty 25 O.R.	
	19/6/15	6.15 p.m	Adm. 1 Off. 4 O.R. to CCS 2 O.R. to 2/1 Wessex F.A. 1 Off. to duty 2 O.R. B.R.S. adm 24 O.R.	
			To CCS 2 O.R to duty 13 O.R	
	20/6/15	5.45 p.m	Adm. 5 O.R. to B.R.S. 1 O.R. 14 " B.R.S. adm 16 O.R. to CCS 2 O.R. to duty 14 O.R.	
			The Envoy was inspected by Lieut General Sir J.C Maxwell K.C.B. N'Cape Commander.	
	21/6/15	5.45 p.m	Adm. 13 O.R. to CCS 3 O.R. to B.R.S. 10 O.R. to ½ F.A. 2 O.R. to duty 4 O.R. B.R.S. adm. 31 O.R.	
			2 CCS 4 O.R. to ½ F.A. 2 O.R. to duty 12 O.R.	
	22/6/15	6 p.m	Adm. 2 O.R. to ½ F.A. 1 O.R. to duty 4 O.R. B.R.S. adm 2 O.R. to CCS 2 O.R. to duty 27 O.R.	
			Lieut Grant proceeded to New Zealand Hospital ship Boras for temporary duty.	
	23/6/15	6.30 p.m	Adm. 11 O.R. to CCS 2 O.R. to B.R.S. 6 O.R. ½ F.A. 2 O.R. duty 2 O.R.	
			B.R.S. adm. 21 O.R. 2 CCS 3 O.R. to duty 17 O.R	
			Capt Perry returned from leave.	

Army Form C. 2118.

WAR DIARY
or
INTELLIGENCE SUMMARY.
(Erase heading not required.)

Place	Date	Hour	Summary of Events and Information	Remarks and references to Appendices
Aulnoit	24	4 P.m.	adm - 14. 6 R. ₮ C.C.S. 2 O.R. ₮ 9 O.R. 3 . ₮ 142 F A 10 R. ₮ duty S. O. R.	
			D.R.S. acdm. 33 O.R. ₮ C.C.S. 10 R. ₮ duty. 16 O.R. Capt Pyncent to pardes to aut from Wimbolen - Mots Crew returned 2 sheep from 14 C.S.S.	
	25	5 P.m	adm - 1 Offin - 4 O.R. ₮ C.C.S. 15 Off - 26 R. ₮ O.R. 2 out 4 - 3 O.R.	
			D.R.S. acdm 17. O.R. ₮ C.C.S. 4 O.R. ₮ duty 23. 6 R. Capt Pyne Pyncent ₮ 49? B.W. R.E.A. to hosp. duty. Capt Boston returned from Leon? ab sent w/o leave -	
	26	1 P.m	adm. 4. O.R. ₮ C.C.S. 1 O.R. ₮ 142 FA 3 O. R. ₮ duty - 10 R. D.R.S. adm 12. 6 R.	
			₮ C.C.S. 6 O.R. ₮ duty. 8. O.R.	
	27	1 P.m.	Capt Boston Proceeds to line duty 32 C.C.S. Adm - 10. O.R. ₮ C.C.S. 1 O.R. ₮ duty 5. O.R	
			D.R.S. adm 21. O R ₮ C.C.S 4 O R ₮ duty 14. O R	
	28	1 P.m.	adm - 1 Off - 3. O R. ₮ C.C.S 16 R ₮ 3 R R C 3 O R ₮ 142 F A 10 R - ₮ total 40 R ₮ 2/2 arrive ₮ 1 Off - D.R.S. adm. 3 O R ₮ C.C.S 4 O R ₮ 142 FA 10 R	
			₮ duty 17 O R	
	29	1 P.m.	adm . 13 O R ₮ C.C.S 2 O R ₮ D.R.S 2 O R. ₮ duty 8 2 6 R. D.R.S adm 40 O R ₮ C.C.S. 4 O R ₮ duty 6. O R.	
	30	1 P.m.	adm. 13 O R ₮ C.C.S. 1 O R ₮ D.R.S 12 O R. ₮ duty 2 O R. D.R.S. adm. 13 O R ₮ C.C.S 10 R ₮ duty 12 O R	

July
44 & Aus
Vol 15

14/

War Diary

of

4th Field Ambulance

JULY 1-31

1916

Army Form C. 2118.

WAR DIARY
or
INTELLIGENCE SUMMARY.
(Erase heading not required.)

Instructions regarding War Diaries and Intelligence Summaries are contained in F.S. Regs., Part II. and the Staff Manual respectively. Title pages will be prepared in manuscript.

Place	Date	Hour	Summary of Events and Information	Remarks and references to Appendices
Lens Govt	1/4/16	5.p	Admn Q.O.R. & C.C.S. 1.O.R. Evacd S.O.R. D.R.S. ordn 5.O.R. & C.C.S. 3.O.R. Evacd 15.O.R.	JR
Luc Caul	2/4/16	2pm	admn 17.O.R. & C.C.S. 1.O.R. & 42 FA 6.O.R. Evacd 3.O.R. D.R.S. ocen 20.O.R. & C.C.S. Y.O.R. & clug.	JR
"	"	2 S.O.R.	Capt. Speel. Reine. Dental Reinforcements 549 Bac R.F.A.	JR
"	3/4/16	6pm	admn 13.O.R. & C.C.S. 2.O.R. & D.R.S. 4.O.R. Evacd. 1.O.R. D.R.S. ocen 3.O.R. & C.C.S. S.O.R.	JR
"	"		Evacd 13.O.R.	
"	4/4/16	7pm	am 13.O.R. & C.C.S. 2.O.R. Evacd 2.O.R.S. 2.O.R. Evacd 6.O.R. D.R.S. ocen 2.O.R. & C.C.S. 4.O.R.	JR
"	"		Evacd. 17.O.R.	
"	5/4/16	6pm	am 15.O.R. & C.C.S. 2.O.R. Evacd 42 FA 1.O.R. Evacd 10.O.R. D.R.S. ocen 23.O.R. & C.C.S. 9.O.R.	JR
"	"		Evacd. 18.O.R. Cast Bood Il Wheelin to evac. from RE Pool DUISANS.	
"	6/?	9?m	adm S.O.R. & C.C.S. 3.O.R. & D.R.S. 2.O.R. Evacd. 7.O.R. D.R.S. ocen 14.O.R.	JR
"	"		& C.C.S. S.O.R. & Evacd. 18.O.R.	
"	7/?	2pm	adm 8.O.R. & C.C.S. 3.O.R. & D.R.S. 4.O.R. & 43 FA 20.O.R. Evacd. 3.O.R. D.R.S. ocen 20.O.R. & C.C.S. 4.O.R.	JR
"	"		Evacd 14.O.R. had over A.D.S. ARROS from 42 FA - Capt Reeves return 2 pm duty at -	
"	"		(M.Nicolas—	
"	8/?	6pm	adm 44.O.R. & C.C.S. 6.O.R. & 43 FA 34.O.R. Evacd. S.O.R. D.R.S. ocen 12.O.R. & C.C.S. 30.O.R.	JR
"	"		& Evacd 16.O.R.	
"	9/?	6pm	adm 54.O.R. & C.C.S. 7.O.R. & 43 FA 3.O.R. Evacd. 1.O.R. D.R.S. ocen 16.O.R. & C.C.S. 40.O.R.	JR
"	"		Evacd 8.O.R.	

WAR DIARY
or
INTELLIGENCE SUMMARY.
(Erase heading not required.)

Army Form C. 2118.

Place	Date	Hour	Summary of Events and Information	Remarks and references to Appendices
Sain Crug.	15/7/16	6 pm	adm. 1 off. 36 OR. CCS. 9 OR. to An. 7 OR. to Sound Hosp. of Port 1 OR. to 43 FA.	A.P.L.
	14/7/16		1 off. 18 OR. to dut. Y.OR. DRS. ocen 13 OR. to CCS. 4 OR. to dut. 12 OR.	A.P.L.
	11/7/16	6 am	ocen 10 off. 249 OR. to CCS. 1 off. S.O.R. to 43 FA 14 OR. to dut. 3 O.R. to R.S. ocen	A.P.L.
			6 OR. to CCS. 20 R. to dut 7 OR.	A.P.L.
	12/7/16	6 pm	ocen 3 off 300 R. to CCS. 6 OR. to An. 1. 2 OR. to 43 FH. S off. 290 R. to dut. 46 R.	A.P.L.
			DRS. ocen 20 OR. to CCS. 1 OR. to 43 FH 1 OR. to dut. 20 OR.	
	13/7/16	6 pm	ocen. 1 off. 31 OR. to CCS. 3 OR. to DRS. S.O.R. to 43 FH 10 off. 26 OR.	A.P.L.
			to dut. 10 OR. DRS. ocen S.OR. to CCS. 4 OR. 6 dut. 2 OR.	
	14/7/16	6 pm	adm. 2 off. 61 OR. to CCS. 2 off. 12 OR. to DRS. 3 OR. Engham w 1 to h Hosp.	A.P.L.
			3 OR. to 43 FH. 28 OR. to dut. 4 OR. DRS. ocen 19 OR. to dut. 146 R.	
	15/7/16	6 am	ocen 3 off. 43 OR. to CCS. S.OR. to ANS 20 R. Pris Hosp Herbert 4 6 R.	A.P.L.
			43 FH. 3 off. 27 OR. to dut. 4 OR. DRS. adm. 21 OR. to CCS. 10 R. to dut. 14 OR.	
	16/7/16	6 am	ocen S6. OR. DRS. adm. 6 OR. to CCS. 20 R. to dut. 7 OR. to dut 7 OR. 2/1 wagons. 1. 66. 47 FH. 2 OR.	A.P.L.
			to dut. Y.OR. DRS. adm. 6 OR. to CCS 20 R. to dut 7 OR. Lt Pauls Hosp to when from New Zealand	
	17/7/16		Tunnell Corks. Capt A.T. Todd Medical Us. Used & Attendance for Turk Ambul & Med Sentinel Tunkin Corks	

WAR DIARY
or
INTELLIGENCE SUMMARY.

Army Form C. 2118.

Place	Date	Hour	Summary of Events and Information	Remarks and references to Appendices
Lucheux	17/16	6 PM	adm 2 off. 87 O.R. & CCS 6 O.R. & 43 F.A. 10 ff. 22 O.R. Evac 1 off 46 O.R. D.R.S. adm 23 O.R. & CCS 3 O.R. Evac 6 O.R.	R.L.
"	18/16	6 PM	adm. 20 ff. 47 O.R. & CCS 6 O.R. & 43 F.A. 2 off. 39 O.R. to Stat Hosp Hardy 2 6 R & adm 7 O.R. D.R.S. adm 1 O.R. & CCS 2 O.R. & evac 8 O.R. Corp Board Vyern Sol. church died as to Mil. cont Euclean 42° F.A.	R.L.
"	19/16	6 PM	adm 41 O.R. & CCS 4 O.R. & 43. 28. O.R. to 14 D.R.S. 6 O.R. Evac 30 R. D.R.S. adm 23 O.R. & CCS 3 O.R. & 43 F.A. 1 O.R. & evac 12 O.R.	R.L.
"	20/16	5 PM	adm 47 O.R. & CCS 8 O.R. & Stat Hosp Harbon. 1 O.R. & 43 F.A. 3 6 2. & evac 3 1 O.R. D.R.S. adm 4 O.R. & evac 2 O.R.	R.L.
"	21/16	5 AM	adm 3 ff. 41 O.R. & CCS 2 off. 9 O.R. & D.R.S. 4 O.R. & 43 F.A. 10 ff. 20. O.R. & evac. 4 O.R. D.R.S. adm 17 O.R. & CCS 2 O.R. & evac. 7 O.R.	R.L.
"	22/16	5 PM	adm 26 ff. 28. O.R. & CCS. 10 ff. 6 O.R. & D.R.S. 4. O.R. & 43 F.A. 10 ff. 20. O.R. & evac 13 O.R. Capt Boult & H. Benn Rynn D.R.S. adm 9 O.R. & CCS 5. O.R. & evac 3 O.R. to Achicourt by 33° F.A. H + T. Sections returning by	R.L.
"	23/16	6 PM	adm. 10 ff. 60. O.R. & CCS 9 O.R. & 43 F.A. 19 ff. 37 6 R. Evac. 3 O.R. D.R.S. adm 24 O.R. & CCS. 4 O.R. & evac 4 O.R. Capt Pense return 9 O.R. Capt Pense return East thou Rynn & 4 O.R.	R.L.

WAR DIARY
or
INTELLIGENCE SUMMARY.
(Erase heading not required.)

Army Form C. 2118.

Instructions regarding War Diaries and Intelligence Summaries are contained in F. S. Regs., Part II. and the Staff Manual respectively. Title pages will be prepared in manuscript.

Place	Date	Hour	Summary of Events and Information	Remarks and references to Appendices
Div Compt	24/4/16	6 p.m.	adm. 3.O.R. & CCS. 26.O.R. & 43 F.A. 24.O.R. admid 10 R. & dich 2.O.R.	J.P.
"	25/7/16	6 p.m.	D.R.S. occu. 8.O.R. & CCS. 1.O.R. & dich. Y.O.R.	J.P.
"	"		adm. So ff 38 O.R. & CCS. 20ff. 14.O.R. & D.R.S. 9.O.R. & 43 FA. 38 ff. 21.O.R. dich 1.O.R.	J.P.
"	26/7/16	6 p.m.	& dich. 4.O.R. D.R.S. adm. 9.O.R. & CCS. Y.O.R. & dich 21.O.R.	J.P.
"	"		occu 1 off 69.O.R. & CCS. 1.off. 23.O.R. & 43 FA. 21.O.R. & dich. 3.O.R. D.R.S. occu 48.O.R.	J.P.
"	27/4/16	6 p.m.	& CCS. 9.O.R. & 3s. FA. 3.O.R. & canv. 13.O.R. Capt A.T.Boo-Row inverview & 43 FA.	
"			occu. 43.O.R. & CCS. 6.O.R. & 43 F.A. 37.O.R. & canv. 3.O.R. D.R.S. occu. 20.O.R. & CCS R.O.R. Capt Boton reported from	
"			Returns 1.O.R. Returns at A.D.S. ARRAS Bn. 66 FA.	
"			37 CCS for duty.	
"	28/7/16	6 p.m.	v adm 24.O.R. & CCS. 5.O.R. & D.R.S. 3.O.R. & 43 F.A. 13.O.R. & dich. 6.O.R.	J.P.
"			D.R.S. occu 26.O.R. & CCS. 4.O.R. & 3s. F.A. 4.O.R. & 63 FA. 5.O.R. & dich. 12.O.R.	J.P.
"	29/4/16	5 p.m.	adm. 1.O.R. & CCS. 8.O.R. D.R.S. occu. 14.O.R. & CCS. 17.O.R. & dich. 1.O.R. Returns	J.P.
"			at PIENCOURT by 65. F.A. of 2 p.m.	
"	30/4/16	5 a.m.	adm. nil — & CCS. Y.O.R. & 65. FA. 32.O.R. & dich. 13 O.R. marched from	J.P.
"			LIENCOURT 10 A.M. & IVERGNY.	
"	31/4/16	7 p.m.	marched at 11 A.M. from IVERGNY & RORLY. 7A. adm. 10.O.R. & CO.S. 9.O.R. D.R.S. 1.O.R.	J.P.
			& canv. 36 CCS for Recep 7 cent.	

14" Pub. Nov./16
44 F Amb.

War Diary
of
No. 44 Field Ambulance
for the month of August, 1916

August 1916

COMMITTEE FOR THE
MEDICAL HISTORY OF THE WAR
Date -5 OCT. 1916

WAR DIARY
or
INTELLIGENCE SUMMARY
(Erase heading not required.)

Army Form C. 2118.

Place	Date	Hour	Summary of Events and Information	Remarks and references to Appendices
Barly	Aug 1	8 pm	adm - 6.O.R. & C.S. P.O.R. marches to Gezaincourt.	
Gezaincourt	2"	5 am	adm. 3.O.R. & C.S. 3.O.R. Col. Brown & Dr. Gourlay & Dr. Dunning St Ouen to study -	
"	3"	6 pm	adm. 12.O.R. & C.S. 1.O.R.	
"	4"	3 pm	adm. 6.O.R. & C.S. 4.O.R.	
"	5"	5 pm	adm. 10 D.R. & C.S. 10.O.R.	
"	6"	4 pm	adm. 1 off. 3.O.R. & Pers. 1 off. 33 O.R.	
"	7"	5 pm	adm. 3.O.R. & C.S. 3.O.R. Inspection of Corn. J.C.S. & Ambulances	
"	8"		Returned at MERICOURT March to DERNANCOURT out Coll Pub. dur	
			will Col. Boud & H. Breef. & main dressing stations DERNANCOURT.	
DERNANCOURT	9"			
"	10"	6 pm	adm. 19.O.R. & 15 Corps R.B. 19.O.R. inspec collecting posts at FRICOURT -	
			and advanced collecting posts - at Bellair wood.	
"	11"	8 am	adm. 8.O.R. 1 Spiro of Brown in advance to A.D.S. F.& A. 40. 1 Spiro & Aid post BERNAFOY WOOD off	
"	12"	6 pm	adm. 5.O.R. & 13 Corps Main dress Stations 18.O.R. relieved 32" Field Ambulance at A.D.S. F.& A. 40.	
			4 Aid Post at POMIERS REDOUBT QUARRY and BERNAFOY WOOD - Wounded 4 15" Corps Main	
			dress'g Station. 1 off. 3.O.R.	

Army Form C. 2118.

WAR DIARY
or
INTELLIGENCE SUMMARY.
(Erase heading not required.)

Instructions regarding War Diaries and Intelligence Summaries are contained in F. S. Regs., Part II. and the Staff Manual respectively. Title pages will be prepared in manuscript.

Place	Date	Hour	Summary of Events and Information	Remarks and references to Appendices
In the Field.	13	1 A.m	Adm. 9.O.R. to 15th Corps main dress. 9/to 9.O.R. wounded to 15th Corps main dress. Station Off. 2.	9/6.
"	14	"	O.R. 26. Germans D.	9/6.
"	15	"	Adm. 2.O.R. died 2.O.R. wounded to 15th Corps M.D.S. Off. 3. O.R. 31	9/6.
"	16	"	Wounded to 15th Corps M.D.S. O.R.9. Prvt. for evac. of Unit Ch. P.U. wounded.	9/6.
"	17	"	Wounded to 15th Corps M.D.S. Off. 1. O.R. 21.	9/6.
"	18	"	Adm. 10/6. to 15th Corps M.D.S. 9/6. Wounded to 15th Corps M.D.S. 15 O.R.	9/6.
"	"	"	Wounded to 15th Corps M.D.S. 10/6. 115 O.R. Germans 4. Prvts Heslop, Bushell & Mr. Johnston	9/6.
"	"	"	of the Unit Ch. P.U. wounded.	9/6.
"	19	"	Wounded to 15th Corps M.D.S. Offrs. 6 & 14/6.R. Germans 6. Co. Q.M. Sergeant Provost Baden	9/6.
"	"	"	of the Unit killed in action.	9/6.
"	20	5 p.m	Adm. 2.O.R. died 2.O.R. wounded to 15th Corps M.D.S. Off. 2. O.R. 42. Germans 6.	9/6.
"	21	6 p.m	Wounded to 15th Corps M.D.S. Off. 2. O.R. 31.	9/6.
"	22	5 p.m	Wounded to 15th Corps M.D.S. O.R. 16.	9/6.
"	23	"	Wounded to 15th Corps M.D.S. S.2. 16. Provost Banks & Snowbill of the Unit wounded	9/6.
"	"	"	in action.	9/6.
"	24	p.m	Adm. 1. died 1. wounded to 15th Corps M.D.S. Off. 5. O.R. 41. Germans 2.	9/6.

Army Form C. 2118.

WAR DIARY
or
INTELLIGENCE SUMMARY.
(Erase heading not required.)

Instructions regarding War Diaries and Intelligence Summaries are contained in F. S. Regs., Part II. and the Staff Manual respectively. Title pages will be prepared in manuscript.

Place	Date	Hour	Summary of Events and Information	Remarks and references to Appendices
In the Field	24th	6 A.	Capt. Brown & Corpl. McCleod. Placed in charge of Brown for 10 mins -	off
Do	25th		have been to 15 CWn M.D.S. Off. 16. OR. 118. Penman. 12.	
"	26th	2 pm	adm. 2.O.R. died 2.O.R. Wounded Thro' A.D.S. OR 38. Penman. 1.	off
"	27th	6 pm	adm. 3.O.R. died 3.O.R. wounded Thro' A.D.S. Offrs 1. OR.15. Penman 1.	off
"	28th	4 pm	adm. 1.O.R. died 1.O.R. wounded Thro' A.D.S. Offrs 3. OR 22. Penman 2.	off
"	29th	8 pm	Wounded Thro' A.D.S. Offrs 2. OR. 15. Penman 1.	off
"	30th	8 am	adm. 1.O.R. died 1.O.R. Wounded thro' A.D.S. OR.4. Wounded Thro' A.D.S.	off
"	31st	7 pm	+ adm. Loebelwig post. & 42 F.A. Unit Marched to DERNANCOURT. Capt. Penny. Brown. and Lieut Cunningham. Proceed for Temporary duty. to 115 CCS. CORBIE. Unit marched to MERICOURT wid enhanced debauce of ARINES. and marched to SAILLY a MOUCH.	off

Major R.A.M.C
COMMANDING No. 44 FIELD AMBULANCE

140/1734

14th Bg ADS
Confidential

War Diary

of

4th Field Ambulance

September. 1st to 30th. 1916.

COMMITTEE FOR THE
MEDICAL HISTORY OF THE WAR
Date 26 OCT. 1915

Sept. 1916
5

Army Form C. 2118.

WAR DIARY
or
INTELLIGENCE SUMMARY.
(Erase heading not required.)

Instructions regarding War Diaries and Intelligence Summaries are contained in F. S. Regs., Part II. and the Staff Manual respectively. Title pages will be prepared in manuscript.

Place	Date	Hour	Summary of Events and Information	Remarks and references to Appendices
LA RUE EMPORE	1 9/16		Adm. 5 O.R. CCS 5 O.R. Capt Barton detached for temporary duty with 48 Div R.F.A.	247
	2 9/16		Adm. 9 O.R. to CCS 6 O.R. to duty 3 O.R.	247
	3 9/16		Adm 13 O.R. to CCS 7 O.R. to duty 3 O.R.	247
			Reinforcement 3 O.R.	
"	4 9/16	6.30pm	Major Craw departed on leave to England. Adm 11 O.R. CCS 12 O.R. to duty 1 O.R.	247
"	5 "	7pm	Adm 2 Off Y O.R. to CCS 1 Off 7 O.R.	247
"	6 "	6.15pm	1 Sergeant + 5 men reported for duty. In camp field W.E. Adm 9 O.R. CCS 9 O.R. to Sergt Pk	247
"	7 "	6pm	Adm 6 O.R. CCS 16 O.R. to duty 1 O.R.	247
"	8 "	7pm	Adm 1 Off 6 O.R. to CCS 1 Off 10 O.R. (to duty 7 O.R.)	247
"	9 "	6pm	Adm 1 Off 13 O.R. to CCS 1 Off 15 O.R. Motor Transport under Capt Rouse moved to	247
			AILLY-SUR-SOMME	
DERNANCOURT	10 "	7.30pm	Adm 19 O.R. to CCS 19 O.R. Personnel moved by bus to DERNANCOURT	247
			Transport moved from AILLY to DERNANCOURT	
In the Field	11 "	6.15pm	Adm 36 O.R. to CCS 26 O.R. XX Corps Rest Station 10 O.R. about moved to	247
			Reserve Camp FRICOURT	
"	12	7pm	Adm 16 O.R. to Y Corps Rest Station 14 O.R.	247

Army Form C. 2118.

WAR DIARY
or
INTELLIGENCE SUMMARY.
(Erase heading not required.)

Place	Date	Hour	Summary of Events and Information	Remarks and references to Appendices
In the field	13th	6.30pm	Adm 12 O.R. to C.C.S. 1 O.R. to Y Corps Rest Station 13 O.R.; Capt. Willis Bund R.A.M.C. reported his arrival for duty.	24?
"	14th	10.30pm	Adm 1 Off 6 O.R. to Y Corps R.S. 6 O.R. To Off Convalescent Home Etaples 1 Off. 3 Off + 2.2 O.R. returned from temporary duty at S.C.C.S. Corbie 2 Capt Brewster & Lieut Cunningham with Bearer Division moved off at 9.30 A.m. to report to 42nd Inf. Bde at MONTAUBAN. Capt. Brown with an orderly reported to 42nd Inf. Bde to act as division officer.	24?
"	15th	6.30pm	Adm 18 O.R. to Y Corps R.S. 1 O.R.; 20 O.R. (Telegraphs & Brewery Workers) sent out to relieve Bearer Division at 3.30 pm.	24?
"	16th	6pm	Adm 9 O.R. to Y Corps R.S. 13 O.R. To duty, 1 O.R. en list with tetanus sent forward to report to Div. Collecting Station at MONTAUBAN at 1 A.M.	24?
"	17th	7.30pm	Adm 1 O.R. to Y Corps R.S. 1 O.R.; Unit was relieved by 21st Division & moved to DERNANCOURT at 5 pm. Casualties reported 5 killed O.R. 1 O.R. missing. Capt Brown detailed for HALL P., HUNTINGTON W.) 5 wounded O.R. 1 O.R. missing. Capt Brown detailed for Company duty with 9th R.B. Capt Penny detailed for Company duty with 36 C.C.S. Lieut Cunningham detailed for temporary duty with 7th K.R.R., Capt Bund + 23 O.R. detailed for temporary duty with 37 C.C.S.; Capt Garrett

T2134. Wt. W708—776. 500000. 4/15. Sir J. C. & S.

WAR DIARY or INTELLIGENCE SUMMARY

Army Form C. 2118.

Place	Date	Hour	Summary of Events and Information	Remarks and references to Appendices
Juilé	17th	cont.	Pte reported his arrival for duty. 1 N.C.O. & 4 men detailed for duty at Y. Corps R.S. Capt. Leslie HEILLY.	2n 2
DERNANCOURT	18	1.30 pm	Adm. 1 Off. 6 O.R. to C.C.S. 1 Off. to Y. Corps R.S. 6 O.R. 1 N.C.O. + 3 men detailed for temporary duty at tete RIBEMONT.	242
"	19	7 pm	Adm. 3 O.R. to Y Corps R.S. 3 O.R. This Reserve bn this Coy - were on charge of their N.C.O. were sent forward & taken for duty with the 21st Division at MONTAUBAN. Capt GARRETT R.C. was detailed for duty with the 6th SOMERSET L.INFY in relief of Capt COUCHMAN who is temporarily attached to this unit. Capt F FREEMAN R.A.M.C. reported to this unit & transferred as M.O. Ys XV Corps HQ Troops	21 » 24 ?
"	20	6.30 pm	Casualties 1 O.R. killed (Pte Fox) 2 O.R. slightly wounded (one on duty). Service details returned from temporary duty with 21st Division. Capt COUCHMAN reported to Y.Corp R.S. for duty. Adm. 19 O.R. to Y Corps R.S. 9 O.R.	24 ?
"	21	2.30 pm	Adm. 10 Off. 6 O.R. to Y Corps R.S. 1 Off. 15 O.R. to duty 1 O.R. Lieut Mills and Hurter reported for duty. Pte Thwaitet. Transport left under Capt Broster & men and detailed for the night at TALMAS. Tent Subdivision at Y Corps Dressing Station returning. Capt PENNY returned from 36 C.C.S.	24 ?
GOUCHES	22nd	7 am	Adm. 240 O.R. to Y Corps R.S. 4 O.R.; Capt BUND + 23 O.R. returned from 36 C.C.S. 5 O.R. returned	

WAR DIARY
or
INTELLIGENCE SUMMARY.
(Erase heading not required.)

Army Form C. 2118.

Place	Date	Hour	Summary of Events and Information	Remarks and references to Appendices
GROUCHES	22nd Cont		from Bethe HEILLY Unit proceeded by bus to GROUCHES arriving at 5pm. Transport and Capt. BROSTER arrived at 2pm.	247
"	23rd	4pm	Adm 1 O.R.	248
"	24th	6.15	Adm 12 O.R. to C.C.S 4 O.R. Wound recd 12th Div D.R.S. and made arrangements about Makingover.	249
"	25th	7.30pm	Adm 1 Offr T.O.R. to C.C.S. 1 Offr to 12th D.R.S. 15 O.R. Capt BROSTER proceeded on temporary duty as Town Commandant of GOUY. Sergt CORBISHLEY proceeded on temporary duty as Garrison Sergt Major of GOUY. Capt PENNY + 10 O.R. proceeded to take over charge of Officers Rest Camp MANIN from 37 F.Amb. Lieut HURTER + 30 O.R. proceeded on temporary duty to 37 C.C.S. relieving the personnel of the 37th + 37th F.Ambs.; 4 O.R. reported to 41st Inf Bde for duty at 1st BRETENCOURT.	247
BARLY	26th	11am	Adm 13 O.R. to C.C.S. 5 O.R. to 10th D.R.S. 10 O.R. Transport moved to BARLY under charge of Lieut MILLS at 7 am; personnel moved by charabancs from LUCHEUX to BARLY at 145pm; Capt BOOTH relieved Lieut HURTER at 37 C.C.S.	250
"	27th	7.30	Relieved 37 Field Amb at DRS CHATEAU BARLY at 10am, to D.R.S. Adm 12 S. O.R. (transferred from 12th D.R.S.) Officers Rest Camp MANIN Adm 3 (Transfer from 37 F. Amb)	

Army Form C. 2118.

WAR DIARY
or
INTELLIGENCE SUMMARY.
(Erase heading not required.)

Instructions regarding War Diaries and Intelligence Summaries are contained in F. S. Regs., Part II. and the Staff Manual respectively. Title pages will be prepared in manuscript.

Place	Date	Hour	Summary of Events and Information	Remarks and references to Appendices
BARLY	27th Cont.		Lieut H R HURTER & Lieut E A MILLS were dispensed for duty with 12th Division who notified by ADMS 14th Div. that Capt W EGAN had been appointed and will from the 28th inst.	
"	27.9.16	5.30pm	Captain W. EGAN RAMC having previously reported his arrival to ADMS at the Divisional Headquarters arrived at BARLY (Advanced Divisional) of the unit. By arrangement between ADMS of the Division & ADMS IV Corps he has been lent to the latter Corps to assist in the evacuation of the wounded resulting from the actions operations beginning September 25th.	
"	"	6.45pm	were arrived from ADMS ordering Med. Officer for sanitary duty with 8 R.B. Captain BUND attaila for the duty	
			were arrived . Moving a party of 30 O.R. including 4 N.C.O. for permanent fatigue at the Divisional workshops - Klee Schumes. Accommodated & attached for discipline to 61st Field Company R.E. - Party attached	
"	28.9.16	-	Inspected Rest Station during the forenoon. The Rest Station consist of a Chateau with outhouses etc - now for communication purposes Chris huts - a 5' hut - for patients one of these huts is in extremely good one. Accommodation for 168 approximately	

Army Form C. 2118.

WAR DIARY
or
INTELLIGENCE SUMMARY.
(Erase heading not required.)

447A.

Instructions regarding War Diaries and Intelligence Summaries are contained in F. S. Regs., Part II. and the Staff Manual respectively. Title pages will be prepared in manuscript.

Place	Date	Hour	Summary of Events and Information	Remarks and references to Appendices
BARLY	28.9.16	—	Laundry fair — bath house accomodation old, out of repair requires thorough overhauling. The whole place wants thorough cleaning —	
"	"	P.M.	Inspected Officers Rest Hospital at HANN attch in i/c of Captain PENNY. R.A.M.C. He has with him 2 attachment of 1 N.C.O & 11 Men. It is a delightful little hospital. Has accomodation for 16 Officers & other ranks. — Captain PENNY has since made many improvements since he took it over. — Requires a few R.S. Cross Et. 16's skates if possible	Officers Rest Hospital for Vi Corps
"	29.9.16 P.M	—	Saw. A book in reference to disinfection & projectors clothing — Approved so, is the only method by which lice are destroyed — Opened inspect a/c or asked carried on with the ord inspect number at the signal of the first baskin.	
"	"	1 p.m	Went to Red Cross Stores at HEM. Drew Stores.	
"	"	10 p.m.	Orders received from A. D.M.S. Bend 10 more men to 61st Coy R.E. Orders received from A. D.M.S. Bend M.O. to 9 KRR for duty of duty. Captain GRANT Sent. This leaves me now with only one M.O. — 21 N.C.O & 2 men.	
"	30.9.16		The unit is very split up now. — A.D.M.S. Inspected Rest Camp. — On assuming Command of unit	Applied for temporary Sanct. [signature]

140/1814

Confidential

War Diary
of
44 Field Ambulance. 14th Divn

from 1st October, 1916 to 31st October, 1916.

(Volume 18.)

Oct. 1916

COMMITTEE FOR THE
MEDICAL HISTORY OF THE WAR
Date -9 DEC. 1916

WAR DIARY
or
INTELLIGENCE SUMMARY.
(Erase heading not required.)

Army Form C. 2118.

44 FA

Place	Date	Hour	Summary of Events and Information	Remarks and references to Appendices
BARLY	1.10.16	-	Orders Received from ADMS to send a fatigue party of 1 NCO & 10 OR to 61 Coy RE at 9am 2.10.16	
"	2.10.16	-	party details above returned after amp. work	
"	3.10.16	-	Captain BROSTER again assumed the unit	
"	"	-	Reinforcement of 9 privates joined from base	
"	4.10.16	-	Captain BROSTER details for temporary duty with 14th Div. School of instruction	
"	"	-	DDMS XI Corps inspects D.R.S.	
"	5.10.16	-	Lieut VERNON TAYLOR R and No 2 Amb Ambulance attached to D.R.S. for temporary duty during absence of Captain BROSTER.	
"	6.10.16	-	Routine.	
"	9.10.16	-	Recommendations for award & mention for General dispatch forwarded to A.D and Capt BROWN for Military Cross. Lieut D&M FOSTER Hon Mention. Private HERBERT PEARSON for Military Medal & Private CHALKE for Hon Mention.	
"	8.10.16	-	notification received that 14 days F P No 1 awarded to No 34063 L/Cpl P. McKINLAY RAMC whilst undergoing punishment of 28 days No 2 be cancelled (authority Col N.C.D.M.)	
"	9.10.16	-	Authority of GOC received approving of Captain W. EGAN RAMC wearing the badges of rank of Lt Colonel pending publication of temp. of promotion in London Gazette	

WAR DIARY
or
INTELLIGENCE SUMMARY.
(Erase heading not required.)

Army Form C. 2118.

44 FA

Place	Date	Hour	Summary of Events and Information	Remarks and references to Appendices
BARLY	10.10.16	-	Intensive application for special leave to Officers on urgent private affairs submitted. O.C. + Captain BROSTER.	2
"	11.10.16	-	Proposed Military Medaly was awarded to Sergt CORBISHLEY, L/Cpl ATKINSON, Pte RIMMER authority A.M. T6 1107	2+2
"	12.10.16	-	Captain GRANT returned from temporary duty with 9th K.R.R.C.	2+2
"	13.10.16	-	Lt Col EGAN departed on leave to IRELAND, Captain BARTON returned from temporary duty with 44th Bde RFA and departed on temporary duty with 6 K.O.Y.L.I., Lieut TAYLOR reported the 42nd F Amb.	"
"	14.10.16	-	D.R.S. inspected by the ADMS, two support Rl inspected & told on necessary work. Hearing of huts.	2+2
"	15.10.16	-	Routine	2+2
"	16.10.16	-	Routine	2+2
"	17.10.16	-	D.R.S. inspected by Col THOMPSON, DDMS, and by ADMS.	2+2
"	18.10.16	-	Routine	2+2
"	19.10.16	-	10 OR sent to ARRAS under instruction of ADMS in arranging party to 63rd Div 6th & 2 OR sent to Railhd SIMENCOURT under instruction of ADMS CO MACKENZIE PAMS	2+2
"	"	-	reported his arrival for duty	2+2

Army Form C. 2118.

WAR DIARY
or
INTELLIGENCE SUMMARY.
(Erase heading not required.)

44 FA

Place	Date	Hour	Summary of Events and Information	Remarks and references to Appendices
BARLY	20.10.16	—	Capt GRANT departed for duty with 35th Division. Fatigue party of 20 O.R. went under instruction of A.D.M.S. to WARLENCOURT. they returned the same evening	
"	21.10.16	—	Capt BROWN reported his return from temporary duty. Fatigue party of 20 O.R. went under instruction of A.D.M.S. to SAULTY.	
"	22.10.16	—	Capt L.G. BROWN departed to 10 days leave to ENGLAND.	
"	23.10.16	—	Lt. Colonel EGAN returned from leave.	
"	24.10.16 & 10 pm.		Operation Order No 4 & 5 by O.C. R.A.M.C. 14th Division Reserves – 14th Division Relieved Saturday 12th Division on 25th Oct – night 26/27 Oct – No 44 Field ambulance to collect sick from H. Brigade on Oct 26th & from the 41st – 42nd & 43rd Brigade on 27th relieve the Dressing Room from the Area – No 44 Field ambulance the relieved by 37 Field Ambulance on Oct 27th. Divisional H.Q. Close at WARLUS the then LE CAUROY at 10 pm on 27th inst – Additional transport as follows to 44th F.A. 2 horsed M. motor ambulance – from 43 one horsed M. motor ambulance.	
	25.10.16		Routine	
"	26.10.16 2 pm		Handed over charge of Officers Rest Hospital to O.C. 37 C.C.S. Officers transfers – Captain BARTON R.A.M.C. returned from 6 K.O.Y.L.I. – Southern to arrange for buses.	

WAR DIARY
or
INTELLIGENCE SUMMARY.

Army Form C. 2118.

Place	Date	Hour	Summary of Events and Information	Remarks and references to Appendices
BARLY	26.10.16	—	With Staff, Captain HT Brigade — letters arranged for at SOMBRIN	
"	27.10.16	10.30 a.m.	Forwarded over D.R.S at BARLY — 103 transferred.	Movement
			Unit moved 15 mins area as follows. Advance party of 2 NCOs + 30 O.R. under Captain BARTON & accompanied by Interpreter left BARLY at 9.30 a.m. All the transport under command of Captain BROSTER & accompanied by Lt + QM FOSTER left at 10.30 a.m.	Orders
			Remainder of unit under command of O.C. marched from BARLY at 1.45pm.	
"	"	11. A.M.	Captain BOOTH R.A.M.C & party deployed from 37 C.C.S	
			Evacuation of Sick — All A + D booths closes 7.30pm. 26 Oct Mature arriving after that time were shown as directed & evacuated to 37 C.C.S	
SOMBRIN	"	2.45pm	Unit arrived at SOMBRIN — located by H.Q. No. 25 luellis map reference 023 640 Sheet 57C. — Men & Officers billetis in village transport locals in large farm ½ mile S. on road SOMBRIN HUMBERCOURT.	
			No available site for hospital — Fwd Ambulance only collecting	
"	26.10.16	"	43 Field Ambulance opened at GIVENCHY LE NOBLE & sent transfers then lorries bringing cases who go to 37 C.C.S — additional transport running 15 miles	

WAR DIARY
or
INTELLIGENCE SUMMARY.
(Erase heading not required.)

Army Form C. 2118.

Place	Date	Hour	Summary of Events and Information	Remarks and references to Appendices
SOMBRIN	28.10.16	6 PM	Captain WILLIS. B.U.N.D. Reported from 8th Rifle Brigade	
"	29.10.16	11 AM	Conference at A.D.M.S. when questions of training of officers men were discussed	
"	30.10.16	-	Routine training begun - 2 hours route marching in the morning - 2 hr Stretcher drill in the afternoon including Gas helmet practices - duty lecture to Officers at 5 pm	
"	"		Captain BROSTER R.A.M.C. Attached for duty (temporary) to A.D.M.S. VI Corps (authority A.D.M.S. verbal)	
"	"		Captain FLOOD R.A.M.C. Attached for temporary duty with 3rd K.S.L.I. (authority A.D.M.S. 14 Div n)	
"	31.10.16	-	Captain BOOTH Attached for temporary duty with 14 D.A.C. (authority A.D.M.S. 14 Div n)	
"	"		Strength Brought up to War Establishment less 1 Private R.A.M.C.	

Maurice L Graub
a/Lt Col R.A.M.C.
O.C. 44 Field Ambulance

Nov. 1916

War Diary

of

44 Field Ambulance

for month of

November 1916.

Army Form C. 2118.

WAR DIARY
or
INTELLIGENCE SUMMARY.
(Erase heading not required.)

44 Field Ambulance

Place	Date	Hour	Summary of Events and Information	Remarks and references to Appendices
SOMBRIN	Nov 1st	—	Ambn's training continued	
"	"		G.O.C 41st Brigade wrote offering this unit to IVERGNY at earliest convenience.	
"	"		Captain MACKENZIE Attaches for duty with No 18 General Hospital (authority A.G.M.S)	
"	2		3 N.C.O's & the details for course of Inoculation at Divisional School beginning Nov 2nd. (authority A.D.M.S)	
"	"		A.D.M.S wired to look for suitable place for Scabies Camp at IVERGNY.	Q
"	2		Notified A.D.M.S he proposed Hors.	Q
"	Nov 3rd 16.15		Captain BARTON & the whole F.B Section complete with transport up to SOMBRIN as an advanced party to Get. Ready billets at IVERGNY.	Q
"	"		Spent whole morning inspecting site for Brigade baths with Staff Captain & R.E. officer	Q
"	"	2pm	Captain MACKENZIE departed for duty with No 18 General Hospital	Q
"	Nov 3rd	10.17am	Remainder of unit less details men horse teams left SOMBRIN for IVERGNY	Q
"	"		Captain BUND with A.D clerks 2 nursing orderlies Sanitary Squad remained behind to collect Funerals. Brigadier helan up billets.	
IVERGNY	"	12 noon	Field Ambulance closes at SOMBRIN & opened at IVERGNY	Q
			Map Reference N 27 a 8.4 Sheet 57C. A.D.M.S & Staff Captain to offices	

WAR DIARY or INTELLIGENCE SUMMARY

Army Form C. 2118.

444 F.A.

Place	Date	Hour	Summary of Events and Information	Remarks and references to Appendices
IVERGNY	3.11.16	2pm	Relieved Airplane hurt to No 25 Mobile Vet Section.	
"	"	3pm	A.D.M.S. visits & inspects new area - Selects site for scabies hospital in our billeting area.	
"	"	—	Captain BROWN proceeds to Camp P. Duty as D.A.D.M.S. 6¹ Corps. in place of Captain P. Duty Lunby W.E 11² Kings Brostes.	
"	"	10pm	Orders received from A.D.M.S. forward H.Q. for Camp Y Lunby W.E 11² Kings Liverpool Reg	⊘
"	4.11.16	9pm	Captain BUND attached Reports for Duty with 11² Kings Liverpool Reg	
"	"	"	Sgts BRYANT, CORBISHLEY & REES proceeded to Corps/Corps LIGNEREUIL & are attached to 43 F. Ambulance	⊘
"	"	"	I Walter Corp sent to Laundry at AVESNES (attached to 23 F.A. (authority A.D.M.S.)	⊘
"	5.11.16	—	Routine	⊘
"	6.11.16	.	No 57403 Pte HOLDEN W. R.A.M.C. awarded 21 days F.P. No 2 for a Drunkness & w Creating a disturbance in the public thoroughfare	⊘
"	7.11.16	—	Routine	⊘

Army Form C. 2118.

WAR DIARY
or
INTELLIGENCE SUMMARY.
(Erase heading not required.)

Place	Date	Hour	Summary of Events and Information	Remarks and references to Appendices
IVERGNY	8.11.16		Lt. Q.H. FOSTER - R.A.M.C. & Rev. Fr. McCANN. C.F. proceeded on 10 days leave to England	
			A and C cars & rations unit & early morng to LIENCOURT & rec SBS	
		9.30 p.m	Movement Order received from A.D.M.S.	Movement Order
			1. Motor Ambulances made with 11 Corps for an 15 more from IVERGNEY to LIENCOURT, to take over from a Divisional Rest Station.	
			2. Move to be made on Nov 9th, finally completed by noon on Nov 10.	
			3. Officers and Advance Party & Lorries at LIENCOURT Thursday morning & two & later morn from 35th Division Field Ambulance and the remainder	
			of the Ambulance will be arrive at LIENCOURT at 2 p.m.	
			4. About 15 cars will be left at D.R.S. by 35th Division rations 75" Cars will be transferred from 145 F.A. at GIVENCHY LE NOBLE during the afternoon arriving at ours after 2-30 p.m. — Div Orders Received and Billets kept henceforth from 42 Brigade Area.	

WAR DIARY or INTELLIGENCE SUMMARY.

Army Form C. 2118.

Place	Date	Hour	Summary of Events and Information	Remarks and references to Appendices
IVERGNY	9.11.16	9am	Arrival at A.D.S LIENCOURT. Was informed by O.C. A.D.S. that movement was cancelled as for the present. Reported same to A.D.M.S. who asked he to ring up A.D.M.S. Corps. He confirmed the cancelling of orders. Orders to stand fast.	
"	"	4pm	Orders received from A.D.M.S. to take over LIENCOURT by noon 10.11.16	
"	10.11.16	8.20	Captain BARTON & 2 men early (to left) for IVERGNY for LIENCOURT	
"	"	11pm	Remainder of Unit left IVERGNY for LIENCOURT	
LIENCOURT	"	12 noon	Took over A.D.S LIENCOURT from O.C. 107 Field Ambulance. Map reference 1.31.a.97 Sheet 57C.	
"	"	5pm	Took over 45 Check 1 wounded. 66 Sick hairspring from 43 Field Ambulance. 11 sick " 42 Field Ambulance. Captain BOND ROME returned from temporary duty with 11 Divisional Train. Captain FLOOD returned do do " 5KRRL ARMS Mobile Hospital Captain FLOOD & Sgt RICHARDSON. SUTTON & SWINN Wales Station Corps School	
"	11.11.16	—		
"	12.11.16			

WAR DIARY
or
INTELLIGENCE SUMMARY.
(Erase heading not required.)

Army Form C. 2118.

Place	Date	Hour	Summary of Events and Information	Remarks and references to Appendices
LIENCOURT	12.11.16	-	9 motineles. Captain BARTON & Sgt BAILEY battle on was of small pox hospitals or 18th inst. Admd sanctioned following attach following blue Ouenfield Daily at Divisional Foden. to blanket Parties undertaking	2
"	13.11.16		Captain BUND proceeded on 14days leave to ENGLAND	
"	"		Captain BOOTH returned from temporary duty with D.A.C	2
"	"		Artist promoner from Admd to Actual Captain BOOTH motion of Captain FLOOD for duty at depot of Instruction promotion granted —	2
"	14.11.16		Tr/937 Acting S Major M.L CORPS A.V.C. Promoted to be Substantive Rank Relief Sergt Major took effect from 1st September 1916 —	2/
"	"		Dentist visited A.R.V. Monday & Wednesdays Holidays	2/
"	15.11.16	10 am	Veterinary Chief Corbra brined fires admitted from Divisional & shot - Saw the Case but did not concur in a holy cure. Dorales hui in Bee link -	2/
"	16.11.16		One this morning looks more improving - Privately hospn Admd kind to Queck no 12 Stationary Hospital St Pol with lumbar puncture was performed - Clear fluid's was found to cure a probably but Not specific	2/

WAR DIARY
or
INTELLIGENCE SUMMARY.
(Erase heading not required.)

Army Form C. 2118.

Place	Date	Hour	Summary of Events and Information	Remarks and references to Appendices
LIENCOURT	16.11.16		Reinforcement - 3 R.m.a.b's arrives from base	
"	17.11.16		Stretcher carrying parade as usual	
"	18.11.16		Captain BROSTER returned from leave - DDMS conference	
"	19.11.16		Captain BROSTER details for duty temporary pro DADMS. 16.th Divison	
"	"		Large hospital tent erected - ADMS conference	
"	"	7pm	Divil service for men before an Comielh with Capt. GRANT RAMC	
"	"		this officer is present doing duty with 3.F. Division to this Division since	
"	"		the temporary measures placed in service during that by God month	
"	"		"	
"	"		M. wrote 'to take Murray's picture -	
"	"		The twin got 2nd place in Pongelle Cross country Race	
"	"		Captain F. LOOD NAES as acting IC for next (during M.'s leave)	
"	20.11.16	"	Denhal Kathro at DRS. Monday Wednesday Friday	
"	"		LIEUT & Mr FOSTER returns from leave in ENGLAND	
"	21.11.16	"	NO 32922. Pte F. FILDES evacuated sick	
"	"		Routine - Sports Club formed - Subscriptions voluntary	
"	22.11.16	9.30pm	Captain G.NANT RAMC arrives from 105th Field Ambulance 3.F. Division	

WAR DIARY
or
INTELLIGENCE SUMMARY.
(Erase heading not required.)

Army Form C. 2118.

Place	Date	Hour	Summary of Events and Information	Remarks and references to Appendices
LIENCOURT	22/11/16		By order of the Army Commander Sr. Callan GRANT RAMC was placed in open arrest (Third Army DAO 646) on the following charges a copy of which was given to him at the time.	
			1st Charge Sec 40 AA — Neglect to the prejudice of good order & military discipline in that he in the field on the 10th October 1916 when acting as Medical Officer to the 9th Battalion Kings R.R. Corps did not make proper arrangements for the safe disposal from issue of drugs issued at his Regimental aid post	
			2nd Charge Sec 40 AA — Neglect to the prejudice of good order & military discipline in that he in the field on the 17th October 1916 when acting as Medical Officer to the 9th Battalion K.R.R.C did not exercise a stricter supervision over the administration of drugs to No 13529 Rifleman Curran of the 9th Bn K.R.R.C.	
			3rd Charge Section 40 AA — Neglect to the prejudice of good order & military discipline in that he in the field on the 17th	

WAR DIARY
or
INTELLIGENCE SUMMARY.
(Erase heading not required.)

Army Form C. 2118.

Place	Date	Hour	Summary of Events and Information	Remarks and references to Appendices
LIENCOURT	22/1/16	10am	October 1916 When acting as Medical Officer to the G.C.Dr. K.R.R.C. having been informed that Rifleman CREAM of that unit had delayed on the floor, I was forming, at the time, unjustifiably delayed his personal attention to Rifleman CREAM on the fact that these charges as appears to be delaying after the Summary has been taken. No notices to the accused Officer.	
"	"	11am	Began taking the Summary/ Evidence & examined the following in this order. Sgt. McKEON. Cpl. WATSON. OFFRED. Nurse Mr Dooper, 43 Field Ambulance - Lt. BARNETT & Sergt 4/m. BESSANT & Corpl. ADCOCK. Adjourned for W.D. for lunch- Summary Evidence - 4p.m.	
"	"	1.1.Pm	Miles was taking Summary Evidence to the D.M.S. 3rd Army accompanied by D.A.D.M.S. (Sanitary) in which he D.A.D.S. & Appendix returns with what they saw.	
"	"	7pm	Took Ambulance Summary of Evidence in lieu of Captain GRANT R.amc handed them over to A.D.M.S.	

WAR DIARY
or
INTELLIGENCE SUMMARY.
(Erase heading not required.)

Army Form C. 2118.

Place	Date	Hour	Summary of Events and Information	Remarks and references to Appendices
LIENCOURT	23.11.16		No 6300 Pte ARTHUR details for course Instruction at 3rd Army School of Instruction. - Captain BOOTH details to see men at ETREE WARIN 9th & DEVONS	
"	24.11.16		Nine O.R's selected on leave to ENGLAND	
"	25.11.16		Changing QMStores to Convent hut with ward	
"	26.11.16 2.45pm		DDMS & ADMS inspected Camp.	
"	27.11.16		Rations - Captain L.G. BROWN RAMC reported from "Temp" duty in DADMS to Corps HQ Collection of lice from 41st Brigade began. - Received her revert visit from D.D.	
"	28.11.16		Captain WILLIS BIND returned from leave - admitted 37th CCS with	
"	29.11.16 8pm		R inguinal Hernia & evacuated to 37 C.C.S.	
"	30.11.16 2.30pm		ADMS 1st Division inspected the Unit	
			- Went to the BRC at HQ M Fruato arrangements for Xmas Chemists for future	

Bompe
ADMS

Dec 1916

14th Div

140/95 Vol 20

4th Field Ambulance

War Diary

for period — December 1 to 31. 1916

COMMITTEE FOR THE
MEDICAL HISTORY OF THE WAR
Date 31 JAN. 1917

WAR DIARY
or
INTELLIGENCE SUMMARY.

(Erase heading not required.)

Army Form C. 2118.

Place	Date	Hour	Summary of Events and Information	Remarks and references to Appendices
LIENCOURT	1.12.16	7pm	Captain GRANT R.A.M.C. moved for Courtmaline by M.T. to be held on Decr 5th	
"	2.12.16	—	Kerwala. Captain FLOOD (8.20th) sent to proceed on leave to England	
"	3.12.16	—	Proceding — Dr WINGHAM M. Cancelled 28 days T.O.M.O.2 for Drunk on duty Cpl. Pepiro arrived for Captain GRANT - gave him 3 hrs forward trenches.	
"			+ A.D.M.S. 14th Div (for standard)	
"	4.12.16	2.30pm	Concert for patients in Recreation hut - Lilkerkerdo furnish rheavy forces. ortho secured transport store to town major charge.	
"			CAPTAIN BROSTER relieved from Lieutenant Auley [?] as A.D.V.T.S. 4th Div	
"	5.12.16		Routine	
"	6.12.16	10am	G.C.Martial held at the Field Ambulance on Captain GRANT R.A.M.C.	
"			The accused officer was found "Not Guilty" was immediately acquitted.	
"	7.12.16	—	5:O.R proceeded on leave to ENGLAND	
"	8.12.16	"	14th Div. ARTILLERY arrived in area and collected by unit -	
"			OO5 inspection parade on parade -	
"	9.12.16	"	Collection parade 42nd Inf.y Brigade begun.	
"	10.12.16		Routine.	

WAR DIARY
or
INTELLIGENCE SUMMARY.
(Erase heading not required.)

Army Form C. 2118.

(2)

Place	Date	Hour	Summary of Events and Information	Remarks and references to Appendices
LIENCOURT	11.12.16	—	No 3 24440 Serg: RICHARDSON, A.S. R.A.M.C. proceeded to ENGLAND to select a Cadet unit. to shoot off to Strength of the unit. Orders received from A.D.M.S. 11th Div for Captain GRANT R.A.M.C. to Relieve (the unit — is 107 Field Ambulance 36th DIV. 7.O.R. proceeds on leave to England) 3 Privates awards 2 days F.P.No 2 & 1 Private (minor Sentry) awarded 3 days F.P. No 1 for Irregular Conduct. Absenting themselves from duty without leave —	⚡ ⚡
"	12.12.16	—	Captain GRANT Assumed his unit — Captain R.H.C. GOMPERTZ. R.A.M.C. arrived for duty & taken on the Strength	⚡⚡ ⚡
"	13.12.16	—	Captain BROWN R.A.M.C. Sg. CORBISHLEY & 1 Private proceeded on temporary duty to Vd Corps	⚡
"	14.12.16	—	Captain BARTON R.A.M.C. proceeded on permanent Attach:to M.O. 478th Siege to Shuck off the Strength — Horsemen Others No 30 received. Unit b— Orders from G.1H Section Advanced Dressing Station of Convoy ARRAS & M/S at WANQUSTIN Accompanied by O.C. 36 Field Ambulance Inspected Collecting Post A.D.S. & M.D.S.	⚡

Army Form C. 2118.

WAR DIARY
or
INTELLIGENCE SUMMARY.
(Erase heading not required.)

(4)

Place	Date	Hour	Summary of Events and Information	Remarks and references to Appendices
LIENCOURT	15.12.16	—	Capt Broster departs for permanent duty at 3rd Army HQ's like B/Wright	Q
"	"		Capt W.A. Brown arrived for permanent duty returning. Take over charge of 42nd & 43rd Brigades moving forward. Made arrangements for attaching vets.	Q
"	16.12.16		the taking of Stragglers —	
"	"		Captain Flood returns from leave in ENGLAND	Q
"	"		Mr "Private" Morgan S.K.S.L.I. Charges with stealing medals from wheeled & beating of Hospital order - Spoken to C.O.	Q
"	"	5 pm	Capt Flood & answers party (escort) proceed to H.P. & S HQ'rs res- forward area -	Q
"	17.12.16	8 am	Captain GOMPERTZ Remainders party for A.D.S. & forwards area departs	Q
"	17.12.16	2 pm	The following have taken over in the forward area from 36th Field Ambulance -	
			A.D.S. (Convent at ARRAS) map reference Sht. 51B — G.76.b.97	
			Collecting Post (ACHICOURT) " " " G. 32.a.40	
			(H₁) H. 3.a.4.H	
			(H₂) G. 28.c.8.4 +	
			B.O.R. at follows up air posts	Q
			$(G_2) = M56.53 - (G_3) = M56.82 + (G)_3 = M6a.44$	

Army Form C. 2118.

WAR DIARY
or
INTELLIGENCE SUMMARY.
(Erase heading not required.)

Instructions regarding War Diaries and Intelligence Summaries are contained in F. S. Regs., Part II. and the Staff Manual respectively. Title pages will be prepared in manuscript.

(5)

Place	Date	Hour	Summary of Events and Information	Remarks and references to Appendices
LIENCOURT	17.2.16	5 p.m.	Captain L.G. BROWN Relieves (temporary) from Lieuty. Ouhy with VII Corps.	2
"	18.12.16		Advanced party arrived at D.R.S. from 37 Field Ambulance & took over. Handed over 140 patients clear A.T.S beds.	2
"		9 a.m.	Main body left from LIENCOURT for WANQUETIN	
"		10 a.m.	Transport left LIENCOURT — Captain L.G. BROWN Reports to 33rd Div. (D.D.M.S)	2
WANQUETIN	"	11 a.m.	Main party arrived took over M.D.P at WANQUETIN from 26 Fd Ambulance Map reference. Sheet 57C = K 32 d 86. Handing over completed 12 Noon - took over 90 patients patients 39 were scabies	2
"	19 March	6 a.m.	Saw following prisoners were authors of 3076 Cpl W DOUGHERTY - Drunk in July - remands for C.M. 30537 Pte CLIST do 28 days FP No 2	
"		11 a.m.	Saw A.D.M.S re notes for FODEN lorry & Ammunition clothing etc at M.M.S.	2
"		3 p.m.	Took Summary of Evidence against Cpl DOUGHERTY Forwarded to A D M S	
"			Captain PERRY admitted 15 F.A. (P.U.O.) & transferred to HANIN (Stretcher bearer)	2

WAR DIARY
or
INTELLIGENCE SUMMARY.
(Erase heading not required.)

Army Form C. 2118.

Place	Date	Hour	Summary of Events and Information	Remarks and references to Appendices
WANQUETIN	21.12.16	—	Six O.R's proceed on leave to England. John Lorry arrived.	
"	21.12.16	—	Inspected A.D.S. & works under construction at RONVILLE — turned the grector arc points as follows:—	
			$G_1 = M8 c 9.1 = (old G4)$	
			$G_2 = M8 c 8.2 = (old G3)$	
			$G_3 = M8 c 7.5 = (old G2)$	
"	22.12.16	—	Inspected works being made in the ARRAS, DOULLENS Road S.E. of DAINVILLE about L.35 b 86.	
			7 Other Ranks proceeded on leave to the United Kingdom	
"	23.12.16		Nr. 054367 Pte SPENCER R.M. (M.T.) A.O.C. Despatched to ENGLAND Base Cadet Corps.	
"	24.12.16		Xmas Mess Canteen hours — 12 - 2 pm & 6 - 8 pm (British beer)	
"	25.12.16		Xmas Day —	
"	26.12.16		6 O.R's proceeded on leave to the United Kingdom	
"	27.12.16		6 Artesian tubes in position handed to 6 O.R's returned from leave — Cellars being completed & fitted with dynamators R.E. ACHICOURT with tees & utilising time for manoeuvres. Report ACHICOURT with trees of utilising time for manoeuvres.	

Army Form C. 2118.

WAR DIARY
or
INTELLIGENCE SUMMARY.
(Erase heading not required.)

Instructions regarding War Diaries and Intelligence Summaries are contained in F. S. Regs., Part II. and the Staff Manual respectively. Title pages will be prepared in manuscript.

Place	Date	Hour	Summary of Events and Information	Remarks and references to Appendices
WANQUETIN	27.2.16	—	Captain PENNY R.A.M.C. discharged from hospital & returns to duty. Captain BOOTH " " " proceeds on leave to ENGLAND	
"	28th		Routine	
"	29.2.16		do	
"	30.2.16		do	
"	31.2.16		Conference at P.D.M.S. VI Corps	

Major McPaul
1 Hatfield Coy Ambulance

14

140/1943 Vol 21

44 Field Ambulance

War Diary

for period

January 1st to 31st

1917

COMMITTEE FOR THE
MEDICAL HISTORY OF THE WAR
Date 13 MAR. 1917

WAR DIARY or INTELLIGENCE SUMMARY

Army Form C. 2118.

Place	Date	Hour	Summary of Events and Information	Remarks and references to Appendices
WANQUETIN	1.1.17		Captain PENNY R.A.M.C. attached as proceeded on leave by Col DOUGHERTY.	
"	2.1.17		32659 Pte ROBERTSON R.A.M.C. & 7/25898 Dr LLOYD W. A.S.C. proceeded to VII Corps workshops	
"	3.1.17		7 O.R's went on leave to ENGLAND	
"	4.1.17		Cpl DOUGHERTY R.A.M.C. tried by Court Martial — wrote to A.D.M.S. regarding Hon. Cpl ELLIOTT R.A.M.C. he adheres to the route for reinforcements. Sgt Major MARTIN R.A.M.C. went on leave to ENGLAND 3 Reinforcements arrived 32487 Pte SHUTTLEWORTH R.A.M.C. & 39673 Pte ROBERTS R.A.M.C. proceeded to VII Corps workshops	
"	5.1.17		Captain VARTAN R.A.M.C. arrives for duty taken on strength 7 O.R's returned from leave in ENGLAND	
"	6.1.17	3.30pm	Small raid & must enemy on H sector — 1 Coy trenches at 3.15 pm. Casualties when known though the A.D.S. were — 4 Officers & 33 Men wounded & 4 Queries	
"	"	9pm	Proceedings of F.G.C.M. on No 32076 Cpl W. DOUGHERTY R.A.M.C. arrived — Sentence of Court is that he be "REDUCED TO RANKS"	
"	7.1.17	12 noon	Sentence of F.G.C.M. on strength Cpl Pte on parade at H.Q.	
"	8.1.17	10 am	4th Division taken over by VII Corps —	

Army Form C. 2118.

WAR DIARY
or
INTELLIGENCE SUMMARY.
(Erase heading not required.)

Instructions regarding War Diaries and Intelligence Summaries are contained in F. S. Regs., Part II. and the Staff Manual respectively. Title pages will be prepared in manuscript.

Place	Date	Hour	Summary of Events and Information	Remarks and references to Appendices
WANQUETIN	9.11.17	—	No. 60275 Pt. WARD R.A.M.C. proceeds to ENGLAND to join Cadet School	
"	10.11.17	—	No. M/04907 S/Sgt HODGKINSON R.A.M.C. do do do	
"	"	—	Captain PENNY R.A.M.C. & 7 D.R.s proceeded on leave to ENGLAND	
"	11.11.17		Captain L.H.L. BELL R.A.M.C. reports his arrival for duty taken on strength	
"	"		Captain S.H. BOOTH R.A.M.C. returned from leave in England	
"	12.11.17		Captain C.S. VARTAN R.A.M.C. proceeded to A.N.L. at ASSEVILLEIS for duty	
"	"		Captain R.H.C. GOMPERTZ R.A.M.C. reports departs for duty with 61 Division & takes off strength	
"	13.11.17		DDMS VII Corps inspects HQ at WANQUETIN	
"	14.11.17		Routine	
"	"		Other hours D. for educative & sports by VII Corps Commander (S.I.B. 3 (2) 47) Authority No 32 307 C.Q.M.S. ELLIOTT R.A.M.C.	
"	"		No 77264 Pte TAYLOR R.A.M.C. evacuated sick	
"	15.11.17		No. 32307 Pt. ELLIOTT R.A.M.C. transferred to 422 F.A. (sickly attack)	
"	"		Rev. I. McCANN C.F. departs to Gen'l HQ in TH Army.	
"	16.11.17		Accompanies ADMS in inspection of forward area —	

WAR DIARY
or
INTELLIGENCE SUMMARY.

(Erase heading not required.)

Army Form C. 2118.

Place	Date	Hour	Summary of Events and Information	Remarks and references to Appendices
Mahaweinin	18.1.17	—	Captain BELL R.A.M.C. Appointed for Temp. duty with 9th K.R.R.C. accompanies D.O.M.S. 1st Corps + returned forward and	
"	"	"	Captain W.A. BROWN R.A.M.C. proceeded to ENGLAND on Sick leave on transfer + struck off strength	
"	"	"	Lieut. D.T.E. EVANS R.A.M.C. Reinforcement for duty taken on strength (from 61st Div. in exchange with Captain BUTLER)	
"	9.1.17	am	Accompanied A.D.M.S. in inspection of Ocean necessitating movt of forward R.A.P.	
"	"	pm	Accompanied A.D.M.S. in inspection of Ambulances billets BAVINCOURT	
"	20.1.17		Lt Colonel WEGAN proceeded on leave to ENGLAND	
"	21.1.17		Captain BartArtin reported his arrival for duty + taken on strength (from 47th Brigade, R.F.A.)	Bnt/S
	22.1.17		Lieut D.T. EVANS detailed for temporary duty with 8th M.A.C.	
			Two N.C.O's + three men proceed home to United Kingdom from Jan 23rd to Feb 2nd	18 H/S
	23.1.17		Capt. the Revd B.E. BOOKER, C.F. reported arrival + was attached to unit. One O.R. reinforcement received	18 H/S

WAR DIARY
or
INTELLIGENCE SUMMARY.
(Erase heading not required.)

Army Form C. 2118.

Place	Date	Hour	Summary of Events and Information	Remarks and references to Appendices
MANQUET.IN	24/1/17		Routine.	
"	25/1/17		One N.C.O. & three men reinforcements received.	Apps
			3192 Pte KYNASTON, A.H. } proceeded to England to form	
			57328 Pte BROWN, W.? } Cadet Unit & on return & strength	Apps
	26/1/17		32258 Pte LILL, C.D. proceeded to England to form Cadet Unit & is taken off strength	Apps
			32659 Pte ROBERTSON, D. transferred to Heavy Branch M.G.C. & is taken off strength	Apps
	27/1/17		Routine.	Apps
	28/1/17		G.O.C. commanding VIIth Corps inspected Main Dressing Station	Apps
	29/1/17		Routine	Apps
	30/1/17		Routine	Apps
	31/1/17		A.D.M.S. 14 Division inspected Main Dressing Station	Apps

B.M. Sutton. Capt R.Army
Officer commanding 43/2nd
Field Ambulance

War Diary

of

4th Field Ambulance.

for month of February 1917.

Vol 22

WAR DIARY
or
INTELLIGENCE SUMMARY.
(Erase heading not required.)

Army Form C. 2118.

Place	Date	Hour	Summary of Events and Information	Remarks and references to Appendices
WANQUETIN	12.17	—	Lt Col W. EGAN. RAMC Returns from leave in IRELAND	
"	2.2.17	—	38045 C/L EDWARDS. RAMC - charged with being by higher Authorities forto-orders to have good attno own scheme	
"	3.2.17	—	Captain VARTAN. RAMC Wounded at A.D.S. by Captain BARTON. RAMC Captain BELL. R.A.M.C Returns to Unit from temporary duty w/T. 9 KRRs. Sent confidential report on Sqn Major MARTIN, RAMC to remove. Sent away report. The WO have received Court but to note strong enough the matter now for full investigation but I read out The weak three —	
"	"	4.45 pm	Reports (both an RC officer) The Enemy at towciree which is going to be considered with one A.D.S.	
"	"	"	ADMS visited MO interviewed Sq. Major MARTIN & has to execute on my report -	
"	"	"	Child's attention of A.S. & S/o Officer to Kuring arrangements & weekly Status Care have to bath with new refrects turn = in the Bath MAS hard to Station Camp Day —	

WAR DIARY
or
INTELLIGENCE SUMMARY.

Army Form C. 2118.

Place	Date	Hour	Summary of Events and Information	Remarks and references to Appendices
WANQUETIN	4.2.17	-	Captain BELL R.A.M.C. details for duty at A.D.T. ASSAU (APRAS) orders received from A.D.M.S. (4 DIV) to hand over - R.A.P. in G sector & collecting post at ACHICOURT to 98th Field Ambulance 32nd Div on the 5th inst.	Q
"	5.2.17	-	Promotions - W/c Bruce R.A.M.C. 31867 authority - D.D.M.S. G.H.Q. Ptee alker 50207 " PHILLIPS B/14450/357 dated 1.2-17 to be A/L/c 31868 pte BROOMHEADE authority - A.G. MS.828/6 " 32302 " DUGGAN - W.G. Circular memo to 1.B.	Q
"	6.2.17	-	Orders received from A.D.M.S. (4 Div) 16 " to be in my relief to M.S. all other Cars Flee vehicle to G.O.V. Action by A.D.M.S. that Lt. D.T. EVANS proceeds permanently to S.H.A.G. as from 3.2.17 - Struck off Strength Information received from A.D.M.S. that Visit has been issued to Captain PENNY R.A.M.C. (5 FEB. 4 TH 17) No. 34,981 Pte HARRISON-R. details as servant to A.D.M.S. Orders to hold until in absence (M.S. only) Smith at very controller	Q

WAR DIARY
or
INTELLIGENCE SUMMARY.
(Erase heading not required.)

Army Form C. 2118.

Place	Date	Hour	Summary of Events and Information	Remarks and references to Appendices
WANQUETIN	6.2.17	-	HANDED OVER B. Sector Holding post at ACHICOURT to 98 Field Ambulance	2
"	7.2.17	-	No 31529 Pte ADAMS F RAMC (Chocolate Dispenser Operator) transferred Class W in his	
			and this morning. Court of Inquiry respecting from totts	
			Captain Bell RAMC delays for Enquiry duty with N Kings Liverpool	
		3/pm	Court of Inquiry held to investigate circumstances under which Pte Norris met his	2
			death. Lt Col. EVES. 43rd FA President.	
	8.2.17	-	Unit moved from WANQUETIN as per chart - Innox H Ethel proceeded out	
			20 OR RAMC moved Supply with Captain MARTIN RAMC in charge,	
			accompanied by Lt MM FOSTER. O Kew QM Stores etc.	2
			Remainder of Unit with HQ moved to Convent S Sacrament - ARRAS.	
			(Map reference G.21.C.20)	
ARRAS	"		Captain BOOTH RAMC attached to Field Ambulance & proceeds	
			to Stationary St Pol with Major Ernest J Stingt	
	"		Captain GREVILLE PENNY RAMC reports arrival from Rest Camp	
			in England	

Army Form C. 2118.

WAR DIARY
or
INTELLIGENCE SUMMARY.
(Erase heading not required.)

Instructions regarding War Diaries and Intelligence Summaries are contained in F. S. Regs., Part II. and the Staff Manual respectively. Title pages will be prepared in manuscript.

Place	Date	Hour	Summary of Events and Information	Remarks and references to Appendices
ARRAS	9.2.17	—	Captain VARTAN RAMC attached for duty with Dir School G.d Russians. Are temporary measure.	
"	"	"	Captain PENNY detailed for temp duty as DADMS to Division	
"	"	"	89 Coy RE's Bivouies hut on ADS Rouville (roa) from RONVILLE b ACHICOURT - Party details 60 ors	
"	10.2.17	"	Routine	
"	11.2.17	"	80 ors attached from 43 FA for working party	
"	12.2.17	"	Accompanies A.D.M.S in selection of RAPs left hay plain — No 4 i/c of NCWs details to go around trench	
"	13.2.17	"	Accompanies A.D.M.S in selecting sites for RAP on Right hay plain	
"	14.2.17	"	Going round forward are selecting work to be done for RAPs	
"	15.2.17	"	RAP in left hay & line selected work put in to 61 Coy RE's hands — map references G35.C.9.8 — all RAP for 2 Battn	
"	16.2.17	"	Obtained permission from C.R. Division Smoil Gallows etc below RAPs at Gallows officers superficial Cars in "Christ" Church. 5.0 ors from 42 & 43 FA (attached to NZTC) attached to 2w for work in	

Army Form C. 2118.

WAR DIARY
or
INTELLIGENCE SUMMARY.
(Erase heading not required.)

Instructions regarding War Diaries and Intelligence Summaries are contained in F. S. Regs., Part II. and the Staff Manual respectively. Title pages will be prepared in manuscript.

Place	Date	Hour	Summary of Events and Information	Remarks and references to Appendices
ARRAS	16.2.17	—	for work in R.A.P. left — 3 lumbers from 42 F.A. & 2 from 43 F.A. also attached for making road —	
"	17.2.17	—	Accompanied A.D.M.S. r/Brigade Major 43rd Bgde. in road to Church Church. Area visited & approved.	
"	18.2.17	—	Consultation with O.C. 179 Tunnelling Co. R.E. in whose hands R.A.P. of Church Church is placed.	
"	19.2.17	—	Captain BELL R.A.M.C. taken from WL Strength from F.2.T. (authority A.D.M.S. 12th Div)	
"	20.2.17	—	Took our oil factory on ACHICOURT ROAD for Medical purposes. obtained verbal authority from G.O.C. 43rd Brigade. Received notice. Heads up.	
"	21.2.17	—	Captain S. H. BOOTH R.A.M.C. returned from Hospital at ST B. & taken on the Strength. — Apparatus for Temp. duty w/z 10 R DUBH M.L. INFY 48. O.R's. details as working party w/z No 179 Tunnelling Coy R.E. for not on R.A.P. left (Church Church)	
"	"	—	Accompanied A.D.M.S. & was present when he Censured L. Cpl in Solo R.M.C. for ignorance of Div. Orders re Leave in regard to the Clock	
			D Private A.D.M.S.	

WAR DIARY
or
INTELLIGENCE SUMMARY.
(Erase heading not required.)

Army Form C. 2118.

Place	Date	Hour	Summary of Events and Information	Remarks and references to Appendices
ARRAS	21.2.17	-	ADV S. O. C. TRAN. wakefield transfer. Thanks at BARLY. Asks permission of Town Major to occupy Cellar as Orderlies as left of Rue Emile Lenglet. The Cellar is quite close to very good R.A.P. made by Sergt. Kirkpole in Vaus S' Paul. Q.M.S. Cattrall + Sergt. Watson recommended for awards. The former for a meritorious service medal. The latter honourable mention.	
"	"	-	Routine	
"	22.2.17	-		
"	23.2.17	-	The following acts appointments approx. supply 14th Div Supply Column from W 22.1.17. Maj. 0557169 a. Col. Burn G.H. K.C. MT Rtn Adj: with Bay. No 57285 Pt. Pickens. T. " " " a Col " "	
"	24.2.17	-	Captain Flood R.A.M.C appointed Sanitary Officer Ronville (formerly Army R). Captain Booth " " Sanitary to HQ from Lupiauchy with 7.5 D.L.I. Received order from A.D. Med. to make arrangements to keep beds at H.A.L.	
"	26.2.17	-	Whole days place was unsuitable - Army conveners place unsuitable	
"	27.2.17	-	All Cases blue sent to 42 F.A. Barly	
"	28.2.17	-	43.F.A. took over sick from back area	

COMMANDING No. 64 FIELD AMBULANCE
R.A.M.C.

140/2042. Vol 23

War Diary

of

No. 44. Field Ambulance.

for month of

March. 1917.

COMMITTEE FOR THE
MEDICAL HISTORY OF THE WAR
Date 11 MAY. 1917

Mar 1917
S

Army Form C. 2118.

WAR DIARY
or
INTELLIGENCE SUMMARY.
(Erase heading not required.)

Instructions regarding War Diaries and Intelligence Summaries are contained in F. S. Regs., Part II. and the Staff Manual respectively. Title pages will be prepared in manuscript.

Place	Date	Hour	Summary of Events and Information	Remarks and references to Appendices
ARRAS	1.3.17	—	Captain PENNY, R.A.M.C. returned from temporary duty as DADMS 4th Div.	2
"	2.3.17	—	Routine work in the forward area progressing by construction of R.A.P (H.Q.r. Regt) touching of Arterie in ACHICOURT Rd. — Emergency road almost complete.	2
"	3.3.17	"	Work on Reserve line begun 20a0b. made it fit for stretcher cases between HETSAS STREET & WHITE CHATEAU which is going to be used as the R.A.P	2 / 2
"	4.3.17	"	Routine	
"	5.3.17	"	Captain SHEPHERD, R.A.M.C. goes lecture on Gas	
"	6.3.17	"	No 72 & 67 Pk Harvey R.A.M.C. of the unit sent to No 12 Stationary as C.S.M.? Contacts noted.	2 / 2
"	"	"	Both shafts — entrance reached — way through to Christ Church (R.A.P. right) Contacts of C.M.O. enabled by O.C 20 Mobile Laboratory. accompanied D.A.D.M.S. 3rd Army, D.A.D.M.S VII Corps. in inspection of R.A.P forward area. —	2 / 2
"	7.3.17			
"	8.3.17		Accompanied A.D.M.S. D.A.D.M.S. in quest of good road between WAILLY — WAILLY — ARRAS DOULLENS Rd. for watching of wounded (surfaces) None.	2

WAR DIARY
or
INTELLIGENCE SUMMARY.
(Erase heading not required.)

Army Form C. 2118.

Place	Date	Hour	Summary of Events and Information	Remarks and references to Appendices
ARRAS.	9.3.17	—	Horton R.A.S. Emergency Road & Huilerie almost complete	
"	10.3.17	"	O.P. Hotel laboratory notified us that on contact No 32659 Pte ROBERTSON was carried - sent him to 42. F.A. Relieved surrounding florists	
"	"	"	Captain A.V. WEBSTER R.A.M.C. attached to unit from 43 F.A. aoa. Surgical specialist which nears nothing the forward area	
"	11.3.17	"	1st O.R. reinforcement arrived - Captain BOOTH R.A.M.C. depaired for duty as R.M.O. 47 Brigade R.F.A. Hoiten at strength	
"	12.3.17	"	R.H.P now ready for lucking etc. Ron RAS complete HUILERIE almost to my awaiting R.E.S. b/os of junct of R law of bicycle with new Enlarging RAP. Rt. wg. Phasing & entails for A.D.S on Cau Bastanes.	
"	"	9pm	Small area on enemy lines by No V L I (6 Battry) - Lieut CAPLANO FLOOD + BRETON + 24 OR (6 Platoon were laid a startfied district - RAO - All the working to front have how been under fire	
"	13.3.17	"	Routine.	
"	14.3.17	"	Routine.	

WAR DIARY or INTELLIGENCE SUMMARY

Army Form C. 2118.

Place	Date	Hour	Summary of Events and Information	Remarks and references to Appendices
ARRAS	15.3.17	—	Captain J.B. BAIRD Rome reported his arrival for duty later on the 15.3.17. Captain PENNY departed for Cavalry duty with 9th K.R.R.C.	
"	"	—		
"	16.3.17	—	Routine —	
"	17.3.17	—	6 Trau MAPS received transport this as BARLY. The following promotions authorized to complete establishment: No 50202 L/Cpl. PHILIP, R.S. Promoted to be acting Sergt. W.E.F. 15.3.17. No 31419 a/L/Sgt MACDONALD, J. Promoted the acting Cpl " " 2.3.17. Authority D.G.M.S. B/14505-58 —	
"	18.3.17	—	Proceeds R42.CCL by motor stretcher — During the night 18-19 - enemy raided first line which was taken out by Germans	
"	19.3.17	9 a.m.	42nd Infantry Brigade held lines — G36 C45 to M5-6.45 (roughly 3rd "German line") 5th K.O.L.I. in line with 9th RB in support. 110th photo Battalion and RIP, Ronville but across the K.S.L.I. in support, forward B.R.A.P. left about B raw 43rd Brigade held lines — from Oppy to M6 C.TM11d 7] The line is held by 6 Somerset L.I. with 6 D.C.L.I. in support, No Convoys has moved forwards — MSCaH. NCO on leave attacks their...	

WAR DIARY or INTELLIGENCE SUMMARY

Army Form C. 2118.

Place	Date	Hour	Summary of Events and Information	Remarks and references to Appendices
ARRAS	19.3.17	8.0am	Cars brought to Cars Ablain Ame de Bapaume & there they are shewn by MO DCLI Hunt to Collecting post. MO Somervell had cells to clean up German dugout to use as RAP. Collecting Post ADS at 8.2 (Browny) Ronville as Collecting Post where wounds from 43 Brigade are brought. where MO at 5.1.2. Went up his wounded were also be taken thru. Cars wounded from Collecting post to CONVENT	
"	20.3.17		Sinclair. Same as yesterday — MO 5.T.SL1 moved up to Rly left. Captain A.V. STOCKS. RAMC reported his arrival for duty. Taken on the strength.	
"	20.3.17		Colonel GRAY. C.B. RAMC. Surgical Specialist to 3rd Army. Visited ADS. Forward area & afterwards gave a lecture on various ADS. to the MOs	
"	"		nursing staff of the Unit.	
"	19.3.17	"	Captain BAIRD RAMC. details for temporary duty vice 4/1 B. Rt. 8.F.a during the absence of Captain BOOTH on short course of Instruction at S.T.S.	
"	22.3.17		C. Section packs ready wt Complete transport at the Central ARRAS. (orders received from Home.)	

Army Form C. 2118.

WAR DIARY
or
INTELLIGENCE SUMMARY.
(Erase heading not required.)

Instructions regarding War Diaries and Intelligence Summaries are contained in F. S. Regs., Part II. and the Staff Manual respectively. Title pages will be prepared in manuscript.

Place	Date	Hour	Summary of Events and Information	Remarks and references to Appendices
ARRAS	22.3.17	—	No 31490 Pte Le MARINER. W.H. R.A.M.C. Reports for duty with Railway Construction Coy R.E. — Struck off Strength.	
"	"	—	No 30808 Pte RIMMER. J. R.A.M.C. Rejoined A/c with Ray from 21.3.17	
"	23.3.17		No 31809 Pte WARDA. & 35324 Pte GEE. B.C. R.A.M.C. Posted to Railway Coy R.E. Struck off Strength	
"	"		Captain D.S. GRAHAM R.A.M.C. Reports he assumed duties as French Assoc'ts Transport Officer's Funct'.	
"	24.3.17	"	Captain BAIRD P.M.C. returned from Leave/duty with 47 Bde P.H.e.	
"	25.3.17	"	No 50 202 Cpl. PHILLIP J.B. April wounds & evacuated	
"	"		Received Orders Over from A.D.M.S. – Lieut MO. STANLEY LouisB Neulthouse Specialist (San Jac) at P.O.L. — Haemorrage Hems 6 Types Lynne Caused by Shell explosion on 23.3.17. Arrests Discharges delay'd by Small Arms fired Carp Repairing Forms No 9966 + 14385 assured Later	
"	27.3.17	"	Burial Party — LOFTHOUSE + ENDIE Pouling — Worky no R.A.P's almost finished	
"	28.3.17	"	Pouling —	

Army Form C. 2118.

WAR DIARY
or
INTELLIGENCE SUMMARY.
(Erase heading not required.)

Instructions regarding War Diaries and Intelligence Summaries are contained in F.S. Regs., Part II. and the Staff Manual respectively. Title pages will be prepared in manuscript.

Place	Date	Hour	Summary of Events and Information	Remarks and references to Appendices
RUES	29.3.17	—	Lieut. Mitchel & A.H.S. - went to B.E.A.S Doullens.	
	30.3.17	—	Captain Karth N Rowe returns from Div School at Ruvicourt.	
	31.3.17	—	Captain Karth & Captain Martin to Albert for duty G.H.O. Simencourt.	

COMMANDING No. 44 FIELD AMBULANCE

No. 44 FIELD AMBULANCE
ROYAL ARMY MEDICAL CORPS
DATE 31/3/17

140/2086

COMMITTEE FOR THE
MEDICAL HISTORY OF THE WAR
Date −6 JUN. 1917

WAR DIARY or INTELLIGENCE SUMMARY

Army Form C. 2118.

Place	Date	Hour	Summary of Events and Information	Remarks and references to Appendices
ARRAS	1.4.17		Accompanied Brigade Major 43rd Brigade. Relieved 2nd German August (H.E.Bat) off LONDON TRENCH - map ref:- H5.a.80.50 57.B for an R.A.P. it's available before "Zero" Also a Cellar in BEAURAINS H.11.a.20.50 as a divisn R.A.P.	
"	2.4.17		Serg. Major MARTIN R.A.M.C. admitted to F.A. & transferred to Div. REST STN. (4n.F.) Captain R.R.G. ATKINS R.A.M.C. (S.R.) reported his arrival & taken on Strength of Unit	
"	3.4.17		Operation Order No 55 received from ADMS 14th Div	
"	4.4.17		Captain C.H.G. PENNY. R.A.M.C. (S.R.) returned from temp.y duty with 7th K.R.R.C. Roulins	
"	5.4.17		"Zero" postponed for 24 hours	
RONVILLE	7.4.17	3pm	X-day - Head Quarters Punit- moved to "BRASSERIE RONVILLE" - the ADS for actuis. 7pm A Tent Subdivision t/c Captain FLOOD left at Convent St. SACREMENT live Y day.	
"	8.4.17	12 Noon	Y day - Captain FLOOD reports HQ. A Tent Subdivision t/c Captain McDOUGALL RAMC (att. 179 Coy RE) proceeds to look over charge of HULERIE ACHICOURT Road - Prepare Plans for the Collection & evacuation of wounded a of today - Position of Brigades. - 42nd Brigade left of the line. 2 batt.s in line & 2 in Support	
			43rd " "	
			41st " " Right of the line - " " " " in the Caves at CHRISTCHURCH Tunt	

WAR DIARY
or
INTELLIGENCE SUMMARY.

Army Form C. 2118.

Place	Date	Hour	Summary of Events and Information	Remarks and references to Appendices
RONVILLE	8.4.17		"Man of Collection" Evacuation cont?... but known not up to usual supply between HETSAS ST. HODGE E.S. at Zero + 2 hrs + 2 hrs + 2 hrs. — Refers to trouble 42nd Bgde Bearer Divn by 42 F.A. — Bearer Officers Captains CRAIG & EVANS	
			" 43rd " " " 44 F.A. " FLOOD & SMITH	
			" 41st " " " 43 F.A. " BACH, ALLGOOD & HAMNETT	
			Proportion of bearers at Zero + 2 hr (Div Z+10) as follows —	
			42nd Brigade — 12 bearers to each R.A.P. in the line —	
			2 " " Advance Brigade H.Q.	
			(or Divy H.Q.) 1 " " Advance Each R.M.O.	
			Remainder placed less the complete bearer subdivision in reserve at R.H.Q. (33rd R.A.M.C.)	
			43rd Brigade — 16 bearers to each Bn No. 1 R.A.P. in the line	
			2 " Advance Brigade H.Q.	
			1 " Advance to each R.M.O.	
			↑ This proportion bore up all available bearers of this unit to some few (behind our A.D.S. RONVILLE — 8 Z Bearer Officers accompanied remainder placed which were distributed as follows.	

WAR DIARY or INTELLIGENCE SUMMARY

Army Form C. 2118.

(Erase heading not required.)

Instructions regarding War Diaries and Intelligence Summaries are contained in F. S. Regs., Part II. and the Staff Manual respectively. Title pages will be prepared in manuscript.

Place	Date	Hour	Summary of Events and Information	Remarks and references to Appendices
RONVILLE	8.4.17		Coll A 1 Officer + 32 bearers to R.A.P Left (RA-1 60.50)	
			1 Officer + 36 " " to " Right (M11 a 20.80)	
			41st Brigade — 1 Officer + 36 bearers locate in dug-out in experts-hive near	
			HALSTEAD ST. also in bomber midnight Y–Z –	
			This left a reserve of a complete bearer Div (1 Section + 2 + 2 from 42 F.A.) at HOUDAIN	
			Reserve of Stretcher blankets 1 249$ ground at each R.A.P by 3RD	
			H.Q.s RONVILLE staffed by 2 tent subdivisions assisted by DIV's B & D	
"	9.4.17	5.30am	ZERO –	
"		7.30am	Div's ZERO – Bearer Subdivisions R + B 2nd F.A. brought up to RONVILLE	
"		10.30am	First objective reported taken. Ambulance Car able to move up to R.A.P.s	
			G 35.a.25.85 also up to BONVILLE – Forks + horses ambulances used to	
"		1.30pm	R.A.P became a Collecting post for R.T.O's moved up to M.112 G 60.50	
			with DADMS in Corps for 10 M.T. cars + 50 Stretchers 700 blankets – obtain	
			Same from Corps M.D.S.	
"		4pm	R.A.P Right (M11 a 20.80) Neurelia Clear – Wired notified that 3 or "Special"	
			7 wounded + R.A.P Flea Ambulance – Relief of 10 men sent to RAP	

T2134. Wt. W708–776. 500000. 4/15. Sir J. C. & S.

Army Form C. 2118.

WAR DIARY
or
INTELLIGENCE SUMMARY.
(Erase heading not required.)

Instructions regarding War Diaries and Intelligence Summaries are contained in F.S. Regs., Part II. and the Staff Manual respectively. Title pages will be prepared in manuscript.

Place	Date	Hour	Summary of Events and Information	Remarks and references to Appendices
RONVILLE	July 9/17	9am	No% of O.R. P.R.C. reported that field and H.Q. P.R.Ob. H.C. 2×10 reports all casualties 63% in 42 Brigade front.	
		4pm	Officer who has been went up reinforced trench relief to 43rd Brigade.	
		5pm	3 bearer divisions for 41st Brigade and trenches 4 2/0.	
			No % of I.H.C.C. reports all cases dress on Brigade front.	
	1.45pm		During the day the German shewn greatly exceeded in closing the first	2
			aid mounted chairs from H.D.S.	
	10.4/17	5.30am	Informed that 41st Brigade were moving up to relieve 120 Brigade in line	
		9pm	accompanied H.D.M.S. moved R.A.P. forward area — Cap/s 20	2
		3pm	Information from us — wounded lying out	
			41st Brigade trie without success to take W.N.CO. O.P.	
	11.4/17	8am	Cap. G.O.C. 41st Brigade the use of two impossible Echos any move to	
		12noon	who may be lying out during day long being to suebes	2
			during afternoon retiring heavy enemy gunfire	
		3pm	Asked for reinforce 20 extra bearers blankets from L. Corps H.A.	2
			Herr Officer reports 80 stretcher cases injured in 1st/1st Wancest	2
			Private CHAFFEY (No. 31462) wounded ruracuatis on to N.R. unit	2

WAR DIARY
or
INTELLIGENCE SUMMARY.
(Erase heading not required.)

Army Form C. 2118.

Place	Date	Hour	Summary of Events and Information	Remarks and references to Appendices
PONVILLE	12.4.19	3 P.M.	Brig. officers wrote all chat infant of Manoeuvre	
		8.30am	all ranks + officers paraded. F.A.s brought in.	
		"	Midnight sanders over A.D.S forward area 6. Y/1 Northumbrian F.A. relieved 6-	
			Ament MS+C+EMENT AREAS Personnel (manual) total on by on	
			Numbers of field wounded— 323 a/c/c Bromhead S/888	
			9-10 " 131 { 656	Q
			10-11 " 202 Cox 34450	Q
			11-6 This 19R.	Q
ARRAS	13.4.19		Captain Flood + C. Tent out aureous were to HARBACR	Q
			" Partan Parol check off through in 9 feet. 1 transfer to HQ-DH.	
			Captain ATKINS joined Captain FLOOD at H.A.R.B+C.Q.	
"	14.4.19		Met above personnel boating	Q
	15.4.19			
"	16.4.19		Following recommendations for immediate reward towards to A.D.M.S	Q
			Hilary Ord. – Captain Flood. BARTON. CRAIG	
			DCH – Sgt WATSON 4/4 F.A. + Sgt JOHN SMITH + 2 F.A.	

Army Form C. 2118.

WAR DIARY
or
INTELLIGENCE SUMMARY.
(Erase heading not required.)

Place	Date	Hour	Summary of Events and Information	Remarks and references to Appendices
ARRAS	15.4.17	—	Military Medal -	
			44 FA Privates - Chalke, Burkhardt, Painter, Johnstone, (all Pte)	
			42 FA " Palmer, Edmonson, Rawnsley & Dr Hamilton, QSSM	
			43 FA Sgt Blandford, Pte Birse	
BERNEVILLE	16.4.17	12 noon	Unit less transport arrived at BERNEVILLE (Sheet 57C D.6)	
"	17 "		Unit also closed.	
"	18 "		do	
"	19 "		do Transport took over So A.W. T&A at BARLY	
"	20 "		do i/c of Captain GRAHAM & 2nd Lt FOSTER	
"	21 "		do	
"	22 "		do	
BARLY	26.4.17	4 pm	HQrs Personnel (omit transport) HQrs at BARLY. Came up to 7th B'gd + 8 B'gds &	
"	29.4.17	7 pm	left BARLY with 42 Brigade. Surplus Equipment dumps etc at BERNEVILLE	
BELLACOURT	"	11 pm	arrived here -	
"	"	6 pm	42nd Brigade horse with forward area. Supplies Stores, Cookhouses	
			& to pick up Stragglers – Billets West of Brigade + awaits orders	

WAR DIARY
or
INTELLIGENCE SUMMARY.
(Erase heading not required.)

Army Form C. 2118.

Place	Date	Hour	Summary of Events and Information	Remarks and references to Appendices
BELLACOURT	24.4.17	—	Captain BAIRD RAMC arrived to M/c 6th KOYLI relief of the things 23.4.17	
"	8.4.17	3pm	Captain STOCKS " " sick relieved by the 1/4 HLI. Orders received to take over Corps walking wounds Camp (MERCATEL – MQUEEG) 578.	
"	"	3.30pm	Forces at once to arrange for taking over	
"	"	3.30pm	Went to MERCATEL to arrange	
"	26.4.17	8.30am	Advance party H/c R. Captain DENNY departed to H.R. Camp.	
"	"	12.45pm	H.Q. Remainder of Unit left BELLACOURT for MERCATEL. State over.	
MERCATEL	"	3pm	Unit arrived taking up for reception of sick -	
"	"		R. remained behind at BELLACOURT (sick in billet)	
"	27.4.17	—	OC. went to CDRS. BARLY for rest	
"	"		Sick phones (military midday) (mid/eve) (evening) — all men recommended have an everaders Military meals	
"	28.4.17	—	Ambulance — 2 bearer officers - 20 O.R.s mid-up to form aux — attached	
"	29.4.17		42nd Field Ambulance -	
"	"		No 78302 Pte. HALL R.A.M.C. wounded in action, evacuated to Reserved Unit.	

Army Form C. 2118.

WAR DIARY
or
INTELLIGENCE SUMMARY.
(Erase heading not required.)

Place	Date	Hour	Summary of Events and Information	Remarks and references to Appendices
MERCATEL	29.4.17		Sgt SMITH - RMC (142 FA) awarded a Military Medal (recommended for DCM) Captain ATKINS RAMC detailed for temporary duty to 140 F.A.y LIEUT MORRIS M.C the Sleigh to the Unit from this date. Bearer Officers mainly returned to Rear Quarters	2
"	30.4.17			2

B.E.F.

SUMMARY OF MEDICAL WAR DIARIES FOR 44th F.A., 14th Divn. 7th Corps, 3rd Army.

WESTERN FRONT. April- May. '17.

O.C. Lt. Col. W. Egan.

SUMMARISED UNDER THE FOLLOWING HEADINGS.

Phase "B" Battle of Arras- April- May. '17.

1st Period Attack on Vimy Ridge April.

2nd Period Capture of Siegfried Line May.

B.E.F.

<u>44th F.A. 14th Divn. 7th Corps.</u>   <u>WESTERN FRONT.</u>
<u>O.C. Lt. Col. W. Egan.</u>   April- '17.
<u>3rd Army.</u>

<u>Phase "B" Battle of Arras- April- May. '17.</u>
<u>1st Period Attack on Vimy Ridge April.</u>

1917. Headquarters. At Arras.

April- 7th. <u>Moves.</u> To Ronville.

8th. <u>Medical Arrangements:</u> A.D.S. Established.

"A" T.D.S. in charge of Huilerie, Achicourt Road.

16 Brs. at each Battln. R.A.P. in line.

1 and 32 Brs. at L. R.A.P. (M.5.d.80.50)

1 and 26 Brs. at R. R.A.P. (M.11 a.20.80) Sheet. 51 B.

9th. <u>Operations.</u> Divnl. Zero 7.30 a.m. First Objective taken. 10.30 a.m.

<u>Medical Arrangements:</u> Br. S.D. 42nd Field Ambulance attached to A.D.S.

R.A.P. G. 35 D.25.85 formed into Coll. P. as R.M.Os. moved.forward.

10 additional M. Ambulances received from C.M.D.S.- 2 p.m.

0 and 10 sent to 42nd Field Ambulance to replace W. 2 p.m.

1 and 60 sent to reinforce Brs. of 43rd Bgde. 5 p.m.

0 and 38 sent to reinforce Brs. of 42nd Bgde. 5 p.m.

<u>Evacuation:</u> Fords and H. Ambulances cleared from R.A.P. G. 35.d.25.85. 10.30 a.m.

German P.O.W. assisted in clearing wounded.

R.R.A.P. cleared 2 p.m.

Bgde Front cleared 6.45 p.m.

<u>Casualties R.A.M.C.</u> 0 and 3 wounded.

B.E.F. 2.

<u>44th F.A. 14th Divn. 7th Corps.</u>　　　<u>WESTERN FRONT.</u>
　　<u>O.C. Lt. Col. W. Egan.</u>　　　　　April. '17
　　　<u>3rd Army.</u>

<u>Phase "B" cont.</u>
<u>1st Period cont.</u>

1917. April.10th.	<u>Casualties: Evacuation:</u> All wounded cleared from A.D.S. 5 am. 9th- 10th 323 wounded evacuated.
11th.	<u>Operations.</u> 41st Bde. attempted to capture Wancourt, without success.
	<u>Casualties: Evacuation:</u> Impossible to collect wounded during day owing to snipers. 10th- 11th 131 wounded evacuated.
	All wounded cleared in front of Wancourt by 3 a.m. 12th.
	<u>Casualties: Evacuation:</u> 11th- 12th 202 wounded evacuated.
	<u>Medical Arrangements:</u> A.D.S. and Forward Area handed over to 1/1st North. Field Ambulance.
	<u>Moves.</u> To Convent St. Sacrement Arras.
13th.	<u>Moves Detachment:</u> 1 and "C" T.S.D. to Harbacq.
16th.	<u>Moves:</u> To Berneville.
17th-22nd.	<u>Operations R.A.M.C.</u> Routine- Unit closed.
23rd-24th.	<u>Moves:</u> To Bellacourt.
26th.	To Mercatel M.29.d.8.8. (Sheet 51B)
	<u>Medical Arrangements:</u> C.W.W.P. opened.
27th.	<u>Decorations:-</u>

　　　Pte. Chalke.　　　)
　　　　　　　　　　　　)
　　　　"　Burkhardt　　)
　　　　　　　　　　　　) awarded M.M.
　　　　"　Painter　　　)
　　　　　　　　　　　　)
　　　　"　Johnstone　　)

B.E.F.

<u>44th F.A. 14th Divn. 7th Corps.</u>   <u>WESTERN FRONT.</u>

<u>O.C. Lt. Col. W. Egan.</u>   <u>April. '17.</u>

<u>3rd Army.</u>

<u>Phase "B" cont.</u>

<u>1st Period cont.</u>

1917.

April. 28th.   <u>Moved Detachment:</u> 2 and 60 to 42nd Field Ambulance to assist in forward area. Returned 30th.

29th.   <u>Casualties R.A.M.C.</u> 0 and 1 wounded.

B.E.F.

44th F.A. 14th Divn. 7th Corps.   WESTERN FRONT.
O.C. Lt. Col. W. Egan.   April- '17.
3rd Army.

Phase "B" Battle of Arras- April- May. '17.
1st Period Attack on Vimy Ridge April.

1917.	Headquarters. At Arras.
April- 7th.	Moves. To Ronville.
8th.	Medical Arrangements: A.D.S. Established.

"A" T.D.S. in charge of Huilerie, Achicourt Road.

16 Brs. at each Battln. R.A.P. in line.

1 and 32 Brs. at L. R.A.P. (M.5.d.80.50)

1 and 26 Brs. at R. R.A.P. (M.11 a.20.80) Sheet. 51 B.

9th. Operations. Divnl. Zero 7.30 a.m. First Objective taken 10.30 a.m.

Medical Arrangements: Br. S.D. 42nd Field Ambulance attached to A.D.S.

R.A.P. G. 35 D.25.85 formed into Coll. P. as R.M.O's. moved forward.

10 additional M. Ambulances received from C.M.D.S.- 2 p.m.

0 and 10 sent to 42nd Field Ambulance to replace W. 2 p.m.

1 and 60 sent to reinforce Brs. of 43rd Bgde. 5 p.m.

0 and 38 sent to reinforce Brs. of 42nd Bgde. 5 p.m.

Evacuation: Fords and H. Ambulances cleared from R.A.P. G. 35.d.25.85. 10.30 a.m.

German P.O.W. assisted in clearing wounded.

R.R.A.P. cleared 2 p.m.

Bgde Front cleared 6.45 p.m.

Casualties R.A.M.C. 0 and 3 wounded.

B.E.F.

44th F.A. 14th Divn. 7th Corps.   WESTERN FRONT.
O.C. Lt. Col. W. Egan.   April. '17
3rd Army.

Phase "B" cont.
1st Period cont.

1917. April.10th.	Casualties: Evacuation: All wounded cleared from A.D.S. 5 am. 9th- 10th 323 wounded evacuated.
11th.	Operations. 41st Bde. attempted to capture Wancourt, without success.
	Casualties: Evacuation: Impossible to collect wounded during day owing to snipers 10th- 11th 131 wounded evacuated.
	All wounded cleared in front of Wancourt by 3 a.m.
12th.	
	Casualties: Evacuation: 11th- 12th 202 wounded evacuated.
	Medical Arrangements: A.D.S. and Forward Area handed over to 1/1st North. Field Ambulance.
	Moves. To Convent St Sacrement Arras.
13th.	Moves Detachment: 1 and "C" T.S.D. to Harbacq.
16th.	Moves: To Berneville.
17th-22nd.	Operations R.A.M.C. Routine- Unit closed.
23rd-24th.	Moves: To Bellacourt.
26th.	To Mercatel M.29.d.8.8. (Sheet 51B)
	Medical Arrangements: C.W.W.P. opened.
27th.	Decorations:-

Pte. Chalke.   )
 " Burkhardt   )
) awarded M.M.
 " Painter   )
)
 " Johnstone   )

44th F.A. 14th Divn. 7th Corps. WESTERN FRONT.

O.C. Lt. Col. W. Egan. April. '17.

3rd Army.

Phase "B" cont.
1st Period cont.

1917.
April. 28th.   Moves Detachment: 2 and 60 to 42nd Field Ambulance to assist in forward area. Returned 30th.
29th.   Casualties R.A.M.C. 0 and 1 wounded.

WAR DIARY

44 FIELD AMBULANCE

MAY 1 – 31, 1917

WAR DIARY
or
INTELLIGENCE SUMMARY
(Erase heading not required.)

Army Form C. 2118.

Place	Date	Hour	Summary of Events and Information	Remarks and references to Appendices
HERCATEL	1.9.17		Enemy nothing party but up 5 forward area -	2
"	2.9.17	6pm	Captains FIELD & BARTON take the buses up to RAP & Field Ambulance for duty during active operations - All Motor Ambulances (then a ford) also sent to DC & 2 Field Ambulance	2
"	"	"	Lorries & buses began journey from hr Corps for wounded & walking wounded	
"	3.9.17	3.45 am	Zero - Artillery barrage & Infantry attack began.	2
"	"	6 AM	Walking wounded begin to arrive - Motors & cars follow - majority clear to CCS slightly wounded & WD walked - Corps Rest Station - Cars start to come lying after attack - Corps train leaving station (Dorser) - Motors Cars evacuate sick & to Railway SRB.	
"	"	Noon	Railway Clearing finished.	
"	4.9.17	6 am	Total casualties (less those sick or died wounds at CHS)	2
			14th Div. 429 ⎫	
			9th Div. 427 ⎬ Total =	
			18th Div. 690. ⎪ 8u Officers 1705 OR s.	
			62 Div. 83. ⎭	
			Corps Troops 62	
			GERMANS 11	

WAR DIARY
or
INTELLIGENCE SUMMARY.
(Erase heading not required.)

Army Form C. 2118.

Place	Date	Hour	Summary of Events and Information	Remarks and references to Appendices
MERCATEL	4.5.17		Brigade Staff. Bearer Officers & NCOs taken for Ref: following Casualties reported during return Operations during the Night. No. 58755 Pte FROXWELL S.F. ┐ " 53699 " LOUND. G. ├ Wounds – Remained " 28117 " WARREN. J.H. ┘ To duty. " 31465 " HADDEN. D. ┐ Slightly wounded To duty.	✓ ✓
"	"	6.30pm	Once early morning, enemy Stragglers attacking – Troops lorries arriving Black Pit	
"	"	6.30pm	Captain F.G. Flood delivers 15 Report & O.C. 42 Field Ambulance for further forward Area	
"	"	10.30pm	1 N.C.O. & 20 bearers sent to O.C. 42 Field Ambulance	
"	"	–	Following awards appeared in Div¹ Orders (4.5.17) Captain F.G. FLOOD 44 Field Ambulance ┐ T/Captain B.H. BARTON do ├ Military Cross No. 31318 Sgt W.D. WATSON do ┘ A.C.M.	✓ ✓
"	5.5.17	5.30pm	1 N.C.O. & 20 bearers returned from 42 Field Ambulance	
"	"	11pm	Corps Commander Inspected Camp	
"	6.5.17	–	Routine – very few wounded coming through	

Army Form C. 2118.

WAR DIARY
or
INTELLIGENCE SUMMARY.
(Erase heading not required.)

Instructions regarding War Diaries and Intelligence Summaries are contained in F. S. Regs., Part II. and the Staff Manual respectively. Title pages will be prepared in manuscript.

Place	Date	Hour	Summary of Events and Information	Remarks and references to Appendices
HERCATEL	7.5.17	—	Police received from O.C. 55 F.A. 1/c S/C O/No M.D.S. pte that Pr No 53699. O. LOUND Pte. on the 5th inst- from G.S.W.	
"	"	—	H.Q. 6th Seaforth L.I. W.Ost- stating he has put his piercer No 40352 Pt MATHIESON under arrest -	2
"	"	3pm	Pte MATHIESON arrived in Camp under Close arrest. awft- for Coy of charge - documents Evidence Enquiries.	2
"	8.5.17	4pm	2 Officers 4 NCO's of Russ (Heavy) reports to - 49" Feet Am Column for duty	
"	9.5.17	—	extraction enquiries in reference to charge for which he was placed under arrest by H.Q. 6th Seaforth - The M.O. had given him to orders re taking Baths during the night then have no evidence or Evidence of Inoculation of Mathieson at Bath area on records at the time. Mathieson' being Killed	2
"	"	7pm	under instructions from HQ MS Captain PENNY R.A.M.C. attached for Temp duty see K 11th King's LIVERPOOLs BOOTHBY.D	
"	"	10pm	7 Lieut ALEXANDER RETIE reports his arrival return to the Group K Bearer officer from scheme B 5th Guards Brigade Poulin-	2
"	10.5.17	"		
"	11.5.17	"	3 Bearer Officers 15 O.R.s attached 542 F.A. for clearing the forward area	2

WAR DIARY
or
INTELLIGENCE SUMMARY.
(Erase heading not required.)

Army Form C. 2118.

Place	Date	Hour	Summary of Events and Information	Remarks and references to Appendices
MERCATEL	11.5.17		M/25898 Dr LLOYD W ASC Aparks for duty out 1B.M.T.D rather of gen hospt	
"	12.5.17		Bearer Officers MRs returned. No.771S7 Pte COVENEY V. RAMC proceeds inacer Forceaux	
			LIEUT A. BOOTHROYD RAMC attacks for Permanent duty with 11 Kings LIVERPOOLS R.	
			Struck off Strength	
"	13.5.17		Captain PENNY reports unit. T2/11376 Dr HART A/Cor deports for duty Veter or thoght	
"	14.5.17		No.66885 Sgt BRYANT.G.W RAMC } wounds to CCS	
			M2/147298 Pte EADIE R AOC MT }	
			NO 31883 Pte CURTIS W.H. RAMC Sent to 1st Stationary H. German Stack. (13 sh)	
			2 Officers + 3 OR's reports for duty with 42nd FA for winter in forward area	
"			T4/843 Dr LOWE.V A/C proceeds in teen.	
"	15.5.17		S/73.17 Pte GREENWOOD.S. April towards (slight) at duty	
			3 Officers + 6 ors returned	
"	16.5.17		Joining	
"	17.5.17		M2/104767 Pte PEARSON H A/Cor.MT reports for duty	
			3 Officers + 52 ORs West 42nd FA for duty in forward area	
"	18.5.17		NO 31257 Pte KNOWLES T RAMC granted 10 days leave to ENGLAND	

WAR DIARY
or
INTELLIGENCE SUMMARY.
(Erase heading not required.)

Army Form C. 2118.

Place	Date	Hour	Summary of Events and Information	Remarks and references to Appendices
HEM(ATEL)[?]	18.5.17	-	T4/241304 Dr STRANG J. AVC(HT) departs Netual Rtn on Charge Bearer party returned	Q
"	19.5.17	"	Routine	
"	20.5.17	"	Captain E.D. LINDON RAMC reports for duty Return to Charge	
"	21.5.17	5.15pm	Relief Directors of 33rd Divison	Q
"	"	"	Relieved toilets to show No 90399 Cpl WILLIAMS. E. RAMC as Cpl'g S'g' from 29.5.15	Q
"	22.5.17	"	Mounted details from 8 am 21.5.17 to 8 am 22.5.17 16 officers 5 to OR'S	E
"	"	"	Bearer party relieved	
"	22.5.17	"	Captain BARTON absence for Neymerun P.41 St Ing & Brigade HQ at Cellus	Q
"	"	"	NO.31371 Pte J. MALONEY RAMC admitted on transfer to ENGLAND.	P
"	23.5.17	-	32337 Pte T. JOHNSTONE Return in 65. Transportation to No Direct RMC? ... ?	Q
"	"	"	Captain J.H. TAYLOR RAMC Reports for duty Rtn on charge	
"	"	"	Ntice 152 OR's Lucien's & 42 PA for work as bearers	
"	"	"	3/863 Pte CURTIS Rtn'l Reports asume for duty return on 1st H'g.R	
"	"	"	77926 Pte BELL A Rtn'l evacuate sick Nomel to charge from 13.5.17	
"	"	"	Mounted Returns from Army Bearer Divison for detached personnel	Q

WAR DIARY or INTELLIGENCE SUMMARY

Army Form C. 2118.

Place	Date	Hour	Summary of Events and Information	Remarks and references to Appendices
MERCATEL	24.9.17	—	Captain PENNY, R.A.M.C. detailed for temp'y duty with 6 N.Y.L.I.	
			30361 Pte POPE }	
			39041 " Knight } proceeded on leave to ENGLAND	
			39375 " PAINTER }	
	"		Bearer party returned from 42 F.A.	
	25.9.17		2 O.R's (57317 Pte GREENWOOD & 31179 Pte CHURCHLAND) sent to 3 Army Rest Camp	
	26.9.17		10 O.R's details to working party with 42 F.A.	
	"		No 64965 Pte RUSSELL R. awarded 5 days F.P. No 2 absence from roll call, same P.	
			6 B.A.M. Shrink - Automatically Abs'd station places to be	
	"	11 AM	No 34463 Pte R°KINLAY sentenced for 5 days L.y. Coy for stealing Boots	
			the property of a Comrade.	
	"	5 PM	Summary of evidence taken in reference of accused forces up not	
			hasoning any documents towards it to H.Q.S.	
	"		2 Officers & 2 O.R's reported 5/42 F.A. for hospital as being	
			5-3 PM received O.O. %6 of 7.D.A.M.C. in reference to their operation of	
			33rd Div'n for the 27.5.17, only these for C.R.S will be taken up at H in Box 26	

WAR DIARY
or
INTELLIGENCE SUMMARY.
(Erase heading not required.)

Army Form C. 2118.

Place	Date	Hour	Summary of Events and Information	Remarks and references to Appendices
MERCATEL	27.5.17	—	Bearer Party relieved from 42 FA	
	28.5.17	"	Bou[...]	
	29.5.17	"	No 528172 Pte T. PRESCOTT Front Schools for Artry. He has not finished course.	
			1 H.L. officer - Lieut Confederation attd to 75 FA in reference to men concussed.	
			R. Shift by Cres	
			Captain GRAHAM Atkins takes place of 246 B.A. R.F.A. duty	
	30.5.17	—	F.G. Court-Martial held at Div. HQ on No 34683 Pte McKINLAY. P.	
	31.5.17	—	Captain BARTON appointed President	
			Orders received to Close training Manuals & return at MERCATEL	
			Schools held at AGNY (115 a 88 sheet 51B)	

[signature]

B.E.F.

SUMMARY OF MEDICAL WAR DIARIES FOR 44th F.A., 14th Divn. 7th Corps, 3rd Army.

WESTERN FRONT. April- May. '17.

O.C. Lt. Col. W. Egan.

SUMMARISED UNDER THE FOLLOWING HEADINGS.

Phase "B" Battle of Arras- April- May. '17.

1st Period Attack on Vimy Ridge April.
2nd Period Capture of Siegfried Line May.

B.E.F.

44th F.A., 14th Divn., 7th Corps.   WESTERN FRONT

O.C. Lt. Col. W. Egan.   May. '17.

3rd Army.

Phase "B" Battle of Arras- April- May. '17.
2nd Period Capture of Siegfried Line May.

1917.

May. 2nd. Medical Arrangements: 2 and Brs, sent to 42nd Field Ambulance for duty during operations.
All M. Ambulances (Less 1 Ford) sent to 42nd Field Ambulance.. Lorries and Buses arrived for evacuation of wounded.

3rd. Operations- Zero. 3.45.a.m. Artillery barrage and infantry attack began.

Casualties:- W.W. began to arrive 6 a.m.

Total admissions:-

14th Divn.   429 wounded.
21st   "   427   "
18th   "   690   "
62nd   "   85   "
Corps Troops.   62   "
P.O.W.   11   "

Evacuation: By lorries and Buses as follows:-
Majority of Cases to C.C.S.
Slightly wounded and N.Y.D. Shell Shock to C.R.S.
Lying cases to C.M.D.S.

4th. Casualties R.A.M.C. 0 and 4 wounded.

Decorations:-

Capt. F.G. Flood   )
) awarded M.C.
Capt. B.H. Barton)

B.E.F.

<u>44th F.A., 14th Divn. 7th Corps.</u>   <u>WESTERN FRONT</u>
<u>O.C. Lt. Col. W. Egan.</u>   <u>May. '17.</u>
<u>3rd Army.</u>

<u>Phase "B" cont.</u>
<u>2nd Period cont.</u>

1917.
May. 4th. cont.
     <u>Decorations:-</u> cont.
     Sgt. W.D. Watson awarded D.C.M.

6th.   <u>Casualties:</u> Few wounded arrived.

11th.   <u>Moves Detachment:</u>
     2 and 52 to 42nd Field Ambulance to assist in
     clearing forward area. Returned 12th.
     <u>Casualties R.A.M.C.</u> 0 and 1 wounded.

14th.   <u>Moves Detachment:</u> 2 and 52 to 42nd Field Ambulance
     for work in forward area.
     Returned 15th.
     <u>Casualties R.A.M.C.</u> 0 and 1 wounded.

17th.   <u>Moves Detachment</u> 2 and 52 to 42nd Field Ambulance
     for duty in forward area.
     Returned 18th.

20th.   <u>Operations.</u> Active operations by 33rd Division
     commenced 5.15 a.m.
     <u>Casualties.</u> 6 a.m.- 6a.m. 21st 16 and 510 wounded

26th.   <u>Moves Detachment:</u> 2 and 52 to 42nd Field Ambulance
     for worked as Brs.
     Returned 27th.

B.E.F.

44th F.A., 14th Divn., 7th Corps.　　WESTERN FRONT
O.C. Lt. Col. W. Egan.　　May. '17.
3rd Army.

Phase "B" Battle of Arras- April- May. '17.
2nd Period Capture of Siegfried Line May.

1917.

May. 2nd.　　Medical Arrangements:　2 and Brs, sent to 42nd Field Ambulance for duty during operations.

All M. Ambulances (Less 1 Ford) sent to 42nd Field Ambulance.　Lorries and Buses arrived for evacuation of wounded.

3rd.　　Operations-　Zero. 3.45.a.m.　Artillery barrage and infantry attack began.

Casualties:-　W.W. began to arrive 6 a.m.

Total admissions:-

14th Divn.　　429 wounded.
21st　 "　　　427 "
18th　 "　　　690 "
62nd　 "　　　85 "
Corps Troops.　62 "
P.O.W.　　　　11 "

Evacuation: By lorries and Buses as follows:-
Majority of Cases to C.C.S.
Slightly wounded and N.Y.D. Shell Shock to C.R.S.
Lying cases to C.M.D.S.

4th.　　Casualties R.A.M.C.　0 and 4 wounded.

Decorations:-

Capt. F.G. Flood　）
　　　　　　　　　）　awarded M.C.
Capt. B.H. Barton　）

B.E.F.

<u>44th F.A., 14th Divn. 7th Corps.</u>   WESTERN FRONT.
<u>O.C. Lt. Col. W. Egan.</u>   May. '17.
<u>3rd Army.</u>

<u>Phase "B" cont.</u>
<u>2nd Period cont.</u>

1917.
May. 4th. cont.   <u>Decorations:-</u> cont.

Sgt. W.D. Watson awarded D.C.M.

6th.   <u>Casualties:</u> Few wounded arrived.

11th.   <u>Moves Detachment:</u>

2 and 52 to 42nd Field Ambulance to assist in clearing forward area. Returned 12th.

<u>Casualties R.A.M.C.</u> 0 and 1 wounded.

14th.   <u>Moves Detachment:</u> 2 and 52 to 42nd Field Ambulance for work in forward area.

Returned 15th.

<u>Casualties R.A.M.C.</u> 0 and 1 wounded.

17th.   <u>Moves Detachment</u> 2 and 52 to 42nd Field Ambulance for duty in forward area.

Returned 18th.

20th.   <u>Operations.</u> Active operations by 33rd Division commenced 5.15 a.m.

<u>Casualties.</u> 6 a.m.- 6 a.m. 21st 16 and 510 wounded

26th.   <u>Moves Detachment:</u> 2 and 52 to 42nd Field Ambulance for worked as Brs.

Returned 27th.

140/2230 Vol 26

War Diary

44 Field Ambulance

June 1917

Army Form C. 2118.

WAR DIARY
or
INTELLIGENCE SUMMARY.
(Erase heading not required.)

Place	Date	Hour	Summary of Events and Information	Remarks and references to Appendices
HERCATEL	1.6.17	—	Working party went to AGNY before entt. (148 d 80 80) 2 Officers (Captains FLOOD & BARTON) & 55 O.R's details for duty as leaves to K 42 F.A. Ree attached to that unit reported by this LIEUT. SAMUEL - VIDOT R.M.C (2/R) reported for duty & later on the strength	
	2.6.17	—	32 302 Sgt DUGGAN R.M.C - 76560 Pte BEAVER R.M.C admitted to F.A. Dismounting Camp - Mob'ld F.A. equipment throughout l/c Captain GRAHAM moved to AGNY.	
	3.6.17	—	Captain ATKINS returned for duty & later on the strength	
		3.25	8657 Pte KNOWLES R.M.C relieved from leave	
AGNY	4.6.17	9am	Move completed, preparing Camp Disc. Recce & News & some Cars & T.C.S. located at ACHIET LE GRAND Inspection & classification of Walts & Burrows	
	5.6.17		Captain LINDSAY attached as M.O. (temporary) to 47 Brigade R.F.A.	
	6.6.17		Inspection & classification of Selich	
	7.1.17		O.O 149 from 41st Brigade - 1 wheel'n oc attached - & M.O.'s staff and Sears relieved from 42 F.A. - 3 O.R's relieved from leave	

Army Form C. 2118.

WAR DIARY
or
INTELLIGENCE SUMMARY.
(Erase heading not required.)

Instructions regarding War Diaries and Intelligence Summaries are contained in F. S. Regs., Part II. and the Staff Manual respectively. Title pages will be prepared in manuscript.

Place	Date	Hour	Summary of Events and Information	Remarks and references to Appendices
AGNY	8.6.17		Handed over Bysline Hosp Note & also all Copo Equip march 16- 55th F.A.	
"	9.6.17		Captain Flood detailed for temporary duty as H.O's. Tomericks Light Infantry	
"	"	10.30 pm	Lulines No 34063 Pte P. McKinlay Rond. promulgated. He was awarded 3 months F.P.No.1 handed over to A.P.M. (Div)	
"	10.6.17	-	Sgt. Major MARTIN Arhib (345-US) sent to Base Depot for dental treatment. 3886 Pte C. Dyson " Transferred to D.D.M.S. 6th Corps School of Hygine Captain Penny Struck off Strength from 25th May 1917.	
"	"		4 OR's proceeded on leave to ENGLAND - Handed over Site at AGNY & Bryline Shelters to 2/5 London F.A.	
AGNY	11.6.17	7 pm	Unit marched out.	
MONCHIER	"	10 pm	Unit arrived. Billeto in Nissen huts	
"	12.6.17	9.45 am	Unit marched out.	
LABBRET	"	10.45 am	Unit arrived. Billeto in Nissen huts	
"	13.6.17	3.40 pm	Unit marched out	
VAUCHELLE	"	10.30 pm	Unit arrived Conveyed to open D.R.S. in the CHATEAU Roads bad near P.R.S. broke timber post in crossing door side	

T1134. Wt. W708-776. 500000. 4/15. Sir J.C.&S.

WAR DIARY
or
INTELLIGENCE SUMMARY.

Army Form C. 2118.

Place	Date	Hour	Summary of Events and Information	Remarks and references to Appendices
VAUCHELLES	13.6.17	-	Submitted application for one month's Special leave - Captain FLOOD terminated 20.6 Shores leave be granted	
"	14.6.17		Sgt Major MARTIN struck off strength from 10.6.17 (Authority ADMS) preparing B.Rd	
"	15.6.17		Training scheme commenced - One O.R. granted leave to England	
"	16.6.17		Routine - Unit photo paid for June's 24 P.R.	
"	17.6.17		Lt. Col. FOSTER granted leave to ENGLAND	
"	18.6.17		Routine -	
"	19.6.17		2 O.Rs proceeds on leave to ENGLAND Captain LINDOW returned from sick pay duty with 4/1 RFA L'COL W.EGAN Royal granted one months Special leave from 22.6.17 to 22.7.17 Authority VII Corps DA&G. A.152/80 Captain Barlow to telow Capt FLOOD who refours Steward and Ment.	
"	20.6.17	-	Captain FLOOD returned to Headquarters Sto& over Command of the unit during the absence or leave of the Officer Commanding	

Army Form C. 2118.

WAR DIARY
or
INTELLIGENCE SUMMARY.
(Erase heading not required.)

Instructions regarding War Diaries and Intelligence Summaries are contained in F.S. Regs., Part II. and the Staff Manual respectively. Title pages will be prepared in manuscript.

Place	Date	Hour	Summary of Events and Information	Remarks and references to Appendices
VAUCHELLES	21/6/17		Lt Col. WEGAN. R.A.M.C. departed on special leave to IRELAND.	
"	22/6/17		4 O.R. reinforcements reported their arrival for duty on night of 20th and are taken on the strength	#97
"	23/6/17		1 other event	#97
"			Routine	
"	24/6/17		1 O.R. A.S.C granted leave 24th June to 1st July. DDMS conferred the DDS.	#97
"			1 Cpl. + 13 plus reinforcements reported their arrival for duty + are taken on the strength of the unit	#97
"			Routine. 1st day of Units Sports	#92
"	25/6/17		3 O.R. granted leave 26/6/17 to 6/7/17; 2nd day of Units Sports	#97
"	26/6/17		CAPT. BARTON rejoined the unit from temporary duty with 6th Somerset L.I.	
"	27/6/17		1 O.R. R.A.M.C. granted leave 27 June to 7th July	#97
"	28/6/17		CAPT. LINDOW detailed for duty with 11th Kings Liverpool Regt + ceases off the strength	#97
"	29/6/17		Lt + Qm. FOSTER returned from leave. Lt VIDOT detailed for temporary attachment for 4 days to S.R.A.M.C	
"			1 O.R. A.S.C. granted leave 30th June to 10th July. On relief by Capt LINDOW, Capt A BOOTHROYD	#97
"			has been taken on the strength of this unit.	
"	30/6/17		Routine	#97

H.G. Hood Capt R A M C
a/o.c. 40th Fd Amb C.

WAR DIARY

44 FIELD AMBULANCE

JULY 1917

Army Form C. 2118.

WAR DIARY
or
INTELLIGENCE SUMMARY.
(Erase heading not required.)

Instructions regarding War Diaries and Intelligence Summaries are contained in F.S. Regs., Part II. and the Staff Manual respectively. Title pages will be prepared in manuscript.

Place	Date	Hour	Summary of Events and Information	Remarks and references to Appendices
VAUCHELLES	1/7/17		CAPT. J.M. TAYLOR granted special leave in event of contract July 2nd – 15th ;	A47.
"	2/7/17		Routine	A47.
"	3/7/17		LIEUT VIDOT returned from 4 days instruction as R.M.O. with the 7th K.R.R.C.; Qm.S. J.E. CATTRALL 40015, mentioned in despatches as per 14th Div. Routine Orders 492 of 2nd July.	A47.
"	4/7/17		16057 Qm.S. S.M. GAWTHORNE reported for duty & is taken on the Strength. 1 O.R. granted leave July 5–25th 72963 Pte A HARRISON awarded distinguishing Badge of the Strength on 3/7/17 Recommendation for Qm.S. GAWTHORNE to be promoted to Sgt Major sent to A.D.M.S. the necessary duties of Sgt Major of Base await from this date	A47.
"	5/7/17		LIEUT S VIDOT transferred for duty as R.M.O. of 6th ROYLI, CAPT C.H. GPENNY transferred from 6th ROYLI and is taken on the Strength of this unit. CAPT D.S. GRAHAM transferred for duty as R.M.O. of 7th KRRC & is struck off the Strength of this unit. T2145 Pte VEC HELLRICH promoted a/Cpl with pay from 11th May 1917 enclosure (authority ADMS 14 Div M.R.O. 3890 4/7/17), 33611 A/L Cpl H.E. BRAITHWAITE promoted a/Cpl with pay from 11th May 17 enclosure same authority enclosure 31474 Pte E W PERRY promoted a/L Cpl with pay from 5th July 17 enclosure (authority D.G.M.S. 7276	
"	6/7/17		Cie. MEND ha 13.)	A47.
"	7/7/17		2 O.R granted leave to England from July 7th – 17th Routine	A47.

Army Form C. 2118.

WAR DIARY
or
INTELLIGENCE SUMMARY.
(Erase heading not required.)

Instructions regarding War Diaries and Intelligence Summaries are contained in F. S. Regs., Part II. and the Staff Manual respectively. Title pages will be prepared in manuscript.

Place	Date	Hour	Summary of Events and Information	Remarks and references to Appendices
VAUCHELLES	8/7/17		1 OR A.S.C. granted leave to England 9-19th July, 90193 Pte R ORMISTON sent to Base Depot ROUEN for transfer to England to enter Cadet Unit.	74?
"	9/7/17		Remaining M.D. patients sent to 7th Corps Rest STATION Gouy + D.R.S. closed	74?
"	10/7/17	7 a.m.	2 OR A.S.C. + 1 OR R.A.M.C. granted leave to England 11-21st July	74?
			Unit left VAUCHELLES at 8.30 a.m.	
BEAUVAL	10/7/17	7 p.m.	Unit arrived at BEAUVAL + moved into Billets Map Ref. E.21 a 6.4 Sheet 57 d	74?
"	11/7/17		CAPT. BARTON + 2 interpreters proceeded with 41st Inf. Bde. Advanced billetting party to own area.	
"	12/7/17		Major BAILEY proceeded by train to own area as billetting N.C.O.	75?
"			Left BEAUVAL at 11.45 a.m. entrained at DOULLENS. 4.19 p.m. detrained at GODEWAERSVELDE	
			11.30 p.m. marched to BOESCHEPE FARM. Sheet 27. R.17.6.5.3. moved into Second Army IX Corps.	74?
BOESCHEPE FARM	13/7/17		Received 3 reinforcements OR, took over camp from the billeting party of 5th Field Amb.	74?
"	14/7/17		CAPT. R.G. ATKINS detailed for temporary duty with C.R.E. 1 OR granted leave to England 15th - 25th July. A.D.M.S. 16th Div. inspected the Camp	74?
"	15/7/17		Camp inspected by D.D.M.S. IX Corps	75?
"	16/7/17		2 OR sent to Second Army Rest Camp AMBLETEUSE. 4 OR granted leave to England 17th-27th. 3rd WACKS	74?
"	—		A.S.C. H.T. evacuated sick on the 10th inst. + struck off strength of the unit. CAPT TAYLOR.	74?

WAR DIARY
or
INTELLIGENCE SUMMARY.

Army Form C. 2118.

(Erase heading not required.)

Place	Date	Hour	Summary of Events and Information	Remarks and references to Appendices
BOESEHEPE	From 16/7/17 cont		returned from leave	292
"	17/7/17		1 NCO + 5 men sent to Licaut being masking school for temporary duty. 2 NCO + 4 men to 37 C.C.S. for temporary duty.	14.7
"	18/7/17		1 O.R granted leave to England 19th – 29th July. 2 O.R admitted to hospital.	14.7
"	19/7/17		16053 Cmd.A.M. HAWTHORNE promoted to be Act. Sergt. MAJOR with pay from 4th July 17 and 31084 Cpl acting Lce Sergt. C. LUSTY promoted to be Act. Sergt. with pay from 24th May 17 authority D.E.M s/8/4450/1145 + 1152; 2 O.R. discharged from hospital.	14.7
"	20/7/17		CAPT TAYLOR sent for temporary duty to 50 C.C.S. + 1 O.R. admitted to hospital	14.7
"	21/7/17		1 O.R admitted to hospital 2 O.R discharged from hospital	14.7
"	22/7/17		Routine	
"	23/7/17	11 am	Lt Col W. Eggar relieved from leave & assumed command of the unit	
"	23/7/17	-	Captain ATKINS R.A.M.C. returned from temporary duty with C.R.E. 14th Divn	
"	24/7/17		42 104767 Pte. PEARSON. A A.o.C. M.T. awarded 8days F.P. No 2. for driving a motor Ambulance at an excessive speed try 30 miles per hour Contrary to	
			Q.R.O 2053 –	
			90399 Cpl. WILLIAMS. E. permanent rank to be Corporal (R.A.M.C. Record B.S.17/1/10 of 14 July 17)	

WAR DIARY
or
INTELLIGENCE SUMMARY.

Army Form C. 2118.

Place	Date	Hour	Summary of Events and Information	Remarks and references to Appendices
BOESCHEPE F.H.E	25/7/17	-	7/1/27 Pt Simpson J. ASC Awarded 8 days C.B. for being in habitual late. 42027 Cpl Moss C.J. AtmC. Severely reprimanded for "answering fatigue party before appointed hour" (+) Feeling fatshoot to Commanding Officer. Captain BARTON departs for 4 days duty with D.D.M.S. 5th Army D.D.M.S. 9th Corps inspects Ambulance	
"	26.7.17	-	Captain FLOOD detailed for 4 days duty with 47th Bde RFA. Lt DUGGAN RAMC sent for course of instruction to New Army School of Cookery. - Sgt BULL ASC MT granted leave 27 July - August 6th	
"	27.7.17	-	One O.R. granted leave to ENGLAND.	
"	28.7.17	-	No 30136 Pte STEWART, G.G. RAMC transferred for duty to 7th Div Supply Column. On (authority DDMS XIX Corps)	
"	29.7.17	-	Warning notice 15 hrs at work in heat wave to men at their posts	
"	30.7.17 9pm	H.Q.grade O.O. No 154. Received. - 20 O.R's. Granted 10 days leave to ENGLAND One O.R. (Cpl DUNHAM RAMC) sent to Sewing Kit Camp Captain BARTON RAMC returned from 4 days duty with out Mats 5th Army	
"	31.7.17	-	Pte ANDERSON (ASC) RAMC Admitted to Hospital	

T/134. Wt. W708—776. 500 000. 4/15. Sir J. C. & S.

WAR DIARY

44 FIELD AMBULANCE

AUGUST 1917

WAR DIARY
or
INTELLIGENCE SUMMARY.
(Erase heading not required.)

Army Form C. 2118.

Place	Date	Hour	Summary of Events and Information	Remarks and references to Appendices
BOESCHEPE FARM	1.8.17	-	2 O.Rs Gauilé leavs to England. 3286 Pte MARSHALL.E. Evacuated for drunkenness. Strength of the Strength 31.7.17	
"	2.8.17	"	1 O.R Gauilé leavs England. Movement warning Order Cancelled.	
"	3.8.17	"	16 O.Rs Gauilé leavs England. - 10 men still in Unit without leave for 18 months - 3246 S Pte HIDDEN. D. Provl. Awards 7 days F.P. No 2 - when on active service (1) DRUNKNESS -	
"	4.8.17	-	LIEUT BOOTHROYD Attached for duty (Temp'y) with A.D.M.S. 37th DIV"	
"	5.8.17	-	41st Brigade O.O. 153 received - Unit Proceeds to HONDEGHEM tomoro' :-	
"	"	-	2) Sheet - V.2.6.3.7. on morning of 6th - Met with the Brigade - Extra received from A.D.M.S. Evacuate Cases not fit for Brs future shelling Hospital Clara.	
"	"	6 pm	Handed over est of Camp B.R.C. Stores etc. to No 58th F.A.	
"	"	6.25 pm	4 O.Rs Gauilé leavs England - All Carts Nos now issued on leavs to England on their 18 months -	
"	6.8.17	8 am	Unit marched out tent transport -	
HONDEGHEM	"	1.15 pm	Arrived in new Camp - No accomodation for batteries in buildings	

WAR DIARY
or
INTELLIGENCE SUMMARY
(Erase heading not required.)

Army Form C. 2118.

Place	Date	Hour	Summary of Events and Information	Remarks and references to Appendices
HONDECHEM	6.8.17	6.30pm	Visit from A.D.M.S. who gave verbal instructions. Fixed all cases of claim as many of Brigade left as possible.	
"	7.8.17		Routine	
"	8.8.17		Captain FLOOD relieved from Corps Duty Work at 47 Brigade R.F.A.	
"	8.8.17		Captain C HELM M.C. R.A.M.C. sholes two days at Hazebrouck	
"	9.8.17		Captain PENNY reported for temp'y duty vice 10 F. DUR. A.T.L. on CR granted leave.	
			Represenatives from Bureau of Plastic Surgery attend - New Cookhouse well supervised.	
			N/c DUGGAN R.A.M.C. returned from Course of instruction in Cookery at Army School.	
	10.8.17		Submitted the following for awards on New Years honours -	
			Infantry G. GEORGE FOSTER - M.C. Sgt FREEBORN - Distinguished Conduct Medal.	
			Sgt Major CORPS - M.C. M.T. Pte MOSSMAN	
			Driver LIDGETT M.C.M.T. Staff Sgt HEGARTY } Hon Mention	
	11.8.17		Typewriter Dr THOMPSON and H.T. awarded 10 days F.P. No. for "chronic slackness"	

WAR DIARY
or
INTELLIGENCE SUMMARY.

(Erase heading not required.)

Army Form C. 2118.

Place	Date	Hour	Summary of Events and Information	Remarks and references to Appendices
HONDEGHEM	11.8.17	—	Order returning from leave "7am 5th August. 7pm 7 August 1917. 3 days - 3 hours	
"	12.8.17	—	3 days pay under £6 drawn.	
"	13.8.17	—	Abelius - reported attachment at 37 CCS	
"			Washing Oders' received from 41st MT Brigade — Phone no dataglass	
"	14.8.17	—	14-15 not	
"	15.8.17	—	Washing Orders received from H1 Brigade had been sent here away morning of 16.	
"		10 am	Orders Mas 156 received - 10 men (hours) with towels & washing carts	
"			Orders 43 F.A. Captain Barton & washing party left for the Bac.	
"		1.30 pm	Transport to Captain Barton MT/NS left	
"		8 pm	Personnel in charge of O.C. Lt Roberts & 2 drivers of CESTRE	
"	16.8.17	4 am	Motor Ambulances at ABEELE.	
LYSSENTHOEK FARM	"	8 am	Arrived & found transport Albany cooked. Days of service	
"	"	—	27.2.23 A 94	
"	"	—	3 Reinforcements arrived camping mush up to 6 Bivouche 400	
"	"	—	Received MOs from ADM Stats 05 NRB 474 Camp	
"	"	—	as DRS for 26 Field Ambulance	

WAR DIARY
or
INTELLIGENCE SUMMARY.
(Erase heading not required.)

Army Form C. 2118.

Place	Date	Hour	Summary of Events and Information	Remarks and references to Appendices
WARATAH CAMP	1/6/16	10 am	Colonel's early Orderly Room. New Camp Major Sgt. 28 G.S.C.O.B Clerk returned from 36 Field Ambulance. Officers r/173 ORs later over from outgoing ship.	
	2	12 nn	Captain HEATH attached by ADMS to 6 no 8 F Corps Ambulance	
			Car Convoy	
			Captain TAYLOR RAMC behind from temp duty at 36 CCS	
			Lieut BOOTHROYD returned from temp duty with 37 Div. Party of 47 ORs returned from 57 CCS 1 OR on leave to ENGLAND	
	18/7		Lieut BOOTHROYD March 6 - 42 FA for temp duty. Gas DADMS # Corps to Cons N.Y.D.N. forum 1 WO a/c a large number from Brigades, about 2 Officers - Captains FLOOD & ATKINS - & 76 ORs moving to altogether. Medical Report to C & 3 F.A. as hearers in the forward area	

WAR DIARY
or
INTELLIGENCE SUMMARY.

(Erase heading not required.)

Army Form C. 2118.

Place	Date	Hour	Summary of Events and Information	Remarks and references to Appendices
WARATAH CAMP	19/8/17		On PR on leave to ENGLAND 352524 Pte A.C. LOBENHOFER Rept to O.C. Reinforcements SYDNEY for dispersal (durably CR No 816=5/165/A Cd 14.8.17 Amick H1 through of will	⊘
"	20.8.17		D.R.I. returned by A.R. and DDMS	
"	21.8.17		The OR proceeded on leave to England.	⊘
			C.R.E. 4 Division sent an officer at my request to show up a scheme to superceded to kitchens between Waylers clayton dressingroom & Commodities of new kitchen & test officers.	⊘
"	22.9.17		During the morning the aviators took the offensive against the enemy.	
		7 pm	No loss in 152 siege slightly increased. 7 gas cases during the day. Gas cases amounted to 5-74 (mustd.) whom were only slightly affected. Supervised Rly/Water closets at the lines. Gas NE table Latrines	⊘
	23.6.17		Had 360 cases in col — Both to O.C. C.M.D.S (sent copy) & A.D.M.S Gas cases whom mostly evacuate today (no duty). Shower hypo. of latent symptoms	⊘

WAR DIARY
or
INTELLIGENCE SUMMARY.
(Erase heading not required.)

Army Form C. 2118.

Place	Date	Hour	Summary of Events and Information	Remarks and references to Appendices
WARATAH CAMP	25.8.17 26.8.17	-	Routine. 20R' Draught leavs for ENGLAND. Bearers injured - following Casualties reported:-	
			31868 L/c. E. BROOMHEAD. RAMC } Killed in action August 29th 1917	
			32721 Pnr.G. H. BRECKELL do	
			53693 " W. COLE do } Wounded in action August 29th - Died at	
			89760 " A. SCALES do } No 3 Canadian CCS on August 23rd 1917	
			354415 " N. MILLER do	
			32984 " G. SOUTHERN do } Wounded in action + evacuated	
			32034 " G. MOORE do } August 29th 1917.	
			31488 " W. LEVETT do	
			335589 - W. LAWSON do	
			CAPTAIN F.G. FLOOD MC }	
			32050 Pte B. ASPLAND RAMC } Slightly wounded August 29th -	
			32087 " A. FRENCH do } at Auby.	
			421037 " W.R. HILL do	
			31257 " T. KNOWLES do	

Place	Date	Hour	Summary of Events and Information	Remarks and references to Appendices
MARATH H.Q.M. CAMP			31315 Sgt W.D. WATSON - RMC - Gassed (LETHAL) admitted to Hosp 23.9.17 77264 Private F.W.G. TAYLOR do. ⎫ 31804 " W. WYKES do. ⎬ Slightly wounded remaining at duty 23.8.17 48813 " DS WILLIAMS do. ⎭ 33056 " CH GROVES do. ⎫ 70702 " E. HARGREAVES do. ⎬ Slightly wounded ret duty 24.8.17 32230 " J.W. JENKINSON do. ⎭ Captain PENNY reported unfit for Trench duty 10 DL I. Col. F. Jones S commanding Adiacha from the Cecelo for sufficiency (S.163(2)H.A.) T/ No 42/027 Capt. C.J. MOSS RAMC A.D.R. specified time. 8 ENGLAND	
"	27.8.17 - 28.8.17		Morning Orders from 43" Infantry Brigade	
"	29.8.17		A.D.M.S operator Nos 58 received. Acknowledged M.O. to 30 M.T. to officers c/o Battery he was transferred from Infantry Brigades 43 Brigade Op Order No 128 received	

WAR DIARY or INTELLIGENCE SUMMARY.

Army Form C. 2118.

Place	Date	Hour	Summary of Events and Information	Remarks and references to Appendices
WARATAH Camp	29.5.17		30361 Pte ROSE L.L.N. Evacuated sick to Chief of things. Notification received from 12CCS that 32.2.30 Pte JENKINSON Wm. And J. Evans D on August 27	
"	" 10.15pm		Wire from A.D.M.S. to take over Rest Camp at BAILLEUL.	✓
"	30.5.17		Advance party under Captain BARTON proceeds to take over Rest Camp at BAILLEUL from 4th Australian Div. Captain ATKINS proceeds to J.K.S.L.I. for temp duty.	
"	"		" TAYLOR do 9 K.R.R. do	✓
"	"		Private SHEPPARD (6116) transfers to unit from 42 F.A. HINDEDON & WARATAH Camp to 29th F.A. 7th Div. R.T.	✓
"	31.5.17		Proceeds to BAILLEUL - Patients handed over officers P28 O.Rs. Reinforcements 6 arrived	✓

[Signature]
R.A.M.C.
COMMANDING No. 44 FIELD AMBULANCE

44 FIELD AMBULANCE

WAR DIARY

SEPTEMBER 1917

Army Form C. 2118.

WAR DIARY
or
INTELLIGENCE SUMMARY.
(Erase heading not required.)

Instructions regarding War Diaries and Intelligence Summaries are contained in F. S. Regs., Part II. and the Staff Manual respectively. Title pages will be prepared in manuscript.

Place	Date	Hour	Summary of Events and Information	Remarks and references to Appendices
BAILLEUL	1.9.17	-	30R Glanded Leave to ENGLAND	
"	2.9.17	1.45pm	Orders received from A.D.M.S. that the RAVELSBERG Rest Station for Other ranks of 12th Australian Field Ambulance & that one Unit Motor Driven at BAILLEUR	
"	3.9.17	9pm	Advance Party of 2 Officers & 50 Ors left for their site — Unit (two lieut. butchers & horse transport) left for RAVELSBERG	
RAVELSBERG	"	10 am	Unit arrived Map reference 28.S.16.c.3.4.	
"	"	11.30am	Captain FLOOD RAMC on duty Rank granted Lieut X ENGLAND 43 by 4th Brigade 1.9.00.	
"	4.9.17	-	Captain HELM & 2 ORs reported from 1 Corps C.H.C. Roches	
"	5.9.17	-	6 ORs evacuated Home off the Strength	
"	6.9.17	-	78531 Pte BUTT E awarded 14 days F.P. No. 2 for "Stating a falsehood to a N.C.O." The following NCO & men awarded Military Medal. 32133 Sgt. W. SMITH R.A.M.C. 5-73-57 Pte J.M. HIND HARCH R.A.M.C. 32147 Pte J.A BURY A 31864 " W WYKES Authority D.R.O. 653 At 29.7.	

WAR DIARY
or
INTELLIGENCE SUMMARY.
(Erase heading not required.)

Army Form C. 2118.

Place	Date	Hour	Summary of Events and Information	Remarks and references to Appendices
RAVELSBURG	6.9.17	—	One O.R. reported arrival for duty station on Rheingh. (32158 Pte HARSHAW E)	
"	7.9.17	—	Captain PENNY R.M.C granted leave to United Kingdom – 8–18.9.11. 3 O.Rs granted leave to England. 9–19.9.17. 90399 Cpl E WILLIAMS R.M.C granted one month Special Leave to England – under. G.R.O 1679. 10/9/17 to 10/10/17. Roulers	
"	8.9.17	—	3 O.R's granted leave to ENGLAND 11–21"–	
"	9.9.17	—	Lieut H.W.SWEENY & Lieut W.A.R CHAPIN U.S.A Med. Officers reported arrival for duty taken on the strength –	
"	10.9.17	—	34652 Pte HADDEN. D R.M.C evacuated sick whilst off strength	
"	11.9.17	—	One O.R granted leave to ENGLAND. 13ᵗʰ – 23ʳᵈ inst.	
"	12.9.17	—	3 O.R's reported arrival for duty taken on the strength (Cpl MOSS – Pte EATON – Pte LESTER. (returned from leave (U-S-O)	
"	13.9.17	—	32517 Pte WHITE W. R.M.C LewS has apptd R.Q.M.Sr for time being vice to England for invalids roll. (authority A.D.M.S 1st Div m/2179) & other of the strength of the unit . Pte HADDEN diagnosis DYSENTRY (FLEXNER)	

WAR DIARY
or
INTELLIGENCE SUMMARY.

(Erase heading not required.)

Army Form C. 2118.

Place	Date	Hour	Summary of Events and Information	Remarks and references to Appendices
RAVELSBURG	13.9.17	-	Captain B.H. BARTON RAMC Attached for temp duty with 8th KRRC	
			Captain R.R.G. ATKINS " reported from temp duty with 3rd KSLI	
	14.9.17		A.D.M.S. granted leave to ENGLAND 15th - 28th September	
			1.O.R. reported for duty. Pte KNOWLES (returned from 50 CCS)	
			43rd Infy Brigade O.O.(30) received	
			Captain BARTON relieved by Captain TAYLOR RAMC. Relieves 8 Thick	
	15.9.17		Captain ATKINS Attached for temp duty with 6 DCLI.	
"			42nd Infy Brigade O.O. No 109 - received -	
			M/63 23 60 DG LOFTHOUSE ARC M.T. sent to HQ A.F.C. whirl off the Strength	
			from 16th inst (authority A.G. circular A 238/721 of 2.9.17)	
			One O.R. reported sick on for duty later on l/singh	
	16.9.17		Captain BARTON 140 R.J. Stewkler 7 Cav's to ENGLAND (7th - 27th inst)	
	17.9.17		D.D.M.S. inspected Camp Baggage many Ambulance	
	18.9.17		A.D.M.S. inspected Camp	
			Lieut. A. BOOTH R.Y.O Kml proceeds reports to ADMS Ambulance	
			having for duty to the strength from the instant (Authority DMS	
			Mc Array 3666(1))	

WAR DIARY
or
INTELLIGENCE SUMMARY.

Army Form C. 2118.

Place	Date	Hour	Summary of Events and Information	Remarks and references to Appendices
RAWELPINDI			42nd Inf Brigade DO 130 Situard. Captain R.R.G. ATKINS RAMC awarded Military Cross authority DRO 873 a/11/9/17. 28977 Pte HOLLINEAUX J.E. & 40322 Pte LIVINGSTONE W. evacuated sick which of the strength from this date.	
"	19.9.17			
"	20.9.17 midnight	Captain FLOOD 2 D.R's proceeds to forward area to revert to the evacuation of wounded from said of R.B. 10R granted leave —	
			42107 Cpl C.J. Moss RAMC reduce to Rank of Private such order 183(b) A.A. authority DAAG S Corps a/19/12 of 17.9.17 - the above private evacuated sick the day only of area — standing that Pass held & Scanned Clarendy when Between 32050 Pte ASPLAND.R evacuated sick which of the Strength Captain ATKINS proceeds in relieving MO 47. Brigade R.F.A. LIEUT SWEENY do do Captain J.H. Taylor (R.A.R) who proceeded to England which of Strength (bomo to Dunked Destroyed)	
	29.11			

WAR DIARY
or
INTELLIGENCE SUMMARY.
(Erase heading not required.)

Army Form C. 2118.

Place	Date	Hour	Summary of Events and Information	Remarks and references to Appendices
RAVELSBERG	22.9.17	—	4 Or Ranked (?) last to ENGLAND	
"	23.9.17	—	10 P.B. men arrived to replace 10 H.T. A/C men	
			2 OR Rank reinforcement & 1 H.T. arrived	
"	24.9.17		10 ORC H.T. departed for HAVRE (H.T. & Base Depot)	
			2 H.T. Ranked last to ENGLAND	
			Colour ATKINS R.A.M.C. returned from Temp/ duty with 17 Brigade R.F.A.	
			Driver SHUTTLEWORTH (T/017042) A.S.C. H.T. evacuated sick Phthisis(?)(Right)	
			1 O.R. M.T. reinforcement arrived	
"	25.9.17	—	Inspection by Col° R.C. Divisional Commander	
"	26.9.17	—	Captain ATKINS R.A.M.C. & 2nd Lt GLANTS(?) leave to British Isles	
			Lieut SWEENY M.O.R.C. USA returned from Temp/ duty with 6 R.R.C.	
"	27.9.17		Captains PENNY & BARTON returned from leave	
"	28.9.17		Captain BARTON departed for Temp/ duty with 6 Somerset L.I.	
			Dr SHUTTLEWORTH A.S.C. returned from 20 C.C.S.	
"	29.9.17		Poulins	
	30.9.17		Captain FLOOD departed for Temp/ duty with 9 R.B & Col° du Penny(?)	

Army Form C. 2118.

WAR DIARY
or
INTELLIGENCE SUMMARY.
(Erase heading not required.)

Instructions regarding War Diaries and Intelligence Summaries are contained in F. S. Regs., Part II. and the Staff Manual respectively. Title pages will be prepared in manuscript.

Place	Date	Hour	Summary of Events and Information	Remarks and references to Appendices
APPELSBERG	3.9.17	—	Departed for temp'y duty w.k. Head Quarters VIII Corps. No 66885 Sg't: BRYANT R.A.M.C. reported for duty & returned to strength.	

Signed
Major
R.A.M.C.
COMMANDING No. 4 FIELD AMBULANCE

WAR DIARY

44 FIELD AMBULANCE

OCTOBER 1917

WAR DIARY
or
INTELLIGENCE SUMMARY.
(Erase heading not required.)

Army Form C. 2118.

Place	Date	Hour	Summary of Events and Information	Remarks and references to Appendices
RAVELSBERG	1.10.17	—	Routine	
"	2.10.17	—	3 O.R's granted leave to ENGLAND — 8 O.R's reinforcement received later on Nivigh	
"	3.10.17	—	1 O.R. reinforcement received. Captain PENNY, R.A.M.C. returns from temp'y duty with VIII H.Q'rs.	
"	4.10.17	—	Lieut. CHAPIN H.O.R.C. USA sent for temp'y duty with 41 C.C.S.	
"	5.10.17	—	1 O.R. reinforcement arrived. Taken on strength - unit now 3 over strength.	
"	6.10.17	1pm	Routine	
"	"	10am	43rd F.A. Bgde. having orders to move	
"	"	6am	Bearers attached to 43rd Field Ambulance dispersed	
"	"		Lieut. CHAPIN H.O.R.C. USA returned from 41 C.C.S.	
"	"	12.5pm	Unit of 43rd F.A. Bgde. O.O. 136 received. Unit to proceed to WESTOUTRE area (No 7).	
"	"	4pm	Unit departed for this area & camp handed over to 101 F.A. 33rd Div. No probationers handed over. 173	
CONQUERORS CAMP	"	7pm	Arrived in this site - no accommodations for batch - personnel in bell tents in field - site shared with 43rd T.M.B. (Map Ref. 28 N.2 a.80)	

Army Form C. 2118.

WAR DIARY
or
INTELLIGENCE SUMMARY.
(Erase heading not required.)

Place	Date	Hour	Summary of Events and Information	Remarks and references to Appendices
CONQUERORS CAMP.	7.10.17	—	Rained all day.	
	8.10.17	12 noon	Morning Orders 43rd Brigade received.	
			O.O. 43rd Brigade No 137 received – Mid Arms 9.10.17 & 2 a.Clyte Ama	
		8.30pm	Captain ATKINS R.H.T.C returned from leave	
	9.10.17	10am	Unit left for new Camp	
CHIPPEWA CAMP	—	noon	Unit arrived. 28 H &47 – No accommodation for heavier Officer	
	10.10.17	—	Received orders take over from 13th F.A. 5th Division the Officers of	
			set & wounded in the lines. also take over Corps Waiting Mortuaries	
			from 15 F.A. at Woodcote House – Saw both Commanding Officers	
			Arranges details	
		8pm	Captain ATKINS r. A.c.: Wears Ambulances left to late over lines.	
			also ambulance party.	
	11.10.17	10am	Captain PENNY ambulance party left to take over Woodcote House	
			from 15 F.A.	
		—	Captain HELM left to late over charge of turns in the line &	
			the new Quarters blue vitriolic at Ecole de Bienfaisance Henin P.	

Army Form C. 2118.

WAR DIARY
or
INTELLIGENCE SUMMARY.
(Erase heading not required.)

Place	Date	Hour	Summary of Events and Information	Remarks and references to Appendices
CHIPPEWA CAMP	11.9.17	4 p.m.	2 NCO's & 26 hears (bearer subsection) left for ECOLE also 2 hears stretchers from 42 & 43 F.A. gives. Captain HELM & Corpl life (escn) returning to Chas tho' lines	
WOODCOTE HOUSE	12.9.17	noon	Unit arrived at his Quarters 28/20 C.5.3 – Head Quarters Staff & White Ho. Lieut R.H. Foster quarters was from 13 $\frac{B}{2}$–23. Captain Flood reports from Tent & duty at K9 F.R.B's sub Stns. Live & Cpls tracking wounded intermediate forward lines – R.A.P.s Orthelies at (A) J.14.B.6.3 (B) J.14.d.94 (C) J.15.a.5.3. (D) J.21.a.5.5. Vlech 25 Collecting Huar post at Clapham Junction – J.13.d.98 HOOCE - TUNNEL - I.18.b.46	
"		"	CRATER Caso go up to the & Cmercy walk & wounds to X Cpls ADS & ECOLE de BIENFAISANCE Walking wounded evacuated by M.C. Cars to Cmbul bureau at GODE WAERSVELDE – Div'l sick Bears by 42 F.A.	

T/2134. Wt. W708–776. 50C000. 4/15. Sir J. C. & S.

Army Form C. 2118.

WAR DIARY
or
INTELLIGENCE SUMMARY.
(Erase heading not required.)

Place	Date	Hour	Summary of Events and Information	Remarks and references to Appendices
WOODCOTE HOUSE	12.10.17		Casualties in action:-	
			No 31084 Pte W. WYKES MM ⎫	
			" 372124 " E.J. FRY ⎬ Killed in action	
			" 421037 - W.R. HILL slightly wounded at duty.	
	13.10.17		Captain BARTON returns from temp duty with 6 Cambs L.I.	
			No 904 3Sr Pte H.E. WILLIAMS - slightly wounded at duty	
			" 57358 Pte A DOUGLAS wounded & evacuated	
	14.10.17		12 nurses sent to Scale Back as Sisters with 70 from each FA	
			Surgeon General MACPHERSON KMO inspected M.N. Station	
	15.10.17		No 316 22 Pte E.C.F. HUMPHRY RAMC slightly wounded at duty	
			TALLEY Cottage Officers Mess hit in cases by recent shelling	
			M/S 001 Pte A.K. LIGGETT AACMT recommended for M.M. Medal	
	16.10.17		77571 Pte G. BLYTH RAMC slightly wounded at duty	
			5 O.R.s granted leave to ENGLAND	
			Captain EVANS returned on Thursday on duty by Captain CRAIG	
			15 O.R.s 43 FA gassed at MULCH & evacuating posts incurred of "London Shyth"	

WAR DIARY
or
INTELLIGENCE SUMMARY.
(Erase heading not required.)

Army Form C. 2118.

Place	Date	Hour	Summary of Events and Information	Remarks and references to Appendices
WOODCOTE HOUSE	17.10.17	11am	No 399 Cpl. WILLIAMS RAMC evacuated sick.	
"	18.10.17	—	2 Ford Cars damaged by shell fire at WOODCOTE HOUSE the Ford Cars damaged by shell fire at ZILLEBEKE 43656 Pte LOVELL RAMC slightly wounded at duty. 31978 Sgt. BAILEY do do	
"	19.10.17	—	LIEUT CHAPIN MORC USA sent for temp. duty with G.R.B. Captain DUNLOP RAMC attached bearers for nobelinal purposes from 43 F.A.	
"	20.10.17	—	Captain ATKINS relieved Captain CRAIG at the Smells. Sgt BLANDFORD 43 F.A. recommended for DCM — immediate rewards Pte BURTON do MM do No 78245 Pte J. BARNETT RAMC wounded in action & evacuated 10.R Blands hosp.	
"	"	9pm	Operation Order (RAMC) No 2 issued — to hand over lines to 14 FA 5th Division. Relief to be complete 9pm 21.10.17.	

WAR DIARY
or
INTELLIGENCE SUMMARY.

Army Form C. 2118.

Place	Date	Hour	Summary of Events and Information	Remarks and references to Appendices
WOODCOTE HOUSE	21.8.17	—	Routine.	
	22.8.17	—	42nd Brigade OO 135 received. Reinforcements Pte GOOLD OC/H attached 42nd F.A. for L Crew (eventual) reporting Casualties occurred. 92295 Pte W GEDDES RAMC } wounds reads & evacuated 101390 " T JONES do. 32634 " A MARSHAL do. } Slightly wounds at duty 76541 Pte E.S. BUTT do transferred for duty to 21 HTG. Chief of things — 36841 Pte S. FLEXON arrives in relief from 24 H.A.G.	
"	23.10.17 Mon		Advance party of 14 F.A. arrives to take over C/o W.W. Stab at WOODCOTE HOUSE.	
"	11am		Advance party of 15 F.A. arrives to take over duties — 42 Brigade OO 8(135/2 received. 31179 Pte A.B. CHURCHLAND RAMC wounds reads reports to 14 F.A. 5738 " F COLLOP do. Slightly wounds at duty	

WAR DIARY
or
INTELLIGENCE SUMMARY.
(Erase heading not required.)

Army Form C. 2118.

Place	Date	Hour	Summary of Events and Information	Remarks and references to Appendices
WOODCOTE HOUSE	23/10/17		Lt. H.W. SWEENY H.O.R.C. U.S.A. rept. 56 Jom L 1 (?) & Munich Rd 42 F43 FA. Wastro returns by lorries. Other Nuc's	
	24.9.9pm		Lieut. Mck. Menzies M. (near Woodcote) left Woodcote House for N.Z. also BERTHEM. —	
	10.40		Nine recruits rec'd D/S. F.H. 1 C.M.M STATION St. 14 F.t. Captain ATKINS 1 Penn. F die out Chelvenia attacks for duty arr. Q.23.C.C.S.	
Q.23 C.C.S.	8/10/17	4pm	Unit arrives at Q.23.C.C.S.	
	26.10.17		Unit being fitly billeting rec by 2nd Bgade.	
		7.30 a.m.	Pte N WAGSTAFF Australia rec'd wheel to thing Q.S. —	
			31409 Cpl. J. MACDONALD R.A.M.C. 5u "also with ear" also etc.	
			31872 Private L.C. CHALKE " J W.S. 73. —	
	27/10/17		1 N.C.O. P.K. leaves rect. R.7th Queen O. F.O. for duty.	
			28405 Pte W NEILSON (Guards) 3 (?) F. ? no 2. Pays Courtecy leg 6 up to 21 Oct.	
			34292 " J. WELSH Co. " leg cut @ bruise	
			6r About Walk out (out) for 5/2 hr. – Open L.P. butto. 85–96	

Army Form C. 2118.

WAR DIARY
or
INTELLIGENCE SUMMARY.
(Erase heading not required.)

Instructions regarding War Diaries and Intelligence Summaries are contained in F. S. Regs., Part II. and the Staff Manual respectively. Title pages will be prepared in manuscript.

Place	Date	Hour	Summary of Events and Information	Remarks and references to Appendices
R.23 C.6.5.	27/10/17	—	A.D.M.S. No. 468. — Distinguishing mark to be worn by each Medical Officer. Strips on each sleeve "12" x ¼" of maroon.	
"	28.10.17	—	3960 Pte A. GEORGE R.A.M.C. arrived via "rest stations" from sick	
			83156 " T. LACKIN do	
			28798 " J.E. MULLINEUX do	
			Captain T.C. BRITTON R.A.M.C.T. sick.	
29.10.17		—	Captain T.C. BRITTON R.A.M.C.T. sick & struck. Captain C. & G. PENNY "S.R." departs for England, on leave & to report to Horse Establishment "Ripon" D/L Sh.104 (authority B.O.)	
"	30.10.17	—	29129 L/Cpl CLOSE R.A.M.C. awarded Mayo C.B. for services in the Field.	
"	31.10.17	—	M/300/1 Pte A.K. LIDGETT A.S.C. M.T. granted M. MEDAL authority ⁴ᵗʰ Div R.O. 728 29/10/17 Routine.	

[signature] Major A.D.M.S.

COMMANDING No. 44 FIELD AMBULANCE.

WAR DIARY

44 FIELD AMBULANCE

NOVEMBER 1917

Army Form C. 2118.

WAR DIARY
or
INTELLIGENCE SUMMARY.
(Erase heading not required.)

Instructions regarding War Diaries and Intelligence Summaries are contained in F. S. Regs., Part II. and the Staff Manual respectively. Title pages will be prepared in manuscript.

Place	Date	Hour	Summary of Events and Information	Remarks and references to Appendices
Q23C65	1.11.17	—	Routine	
"	2.11.17	—	Routine	
"	3.11.17	—	Routine	
"	4.11.17	—	Routine	
"	5.11.17	—	Under instructions from 4 and 4th Divs. Captain BRITTON & Lieut FOSTER RAMC proceeded to X Corps retraining Centre 28H27C57	
"	6.11.17	—	Lt W.AR. CHAPIN transferred to 9th R.B. O.C. provided a team for 5-21st	
"	7.11.17	—	Routine	
"	8.11.17	—	Lt H.M. GILBERTSON reported for duty and was taken on the strength	
"	9.11.17	—	Received 10 O.Ranks reinforcements and received orders from A.D.M.S. to hold an Fit subdivision in readiness to proceed to HALLINES to take over the D.R.S.	
"	10.11.17	—	Capt BRITTON & Lt GILBERTSON and 1 Fit subdivision proceeded to HALLINES. (Started D.F. & D./15)	
"	11.11.17	—	Routine	
"	12.11.17	—	Visit moved to-day to HALLINES and found the Div Rest Station. The main moved off at 8 A.H. and the transport at 3 P.M. Accommodation has been made for the reception of 170 patients	

T2134. Wt. W708-776. 50000. 4/15. Sir J. C. & S.

Army Form C. 2118.

WAR DIARY
or
INTELLIGENCE SUMMARY.
(Erase heading not required.)

Instructions regarding War Diaries and Intelligence Summaries are contained in F. S. Regs., Part II. and the Staff Manual respectively. Title pages will be prepared in manuscript.

Place	Date	Hour	Summary of Events and Information	Remarks and references to Appendices
Abus 36D				
Fld 44	13.11.17		66 OR's Transfers from 43rd F.A. & Mus DAS	
"	14.11.17		Routine	
"	15.11.17		Capt Helm R.A.M.C. proceeded on leave to England 16-30 am	
"	16.11.17		Routine	
"	17.11.17		1 OR proceeded on leave to England 17 mid't - 2nd pm	
"	18.11.17		34292 Pte J Walsh RAMC transferred to Kings F.A. H.S.	
"	19.11.17		Capt R G Atkins detailed for temporary duty with the 8th Reg Bde, 2 OR detailed for instruction in Signal	
"	20.11.17		Work under O.C. Div Signals. 1 OR proceeded on leave from 22 am to 4 pm	
"	21.11.17		437438 Pte H.M. Low evacuated sick + struck off the strength of the unit.	
"	"		1 NCO + 10 Bearers sent for duty with the 8th Div	
"	22.11.17		Lt W.E.Gan RAMC relinquished forton leave in England.	
"	23.11.17		Routine	
"	24.(?)		Routine	
"	27.11.17		Routine	
"	28.11.17		O.O. 42nd Brigade 142 Received /Struck O.O No 3 Received	

WAR DIARY
or
INTELLIGENCE SUMMARY.
(Erase heading not required.)

Army Form C. 2118.

Place	Date	Hour	Summary of Events and Information	Remarks and references to Appendices
HALLINES	28.10.17	—	Routine - Who received Instruct: DRS 5th Div? & made arrangements for taking over from 26 F.A.	
"	29.10.17	11 a.m.	Visited DRS 8th Division Made arrangements with O.C. 26 F.A. re taking over - Transport-Plumb (Capt F.G.FLOOD RAMC 3rd 1/4) Left HALLINES En route for RED FARM - BRANDHOEK - 41st Brigade OO 181 received	
"	30.10.17	1 p.m.	Captain J. Keen RAMC admitted to No.1 General Hospital visit two transport; also 2 officers & 2 O.R's left by train for RED FARM BRANDHOEK.	
"		6.30 pm	H.Q. I Captain PLUMMER RAMC 26 F.A.) arrived Took over charge of lock at D.R.S. HALLINES.	

[signature]
Lt Col RAMC

WAR DIARY

44 FIELD AMBULANCE

DECEMBER 1917

Army Form C. 2118.

WAR DIARY
or
INTELLIGENCE SUMMARY.
(Erase heading not required.)

Instructions regarding War Diaries and Intelligence Summaries are contained in F.S. Regs., Part II. and the Staff Manual respectively. Title pages will be prepared in manuscript.

Place	Date	Hour	Summary of Events and Information	Remarks and references to Appendices
RED FARM BRANDHOEK	1.12.17	—	Taking over DPS from 2/6 F.A.	
"		6pm	Stronger Complete. Officers and 3 ORs taken over	ℓ
"			LIEUT GILBERTSON RAMC detailed for Temp'y duty with DRS	ℓ
"	2.12.17	"	Captain FLOOD RAMC reported for temp'y duty with 4/2 F.A.	
"			Captain HELM RAMC returns from leave in England	
"			1 NCO & 16 ORs reports for duty with CMDS	
"	3.12.17	—	Captain HELM RAMC reports for temp'y duty with 2/2 F.A.	
"			Holding party relieved from HOLMES having handed over ORS here to 2/96 F.A.	
"	4.12.17	—	OC 141 Labour Coy sent out body of ORs men who lay prisoners to case of men in case of men evacuated direct to train but reported in above - Matts reports to FAul	ℓ ℓ
"	5.12.17	—	2 NCO & 950 R'crut 6/42 F.A. for duty in forward area	ℓ
"	6.12.17	—	Promotions 45835 Pte SM TH In (PB) KOYLI — transfers from 4/3 F.A. as tailors who take 43089 Pte SYKES E (PB) KOYLI who transfers to 4/3 F.A.	ℓ

WAR DIARY or INTELLIGENCE SUMMARY

Place	Date	Hour	Summary of Events and Information	Remarks and references to Appendices
RED FARM BRANDHOEK	6.2.17		114179 Pte. J. HALL 19th Lab. Coy. Th. being discharged from hospital was injured in the abdomen - non penetrating - one wound to C.C.V	
"	8.2.17	-	Sent W.O.P.s to Post office for duty in connection with Xmas Mail	
"	8.12.17		LIEUT GILBERTSON. Relieved from duty & duly on R.T.O.'s D.OR's and F22 F.A. as a working party - proceed that Cabaret	
"			ATKINS R.A.M.C. now with Bgl through from 29th ult.	
"	9.12.17		D.DT.S. inspected D.R.S.	
"	10.12.17	"	Lieut Leef rejoining Car to F.22 F.A.	
"	"	"	Captain F.G.FLOOD R.A.M.C (S.R.) proceeds in action (Chin W.D. & Shrapnel & Right humerus) and evacuated - Shunt by through	
"			90435 Pte WILLIAMS A.E. } evacuated Lot Shunt by through	
"			57380 " COLLOP F.G. }	
"			31448 " N.R.CALDER evacuated Lot Shunt by through	
"	11.12.17	-	54872 " T.PRESCOTT R.A.M.C. Reports Revival & return in Shunt	
"			Lt. J.H. PRATT R.A.M.C.(Rmt.V) Reports arrival taken in the through	
"	12.12.17		The following Rt. R.M.C.s take in ambulances as from the 9th inst -	

Army Form C. 2118.

WAR DIARY
or
INTELLIGENCE SUMMARY.
(Erase heading not required.)

Instructions regarding War Diaries and Intelligence Summaries are contained in F.S. Regs., Part II. and the Staff Manual respectively. Title pages will be prepared in manuscript.

Place	Date	Hour	Summary of Events and Information	Remarks and references to Appendices
RED FARM BRANDHOEK	12/12/17		T/5/460.S. Shoeing Smith c/o/Capt. A.E. HOXON Q.M.C. to the Hope	
			H/0557.69 Pte/A/Sergt. O.H. BULL do " Pegs	
			19/0553.215. Pte c/ Cpl. T. PICKIN do " Cope	Jr.
	13.12.17		10. O.Rs Cent to 42 F.A. for work in forward area.	
			One O.R. Sent for duty to M.F.O ABBEVILLE (Employed 31'mos)	Jr.
			1 O.R. Glaulds leave to ENGLAND	Jr.
	14.12.17		Lt PRATT. Cent to 42 F.A. for being duty.	
	15.12.17		Lt GILBERTSON Rtnd Adcleks for being duty & duty with 6 Van Li	
			Chief of the Viringt of the incid-	
			Capt H.W. SWEENY H.Q.R.C. USA reports his assume rotation in the charge	Jr.
			2. O.Rs Glaulds leave to England.	Jr.
			(Answers for Tourist Put for next week reorg B.m.T (noon) to Dec.	Jr.
			5 officers - 159 -	
	16.12.17		Lt GILBERTSON Htd SWEENY left to England	
	17.12.17		Captain SWEENY H.Q.R.C. USA & L/Cut for duty (Emp. to) HCVD	
			5 O.Rs Glaulds leave to ENGLAND	

WAR DIARY
or
INTELLIGENCE SUMMARY.
(Erase heading not required.)

Army Form C. 2118.

Place	Date	Hour	Summary of Events and Information	Remarks and references to Appendices
RED FARM	18.12.17	—	Captain HELM appointed 2nd in command 42 FA Ambce by 1st Bngde C.6118. Private SHEPPARD RAMC transfer to 42 FA Wood by 1st Bngde 32469. Sgt SWINN RAMC slightly wounded at duty.	
	19.12.17		Captain H. SCOTT, 1st Lt W. BAIN RAMC joined for duty. Captain BRITTON relieved from temp'y duty with 6 D.L.I	
"	20.12.17		Routine	
"	21.12.17			
	22.12.17		1st Lt BAIN evacuated sick to CCS. RAMC OO now received (Unit 6) Arrived 5 Til Ques area 9a.1, 28 mst.	
	23.12.17		Captain SCOTT went to Corps School of Instruction. Lt R. O'CONNOR RAMC reported assumed for duty later in charge 42 Inf Brigade OO. SO received.	
	24.12.17		Snowstorm. 2/c Captain BRITTON left for new area. Advance party of 26 FA ssued Flyst nos DK/ complete for Unit Co of BAKER's Huts on5 94.	
"	25.12.17 12.45pm		Section of 42 A.F left RED FARM Captain's Branches for Wilsons B.	

WAR DIARY
or
INTELLIGENCE SUMMARY.
(Erase heading not required.)

Army Form C. 2118.

Place	Date	Hour	Summary of Events and Information	Remarks and references to Appendices
CORINTHE	25.12.17	8pm	Unit ordered Corinthe - Transport arrived in advance (8pm)	
"	26.12.17	-	Capt. Britton RAMC Attd for Temp duty with 9th B.	
"	-	-	Lt. O'Connor do do 9 KRRC	
"	-	-	Captain Barton returned early life estate her B.E.S. HALLINES (acting rear echelon from MOSS church in RIA 19)	
"	27.12.17	5pm	Remainder Forward transport left for HALLINES	
HALLINES	28.12.17	11pm	Unit arrived - ORS very arduous. Evacuates cars to flash light.	
"	-	-	Routine - Great difficulty in obtaining water enough Drying huts	
"	29.12.17	-	Morning Divis HQs (RAMC) visited	
"	30.12.17	-	Routine	
"	-	-	Ambulance orders 4 RAP received. Unit stores etc up Brigade for 2 MGC Bdes 6 Edge Hill by rail	
"	-	-	Captain Greeny MO RC Grenads Guards to ENGLAND	
"	31.12.17	-	Lt O'Connor returned from duty with 9 KRR	

Henry Bell

44 FIELD AMBULANCE

WAR DIARY

JANUARY 1918

Army Form C. 2118.

WAR DIARY
or
INTELLIGENCE SUMMARY.
(Erase heading not required.)

Instructions regarding War Diaries and Intelligence Summaries are contained in F. S. Regs., Part II. and the Staff Manual respectively. Title pages will be prepared in manuscript.

Place	Date	Hour	Summary of Events and Information	Remarks and references to Appendices
HALLOY	1.1.18	—	Lt O'CONNOR R.A.M.C. returning from Trench duty with 9 K.R.R's.	Q
"	2.1.18	—	Capt. BARTON granted leave to ENGLAND 2 – 16th inst.	Q
			Lt O'CONNOR R.A.M.C. invalids sick whilst off duty at	Q
"	3.1.18	—	attaché party proceeds to SAILLY LE SEC.	
			Capt. SCOTT Rt. M.C. returns from VIII Corps School of instruction.	Q
			Unit complete left for NEW ERA. Lands over BRS. to B.E.F.A.	Q
"	4.1.18	Noon	Arrived at SAILLY LE SEC.	
		7 pm	Sgt FREEBORN (35.852) R.M.C. accidentally injured in attending	Q
			Waggon	
SAILLY LE SEC	5.1.18	—	Routine. — No record when or Les in area occurred.	Q
"	6.1.18	—	" "	Q
"	7.1.18	—	Do continued	
			T/4/091402 Dr. A.E. DOLPHIN R.A.C.H.T. awarded 11 days F.P. No 2 for	
			absent without leave. —	
"	10.1.18	—	Lt PRATT granted leave to ENGLAND – 11th to 25th	Q
			No 322209 Dr. W. GUTHRIE awarded Military Medal	Q
			Authority VIII R.O 365. 22/2/17	

WAR DIARY
or
INTELLIGENCE SUMMARY.

(Erase heading not required.)

Army Form C. 2118.

Place	Date	Hour	Summary of Events and Information	Remarks and references to Appendices
SAILLY LE SEC	11.1.18	-	Lt JESSOP M.O.R.C. arrived from 42 F.A. for emp'y & duty.	
	12.1.18	-	CAPTAIN T.C. BRITTON R.H.T.C. detailed for Remount duty with 2nd Cav Div. (12.1.18)	
			O/R's Sergt R.A. Hunt - B⁰ty 27ᵗʰ	
			B⁰ty R's granted leave 18ᵗʰ - 27ᵗʰ Poulins	
	13.1.18	-	3 O/R's granted leave - 15 - 29ᵗʰ Poulins	
	14.1.18	-		
	15.1.18	-	2 O/R's granted leave 17 - 31 "	
	16.1.18	-	Captain BARTON & SWEENY returned from leave.	
	17.1.18	-	2 O/R's granted leave 19 - Brit Feb	
	18.1.18	-	Poulins	
	19.1.18	-		
	20.1.18	-	41ˢᵗ Inf'y Brig: & O.O. No 192 issued - Brigade Group - Poulins -	
	21.1.18	-		
	22.1.18	8PM	Unit moved to FRESNOY en-CHAUSSEE. Lt D.W. FOSTER granted leave to England. 23ʳᵈ to 6 Feb'y. Sg. FREEBORN returns to unit.	

Army Form C. 2118.

WAR DIARY
or
INTELLIGENCE SUMMARY.
(Erase heading not required.)

Instructions regarding War Diaries and Intelligence Summaries are contained in F.S. Regs., Part II. and the Staff Manual respectively. Title pages will be prepared in manuscript.

Place	Date	Hour	Summary of Events and Information	Remarks and references to Appendices
FRESNOY.	23.1.16	4 PM	Visit M.O.s'd 6th ARTILLERS.	
HALLERS	24.1.16	7.30 PM	Visit M.O. Sd 5 TIRLAN COURT a return from tubs - no man feelers - Lewis 41st Brig. & O.O. 193 -	
TIRLANCOURT	25.1.16	9 PM	Visit M.O. Sd 16 JUSSY. A.D.M.S. O.O. No 5 Received	
JUSSY.	26.1.16	11 AM	Took over DRS from 14/14 French Ambulance - inspection of Medical Stores handed over	
"	27.1.16		Preparing Site to suit the requirements of a British F.A.	
"	28.1.16		" "	
"	29.1.16		PAULUS	
"	30.1.16		M/Ms 2384 Private H.B. FUDGE ASC MT sent to Reference Supply Depot R.F.C. South Farnbro street 98 Single (A.G./21 AS/4 - 28.1.16)	
"	31.1.16		Returns	

44 FIELD AMBULANCE

WAR DIARY

FEBRUARY 1918

Army Form C. 2118.

WAR DIARY
or
INTELLIGENCE SUMMARY.
(Erase heading not required.)

Instructions regarding War Diaries and Intelligence Summaries are contained in F. S. Regs., Part II. and the Staff Manual respectively. Title pages will be prepared in manuscript.

Place	Date	Hour	Summary of Events and Information	Remarks and references to Appendices
JUSSY	1.2.18	—	LT. J. H. PRATT RAMC on relinquishing Commission struck off strength 31.1.18. T/01742. Dr. S. F. SHUTTLEWORTH RAMC awarded 14 days FP No 2 + forfeits 31 days pay under RW absence without leave — 6.30 p.m. 2/.1/.18 to 7.5 p.m. 29.1.18	
"	2.2.18	—	Captain C. J. LAMBIE RAMC } Reported arrival for duty station in which Lt. G. C. M. DAVIES do }	
"	3.2.18	—	Routine — Inspecting Billets for H.D.S.	
"	4.2.18	—	Notified O/c RAMC Depots of the absence without leave of No 94053 Pte PETER McKINLAY RAMC who failed to return with ration supplies of his leave to ENGLAND — leave expired 27.1.18	
"	5.2.18	—	Notified by Sanl that a Gas Cenh had The trees up at JUSSY for the Divison — a doctor to HDS.	
"	6.2.18	—	27648.Pte. J. PARKER for fu 3 Mays pay Wells RW absent 6.35 p.m. 2 – 6.30 p.m. 3.2.18 S.J. TREE " 2 days " 6.30 p.m. 3 – 6.30 p.m. 5.2.18 RW 4.NCO's 748 ORs sent 5.R.D.S for duty week 4.3.5.4	
"	7.2.18	—	D.D.M.S III Corps visited Ambulance + told me that he intended to Report only TRENCH FEET + GAS CASES Injured JUSSY.	

WAR DIARY
or
INTELLIGENCE SUMMARY.
(Erase heading not required.)

Army Form C. 2118.

Place	Date	Hour	Summary of Events and Information	Remarks and references to Appendices
Jussy	8.2.18	—	Routine.	
"	9.2.18	—	Capt LAMBIE RAMC sent to 47 Bde FA for temp'y duty. Capt SCOTT RAMC — " " " " " 61 " " "	
"	10.2.18	—	Bearer party returns from 43 FA — 3 reinforcements received	
"	11.2.18	—	Lt G.R. HARRIS MORC joins for duty. Taken on the strength 22 ORs sent to Corps Rest Station. Hospital CHAUNY for temp'y duty 3 ORs sent to 43 FA for temp'y duty	
"	12.2.18	—	L/Cpl G.M. DAVIES RAMC sent for temp'y duty with CRE	
"	13.2.18	—	Routine. Lt KRAMER MORC joins for duty. Taken on the strength	
"	14.2.18	—	Routine	
"	15.2.18	—	32033 Pte PASSMAN RAMC awarded May FP no 2 – Absent without leave whilst returning from leave – 1 day	
"	16.2.18		Routine	
"	17.2.18			
"	18.2.18		Lt G.R. HARRIS MORC posted to 8 NRRC. Struck off strength	
"	19.2.18		Captain GRAHAM RAMC returns for duty. Taken on strength One O.R. returns for duty. Taken on strength	

Army Form C. 2118.

WAR DIARY
or
INTELLIGENCE SUMMARY.
(Erase heading not required.)

Place	Date	Hour	Summary of Events and Information	Remarks and references to Appendices
Jussy	9.2.18	-	Bowling	
"	19.2.18		6 O.R's Reinforcements arrived - (2 B1 & 4 B2)	
"	22.2.18		Lt D.W. KPTHER MORC departed for duty with 22nd Div views	
			Captain C.G. LAMBIE RAMC departed for duty with 47th Brigade R.A.	
			1st Meerut If Plough - Lt F.D. TAYLOR RAMC later on 1st Punjab	
	23.2.18		Captain GRAHAM RAMC Attach for duty with R.C. Appenditeal Group	
			III Corps	
			Took over Adrian hut & occupied by 224 H.G.C. for Conversion into Scabies	
			Place Submitted to A.D.M.S.	
	24.2.18		Lt Col W. EGAN, D.S.O. R.a.M.C departed on 14 days leave to U.K.	AonS
			Capt B.H. BARTON M.C. R.a.M.C assumed temporary command of the unit	
	25.2.18		Capt Hon SWEENY MORC, U.S.a. returned from temporary duty with 14th D.R.E.	AonS
			and sent to RAMC, 24th Division for duty and attach 1/8th R.W.F.	
	26.2.18		Capt A. SCOTT, R.a.M.C returned from temporary duty with 5th Connaught R.I.	AonS
	27.2.18		Routine	
	28.2.18		Capt A. SCOTT R.a.M.C & 1 Tent subdivision departed for temporary duty with 56th	AonS

Army Form C. 2118.

WAR DIARY
or
INTELLIGENCE SUMMARY.
(Erase heading not required.)

Instructions regarding War Diaries and Intelligence Summaries are contained in F. S. Regs., Part II. and the Staff Manual respectively. Title pages will be prepared in manuscript.

Place	Date	Hour	Summary of Events and Information	Remarks and references to Appendices
JUSSY	28/8/18	1.45pm	Message: "Battle zone has been unnoccupied rather received. Capt. GRAHAM Reports, and I had permission and to go walking wounded collecting post at 6BC 115 & 33. Capt PEIRCE RAMC to 2Dr reported to arrival for duty and was sent to report to Capt GRAHAM, two motor ambulances and all available grannies have been sent to 23rd Dr for duty.	Apps
		11.55pm	Message: "Preceunting period in Battle zone is cancelled" received	

RDBarton
Capt RAMC
COMMANDING No 44 FIELD AMBULANCE

War Diary

140/2349

44 Field Ambulance

March 1918

Confidential

COMMITTEE FOR THE
MEDICAL HISTORY OF THE WAR
Date 12 MAY 1918

Army Form C. 2118.

WAR DIARY
or
INTELLIGENCE SUMMARY.
(Erase heading not required.)

Instructions regarding War Diaries and Intelligence Summaries are contained in F. S. Regs., Part II. and the Staff Manual respectively. Title pages will be prepared in manuscript.

Place	Date	Hour	Summary of Events and Information	Remarks and references to Appendices
JUSSY	1/3/18		Lieut F.O. TAYLOR R.A.M.C. reported his arrival on returning from leave to U.K	
	2/3/18		Routine	
	3/3/18		Lieut F.O. TAYLOR OR 24 CR departed to course of instruction at 5th Army Reinf. Sch.	
	4/3/18		Lieut G.C.M. DAVIES posted to 24 CR as he proceeds ahead of Unit.	
	5/3/18		Routine	
	6/3/18		Routine	
	7/3/18		1 reinforcement OR received	
	8/3/18		Routine	
	9/3/18		Routine	
	10/3/18		Routine	
	11/3/18		Routine	
	12.3.18		Orders received forces detaching from hour – Eastern Western known for use	
	13.3.18		Capt Tully proc 4 B.C.C.S. Capt BRITON R.A.M.C. arrived for duty vice F. Tonic L.	
	14.3.18		[illegible] TAYLOR returns from 5 Army Reinf. School	

WAR DIARY or INTELLIGENCE SUMMARY

Army Form C. 2118.

Place	Date	Hour	Summary of Events and Information	Remarks and references to Appendices
Jussy	3-		Shelling weak. Commies of Sqn. was Gas certs & secured	
	17.3.18		Received the Cpt Ricordan of plydome British Portion & maps in accordance with QRO 3246.	
			Captain SCOTT & 4 O.R's proceeded to 5th Army School of Musketry	
		16.3.18	9 O.R's reinforcements (1st Surrender B)	
		19.3.18	Captain SCOTT returned from School of Musketry	
		20.3.18 9pm	Precautionary wire received. "Battle has late Precautionary action". In receipt of wire Divisional waiting wounds but opened up at Moulemont. Guarding of Captain BRITTON, Lt TAYLOR & a Lieut. Subaltern wa Motorcars & holding equipment — Gas certs opened at Jussy & all available wires sent to 43rd FA.	
	21.3.18 4.30am		Enemy barrage began in forward area — Jussy Shelled.	
		12noon	Jussy opened up so ADS very heavy shelling particularly in the area of the canal. Casualties (10 cas) received. Mules Divisional travelling wounds but have during morning – gradually to wounded Coming in. — Office tent blown up by shell fire — no Casualties surgical personnel	

WAR DIARY
or
INTELLIGENCE SUMMARY.

Army Form C. 2118.

Place	Date	Hour	Summary of Events and Information	Remarks and references to Appendices
Jussy	21.3.18	3pm	Divisional training transfer held closed at Hinkercourt — Wire received from Division (4.0.4.G) "MDS at Trefcon(?) & Beaumont). Unit proceeded leaving Captain Barton & 20 O.R.s to deal with local casualties at Jussy — Orders later personally by A.D.M.S to orders to withdraw all personnel —	
"	"	4pm	Jussy evacuated — wounded & personnel & prisoners (wounded cases Stat – 90) proceed —	
Beaumont	"	5pm	Unit arrived at Beaumont — Unit in hours closed —	
"	22.3.18	3pm	Unit orders to move to Guivry —	
Guivry	"	4pm	Unit arrived — Closed in reserve —	
"	"	5pm	Captain Graham. N.O.Rs. with motor Ambulances proceeds to open up A.D.S at Flavy-le-Martel.	
"	"	7pm	Evacuations A.D.S all Quiet — Cases evacuated to T.R.LANCOURT	
"	23.3.18	11am	Unit left for Tirlancourt	
Tirlancourt	"	1pm	News up A.D.S at Tirlancourt Chateau — Barker, Humbert via R. Guiscard - Tirlancourt — Took over the whole of the line from 42. F.A. —	

WAR DIARY
or
INTELLIGENCE SUMMARY.
(Erase heading not required.)

Army Form C. 2118.

Place	Date	Hour	Summary of Events and Information	Remarks and references to Appendices
TIRLANCOURT	28.3.18	7am	Party of wound from FLAVY LE MARTEL - foot wounds mounted cases - Captain BARTON. Shell attacks heavy post at CUGNY. Captain SCOTT a relay post at VILLESELVE - Large Ambulance working between these posts Flesheires Ham & ADS. 34189 Pte MOSS MAN.T wounded in Action & evacuated 66885 A/Sgt BRYANT evacuated sick	
		8.30pm	Sent 10 O.R's to foot at CUGNY.	
		4pm	Reinforced post at CUGNY & VILLESELVE - walked bob.	
	29.3.18	8pm	Walks bob & next day Captain BARTON's post to cross Roads. BEAUMONT leaving post of 4.9. R.M.O. - one ford car, 4 manager & 1 of whom	
		10.30	when ordered orders to move West (Prise) buib ordnance store 7.H.Q.) left Captain BRITTON in charge. Mid Captain BARTON & Lieut Captain SCOTT & so many wounded as could be spared to form headquarters - Captain BARTON - fell back to VILLESELVE	
	11.30		Captain SCOTT & personnel found new headquarters	

WAR DIARY
or
INTELLIGENCE SUMMARY.
(Erase heading not required.)

Army Form C. 2118.

Place	Date	Hour	Summary of Events and Information	Remarks and references to Appendices
TIRLANCOURT	24.3.18	11 A.S.	Received order to move 6" mor. attacks boot from TILLESSEUE to BEINES	
		3.30pm	Received wire from forward Mor. Battery at NOYON to march leaving working party at BEINES + HQ at TIRLANCOURT.	
		4.30pm	Advance part moved back to BOUCHOIRE - party from QUIRY rejoined unit.	
NOYON	24.3.18		Unit reached NOYON + on arriving in Barracks was immediately bombed by enemy Aircraft. (See appendix) The following Casualties:	
			40015 RMS J E CATTRALL R.A.M.C.	
			31848 S.Sgt. M.E. HEGARTY do	
			31581 Pte. A. GORDON do	Killed
			32972 " W. RAINES do	
			M3/077720 " E.P. SIMMONS A.O.C.H.T.	
			M2/155168 " F.G. GIDDINGS do	
			T3/1018 Sgt. A. HARVY A.O.C.H.T. T7/878 Dr. SMURTHWAITE A.O.C.H.T.	Wounded
			T/1006 Dr. J. BROWN do T4/201300 do J. STRANG do	Evacuated
			T2/016774 Dr. A. RAEBURN T2/11601 do W. HUTCHINSON -	

WAR DIARY
or
INTELLIGENCE SUMMARY.

(Erase heading not required.)

Army Form C. 2118.

Place	Date	Hour	Summary of Events and Information	Remarks and references to Appendices
NOYON	24/3/18	6 p.m.	352418 Pte. G. BLAKE R.A.M.C., 89742 Pte. S.E. GAZELEY R.A.M.C. } wounded	
"		"	31772. Pte. G. PAUL ", 31172 " W. ROSE R.A.M.C. } French	
"		"	8357. Pte. C.T. PAKELEY	
"		"	315 25r Pte. W.H. GANHAM, 30833 Pte. E. BOWCOCK. } wounded at duty.	
"		"	28898 Pte. T.A. PARKIN - R.A.M.C.	
"		"	7 Horses killed + 7 mules. 1 ford car wrecked.	
"		6.30	S-23417. Pte. S. GREEN noor. R.A.M.C. wounded machine gun bullets. TIRANCOURT wrecked, total number of casualties collected + Evacuals (23-24) 550 all ranks.	
"		"	Division having being relieved in the line looked at BOUCHOIRE closed up early by own headquarters. Unit moved to LASSIGNY as I did not consider the Barracks at NOYON a suitable place for the unit for the night.	
LASSIGNY	24/3/18	7.30 pm	Unit arrived - closer in reserve	
"			Unit left for RESSONS-SUR-MATZ.	

WAR DIARY
or
INTELLIGENCE SUMMARY.
(Erase heading not required.)

Army Form C. 2118.

Place	Date	Hour	Summary of Events and Information	Remarks and references to Appendices
RESSONS	28.3.16	6.30 pm	Unit arrived — closed in Bivouac. Some info re hot Scouts from #3 F.A. No M/5001 Pte A.F. LIDGETT a&c M.T. is missing presumed captured on the 27/3/16. His large Car (Humber) is also presumed captured at BENAY.	Q
	28.3.16	8.1 pm	Captain GRAHAM & Staff Sergt. freed up HDS at ELINCOURT.	Q
			Unit moved to CLAIROIX — arrived there 6 pm.	
CLAIROIX		6 pm	Parts of Unit at ELINCOURT. Captain BATON Sent to No.16 Hospital	Q
			Reinforced post at ELINCOURT at Compiègne in charge of Capt WEBSTER wounded	
"	2/3.3.16	7 am	Parties posted ELINCOURT & Schus'd partly there	Q
		1 pm or	Post withdrawn & partly reformed unit — Casualties cleared — B."	Q
		2 pm	Unit left for BEAUVOIS, passed at 7/5 pm.	
BEAUVOIS	28.3.16	10.30	Unit moved out. Posted on road near ESTRÉES ST DENIS	Q
			having Capt. BARTON & Capt. SCOTT on main Compiègne–Senlis road. Also HDS at RANTILLERS. no wounded B"ellies"	
			whole unit moved to GINQUEUX passed there 1.30 free	
GINQUEUX	29.3.16	2 pm	Left for NOGENT where infantry of Division embused.	Q

Army Form C. 2118.

WAR DIARY
or
INTELLIGENCE SUMMARY.
(Erase heading not required.)

Place	Date	Hour	Summary of Events and Information	Remarks and references to Appendices
NOGENT	29.3.18	4pm	arrived at NOGENT - 76.3.44 P.C.J. MORGAN wounded feet	B
	30.3.18	to 3pm	Unit left for AIRION resuming their form - Crew on the march.	B
AIRION	31.3.18	11.pm	Unit left for FAY S. QUENTIN	B

Nugent/Lt C

Vol 36

146/2909

WAR DIARY

44 FIELD AMBULANCE

APRIL 1918

Army Form C. 2118.

WAR DIARY
or
INTELLIGENCE SUMMARY.
(Erase heading not required.)

Place	Date	Hour	Summary of Events and Information	Remarks and references to Appendices
FAY St QUENTIN	1.4.18	10.30pm.	Left for HARDIVILLERS. - Arrived here at 3pm. - Men Clad	
HARDIVILLERS.	2.4.18	"	Left for FOSSEMANANT & arrived here at 6pm. do do	
FOSSEMANANT	3.4.18	11.45pm.	Left for BLANGY-TRONVILLE & arrived here 7pm. On arrival received orders	
BLANGY-		1pm.	to take over forward area. - Details as follows.	
TRONVILLE		4pm.	Captain BARTON. MC & 1NCO & 25 bearers with equipment posted in R.A.P.s	
			collecting post. —	
			Collecting post VAIRE-SOUS-CORBIE. 1 officer 16 O.R.S. Relief reported	
			R.A.P. HAMEL 1 NCO. & 8 O.R.S Complete at 8pm.	
			R.A.P. Bois de VAIRE 8 O.R.S Taken 8mn from	
			R.A.P. 1 mile East of VILLERS-BRETONNEUX 6 O.R.s 1st Cav Division	
			Bearer post at BOUZENCOURT from 16th Division — 1NCO & 4 P.s.	
			# large Cab "Stollied" cases from here & out & bring wounded back	
			6 A.D.S at FOUILLOY. -	
	4.4.18	7pm.	Bot over A.D.S. marching wounded post at FOUILLOY from Cav. Div.	
			keeping transport parked at BLANGY-TRONVILLE	
			Immediate wounded began to arrive very rapidly. — Enemy shelling	

WAR DIARY
or
INTELLIGENCE SUMMARY.
(Erase heading not required.)

Army Form C. 2118.

Place	Date	Hour	Summary of Events and Information	Remarks and references to Appendices
FOUILLY	4.4.18	7am	Crossroads 50 yards from dressing station – 20 yds from waiting wounded Collecting Post.	
"		8.30am	10 M.A.C. cars arrived to clear A.D.S.	
"		11.am.	Owing to heavy shelling had to evacuate waiting wounded post & A.D.S. but left 1 Officer & 8 O.R's there (with Equipment) to deal with local casualties. Moved A.D.S. & waiting wounded collecting post to AUBIGNY. – Enemy reported advancing on the Northern portion of front.	
AUBIGNY	4.4.18	3pm	Established bearer post on FOUILLY WARFUSÉE Road – Enemy reported advancing slowly.	
"		4pm	Collecting post at VAIRE closed as the found at HAMELET – bounded owing in quickly. Got 8 more cars from M.A.C.	
"		7pm	Received warning that he (hours) be relieved by F.A. of 5 Div.	
"			Divn. during the night.	
"	5.4.18	2.am	Advance party followed ambulance arrived staff own post in the line.	

WAR DIARY
or
INTELLIGENCE SUMMARY.

Army Form C. 2118.

Place	Date	Hour	Summary of Events and Information	Remarks and references to Appendices
AUBIGNY	5.4.18	3.30pm	Main party of relieving Ambulance arrived — Relief Complete — Officers hereto reported arrival at AUBIGNY — No wounded at any post or A.D.S. on handing over —	
"	"	5.Mx	Total numbers:- Othr. ranks = Officers 32 — ORs 628 Unit opened transport at BLANGY-TRONVILLE	
"	"	4pm	Unit moved to GLISY carries Three to 8.30 pm.	
GLISY	"	6pm	Received orders to establish A.D.S. at BLANGY trucking wounded lost at GLISY. Division holding Support line. AUBIGNY-GACHY. Division did not come into action. There were no casualties.	
"	6.4.18	-	Division not in action — No Casualties — Lt A.R. PEARCE to P.C. reports from Captain B.H. BARTON M.C. — D.S.O. M/85529 Pte P. RIDLEIGH acting F.M Medal.	
"	7.4.18	-	Promulgated recommendation for immediate awards as follows:-	
"	"	4pm	With Div party at 4 A.D.S. moved left for AMIENS. arriving at STACHEUL at 6pm. — Much cloud.	
ST. ACHEUL	"	"	Party from 2/2 Home Counties F.A. opened —	

WAR DIARY or INTELLIGENCE SUMMARY

Army Form C. 2118.

Instructions regarding War Diaries and Intelligence Summaries are contained in F.S. Regs., Part II. and the Staff Manual respectively. Title pages will be prepared in manuscript.

(Erase heading not required.)

Place	Date	Hour	Summary of Events and Information	Remarks and references to Appendices
S¹ ACHEUL	8.4.18	—	Unit (cont) – Transport & Captain Griffith left with Durham DLI	
	9.4.18	—	81318 Sgt Watson DCM evacuated sick	
	10.4.18 9pm		Unit left for new area – arrived at SALEUX at 9pm. Unit trans- at GAMACHES at 7pm. Thence to DARGNIES	
DARGNIES	11.4.18		Unit closed. Transport at FEUQUIERES.	
	11.4.18 12.15pm		Unit marches to FEUQUIERES. DTR's evacuated sick X Transport at FEUQUIERES arrived there at 3.19am. Returned & Athane at HARESQUEL at 7 austm. Unit took train along Marches to CREQUY at 5.30pm.	
CREQUY	13.4.18	—	Unit collecting 41st Brigade Kit & checking equipment	
	14.4.18	—	O.O. 192 (Div) received. Unit moved to CREQUY at 1pm to billet there instead	
CREPY L'OBLOIS WOOD	15.4.18		Unit moved to L'OBLOIS WOOD – under canvas – arrived there Delivering Kit from Polaire at Brigade DUP Office – L/Taylor RAMC evacuated sick struck off strength from 15.4.18.	
	16.4.18		Captain Lort Atkins for troop duty with 41 M.I. Brigade	
	17.4.18		Captain Hunter RAMC reported for duty taken on height	
"	18.4.18		Coy of McQuay held for surredepth coop I personnel including S	

WAR DIARY
or
INTELLIGENCE SUMMARY

Army Form C. 2118.

Place	Date	Hour	Summary of Events and Information	Remarks and references to Appendices
LOBLOIS WOOD	16.4.16		LT COL TOMKINSON AFF to 10th HUSSARS - to which has been be turned. April 4th to April 16th. An Ambulance with FMO's at 9.62 Division Ambulances attached. A posts, Iss e HQ attaches the Unit for duty.	
"	19.4.16		Routine - Collection & evacuation of sick.	
"	20.4.16		Routine	
"	21.4.16		Unit moved to ECQUEDECQUES - arrived 4pm.	
ECQUED- ECQUES	22.4.16		Collection & evacuation of Portuguese sick.	
"	26.4.16		ADMS found truth Unit & informed me that the F.A. had lately been disbanded. In the near future retaining only a Section of Officers & OR's (iii copies 297,7,30) & after received send all motor Ambulances to SMTO XI Corps.	
"	27.4.16	4pm	All motor Ambulances (5 turnbeams & 2 Fords) left to report to SMTO XI Corps.	
"	"		Orders received to collect HQ 5th Mtd Bad & 1st Mtd Equipment	for 20/4/16 found
"	28.4.16	7pm	Captain IRWIN RAMC reports arrival & attached to Unit	
"	"		Routine	

Army Form C. 2118.

WAR DIARY
or
INTELLIGENCE SUMMARY.
(Erase heading not required.)

Place	Date	Hour	Summary of Events and Information	Remarks and references to Appendices
EGUEDEC - AVES	April -		Personnel & Ambulance Cars went to Fr: T.O. XI Corps Hd. Sheet 36 to Strength - Authority OU.G 249 (A.II/24/4.18).- S.B.B. rank L.1 Mid. Equipment handed i/c to A-DMS XI &	
	30.4.18		Orders - Sick collection from Portuguese Brigade R.E + R.F.A	

[signature]

44 FIELD AMBULANCE [stamp]

WO 137
140/3076

WAR DIARY

44 FIELD AMBULANCE

MAY 1918

COMMITTEE FOR THE
MEDICAL HISTORY OF THE WAR
Date 7 AUG 1919

WAR DIARY
or
INTELLIGENCE SUMMARY.

(Erase heading not required.)

Army Form C. 2118.

Place	Date	Hour	Summary of Events and Information	Remarks and references to Appendices
ECQUEDESQUES	1.5.18	—	Captain HUNTER. RAMC. reports for duty ex F.A.D.11.2 which offg (Lieut) authority Lieut. PEARCE MORC. to 55.2 DDMS XIII Captain IRWIN. RAMC (AH.3) reinf & duty with 41st Brigade } J3/167/2 29.4.18 Captain SCOTT RAMC returns from sick & duty with 41st Brigade 32076 Pte W. DOUGHERTY RAMC awarded 7 days FP No.2 for. (1) absent from 2 pm parade till found in his billet about 2.30 pm (28 min) (2) Breaking out of billet whilst under arrest. 19929 Pte B.C. LENTON RMC awarded 8 days FP No 2 (type b 1 day pay and 8 dys) 1 absent from SOL roll call fatigue from till 5 Am. (8 hrs) 30.4.18 Harling.	
"	2.5.18	—		
	3.5.18	—	DGMS-2369/124/17 DMS. No PL/12.92 - asks us - In brief these mobiles are - (1) HQ's of FA's will be withdrawn by GHQ as required for reinforcements that CO of field Ambulance remain "present for withdrawal as detachments" (app V) to the units in Army Area - (2) when the FA Commander leaves American HQs ? Mich. The personnel will be reviewed so to bear the	

WAR DIARY
or
INTELLIGENCE SUMMARY.

Army Form C. 2118.

Place	Date	Hour	Summary of Events and Information	Remarks and references to Appendices
ECQUEDECQUES	3.5.18		Orders for the dispersal of surplus personnel were at the same time issued by G.H.Q. Training Cadre to consist of Commanding Officer Quartermaster Sgt. Major & 1 Staff Sergt. — (for charge of Equipment) 3 Bearer Sergts. 1 Sergt. Clerk (for preliminary training of Americans) 15 Other Ranks — Bearers Cooks ADS — 13 ORs Reserves for 46 CCS	20/1
"	4.5.18		Routine	
"	5.5.18		"	
"	6.5.18		"	
"	7.5.18		84063 Pte P. McKinlay Stret. Sticks off through 29.1.18 (RAMC records 28/1/64/18 D.A.O.C. Reinforcement (Sgt Bull) arrived	
"	8.5.18		1 Sgt Reinforcement (Sgt Bull) arrived	
"	9.5.18		50702 Pvd E.A. PENNEY RAMC arrived — taken on the strength 53083 SGT R.H. RICHARDSON do do	

WAR DIARY
or
INTELLIGENCE SUMMARY.

(Erase heading not required.)

Army Form C. 2118.

Place	Date	Hour	Summary of Events and Information	Remarks and references to Appendices
ECQUEDECQUES	10.5.16	-	ADMS No 12 newsletter. 1 Car & 1 Cycle returns to 42 F.A. (only 1 car left) Pte WALSH (34292) RAMC evacuated & struck off strength	
"	11.5.16	-	1 Car from 43 F.A. arrived for duty	
"	12.5.16		121599 Pte H.E. BRICKELL RAMC evacuated & struck off strength M2/021535 Pte F. BRUCE ASC awarded 8 days FP No 2 for 1. Dangerous & Reckless Driving 2. Exceeding the speed limit of 20 miles per hour	
"	13-14 15.16 15.5.16		Routine - Motor motorcyclists from AA & QMG 14th Div, 4 G.S. Inspector, A.A. Cols for temp duty with 7th R.I. Rig & 7th R.I. Fus. Routine	
"	16.5.16			
"	17.5.16		About airmen returns DM6 No 14. SCWSB - Captain & a Dvr Cr. Party proceeded to BOUBERS Hope mg from 42 F.A. Major BRITTON & remainder F.C. section proceeded to BOUBERS by road	
"	18.5.16	6am	42103 Private HILL W awarded 8 days FP No 2 for (1) Creating a disturbance (2) Striking a brother soldier	
"	19.5.16			

Army Form C. 2118.

WAR DIARY
or
INTELLIGENCE SUMMARY.
(Erase heading not required.)

Place	Date	Hour	Summary of Events and Information	Remarks and references to Appendices
ECQUEDECQUES	19.3.18		Portuguese Ambulance arrived Hate over	
"	20.3.18		Private TREE (31305) awarded 14 days FP No 2. for Drunkenness on active service –	
			Party in charge of the tent had Visitors during the night 19/20th & M/0555-21- Cpl. T. Pickin RAMC 147. transferred to 53rd Division of which he is Strength –	Authority DGMS B1457/2413
			The following promotions are made to supply establishment.	
			32133 Sg. W. SMITH to a/St.Sergt. from 24.3.18	
			31419 a/Sergt. J MACDONALD 15th to a/Sergt from 25.3.18	
			33611 a/Cpl H.E. BRAITHWAITE 1st to a/Sergt from 27.3.18	
			93210 Cpl F. COCKING BMC do do 24.3.18	
			31873 a/L/Cpl P.F. EKE " a/Cpl do 24.3.18	
			31474 a/L/Cpl C.H. PERRY " do do 25.3.18	
			31212 a/L/Cpl F.G. CHALKE " do do 27.3.18	
			30816 a/Cpl J RIMMER " a/L/Sergt to B.S. 18	
			32147 Pte J.A BURY " a/L/Cpl do do	

Army Form C. 2118.

WAR DIARY
or
INTELLIGENCE SUMMARY.

(Erase heading not required.)

Instructions regarding War Diaries and Intelligence Summaries are contained in F. S. Regs., Part II. and the Staff Manual respectively. Title pages will be prepared in manuscript.

Place	Date	Hour	Summary of Events and Information	Remarks and references to Appendices
ECQUEDESQUES M.S.6			87357 Pte J.M. HINDMARCH Rifle Bde a M/cycl. from 20.5.18	
			31228 " A.W. FLETCHER " " "	
			53906 " F. SOUTHWELL " " "	
"	21-23/5/18		Routine. - "Lost bicycle found"	
"	23.5.18		4 O.R's evacuated sick. Col. EDWARDS, Ptes Jones G.A. - Rush H.H. - Young	
"	24.5.18		Routine.	
"	25.5.18		Col. FEARON R.M.C. + Lt. ANTLEY. Evacuated Sick. Lt. Col. Reynolds	
			arrived. Matters in the Straight (Dr. FARMER + Dr. GORMAN)	
			Renewed raining order in connection with Units proceeding to Instruction	
			(Brig.) (ADMS M.007/13/G dr 22.5.18)	
"	26.5.18		Handed over duties in connection (with Dr. La Verpiere Troops & the Etapes	
			Ambulance. - Qual. PENNY R.A.M.C. sent to DDMS XI for Keed	
			as chief Clerk.	
"	27.5.18		Movement order. (First Army No. SC 164/7/1 O. 23/5/18) Ment. to	
			proceed to NIELLES LES BLEQUIN for duty with 36 Div. U.S.A. in the	
			RR look - hauling carts only 6 bso bed - cyclists transport.	

Army Form C. 2118.

WAR DIARY
or
INTELLIGENCE SUMMARY.
(Erase heading not required.)

Place	Date	Hour	Summary of Events and Information	Remarks and references to Appendices
ECQUEDECQUES	2/5/18	—	Motor Ambulance Othnanes & M.T. Equipment. MT15 (Sunb.) M/c rejoined — from Div. having proceeded too far. Relieving the former No 1 Mot. Aut. under charge of Major BARTON. HC Captain Graham. Stood after Parade. Parade attached to the Division in LILLERS Area. SPR Connolly 1 NCO & 7 DR's No 2 Mot. Aut. Forward of Major BRITTON. Capt. SCOTT. 1 NCO 1 Jort. Stood after Parade of 42 & 43 Brigades (Div. Area)	
"	2& 5/16-5PM	Not consisting of having cars upon DG M.S 2, 3 & 9/124/7 Clybarks for U.S.A Div. Complete with safety wagon — One ASC Driver shell made up with P.B Men. — Ambulance Cars not yet arrived.	
THEROUANNE	—	8pm	Ambulance Cars arrived with Cycles. MT complete.	
"	29/5/18	8am	Left for NIELLES LES BLEQUIN.	
"			Reported to ADir. 8th Div. (British) which Div. to Division attached to 28th Div U.S.A. Ord. to go to LART. & await further orders.	
"		noon	HQ. joined up with MTC Section at DRION VILLE & encamped (will assume QL LART Form.)	
LART.				

Army Form C. 2118.

WAR DIARY
or
INTELLIGENCE SUMMARY.
(Erase heading not required.)

Instructions regarding War Diaries and Intelligence Summaries are contained in F. S. Regs., Part II. and the Staff Manual respectively. Title pages will be prepared in manuscript.

Place	Date	Hour	Summary of Events and Information	Remarks and references to Appendices
L.o.T.	20.5.18	—	Abeele S.	
"	21.5.18	—	26 O.R.s surplus personnel of F.C. rejoined the unit.	

[Signature]
CONGRATULATING O.C. 44 FIELD AMBULANCE
R.A.M.C.

WAR DIARY

44 FIELD AMBULANCE

JUNE 1918

WAR DIARY
or
INTELLIGENCE SUMMARY.
(Erase heading not required.)

Army Form C. 2118.

Place	Date	Hour	Summary of Events and Information	Remarks and references to Appendices
L.A.R.T.	1.6.18	-	Poulins	
"	2.6.18	-	Lieut: MACKEY & RENFRO H.C. USA Seconded as/rued for a Corse of Instruction S.S. SMITH. Sergt. MACDONALD & 2/Sergt. RIMMER R.A.M.C. Reported for duty with 169. Inf.y Reg.t USA. - 2 O.A. buses & Div. No 58 Sec.	
"	3.6.18	7.m.d	Unit departed for BOURNONVILLE & arrived there 11.30 a.m.	
BOURNONVILLE	4.6.18	2.30 pm	Unit left for CONTEVILLE & arrived there 5.30 pm.	
CONTEVILLE	5.6.18	-	Poulins - Cellular evacuation of sick of 702 American Div."	
"	6.6.18	-	Poulins. Co.	
"	7.6.18	-	Hon. Lt. & A/L Q. FOSTER R.A.M.C. thanks left in Hon. Ranks & Captain - Authority. A.C.I. London Gazette June 3rd 1918.	
"	8.6.18	-	Lt. MACKEY & RENFRO. M.O. R.C. rejoined this unit - 2 N.C.O. others from unit's attachment to 109 & Inf. Reg.t USA. - 2 Horses Ambulance Cars unit 25 to 2 F.A. 1 Motor Ambulance No. 573 Attached 28th American Div. on the move	
"	9.6.18	-	Captain R. LYN JONES R.A.M.C. attached for temp.y duty from 104 F.A.	
"	6.6.16	-	C.A. Inf Bn O.O. 123 Red. Unit moved to BOURNONVILLE on 10.6.18	

WAR DIARY or INTELLIGENCE SUMMARY

Army Form C. 2118.

Place	Date	Hour	Summary of Events and Information	Remarks and references to Appendices
BOURNONVILLE	11.6.18		Unit left CONTEVILLE. 7am arrived at BOURNONVILLE 10pm	
"	12.6.18 & 13		Routine - Catholic funeral of 78th American Div[n]	
"	14.6.18		62 ORs R.A.M.C + C.P.B non-injured from race - Motor Ambulance returned from duty w.e.f. to 3 F.A.	
"	15.6.18		No 35"483 Pte W. WHITTAKER Royl (RAMC) awarded 14 days F.P. No 2	
"			2 Motor Ambulances returned from duty w.e.f. to 2 F.A.	
"	16.6.18		Major Barber Captain GRAHAM + 12 ORs reported for duty from No1 Field Detachment (14th Divn) - Captain Syrjones returned to Unit	
"	17.6.18		Major BRITTON Capt SCOTT + 80 ORs reported for duty from No 2 West Attachment (14th Divn) - 6 American ORs attached from 28th Divn. for a course of Instruction - Unit was authorised by 39th British Divn Trails April 29th 1918, who informs no more Unit words soon issued to 30th American Div. for duty	
"	18.6.18		Routine - No 58961 Pte HARWOOD R.A.M.C. proceeds to Abbeville Signal School	
"	19.6.18		Influenza broke out in the Unit	
"	20.6.18		6 American ORs returned to their units	

WAR DIARY
or
INTELLIGENCE SUMMARY.

(Erase heading not required.)

Army Form C. 2118.

Place	Date	Hour	Summary of Events and Information	Remarks and references to Appendices
BOORNONVILLE	22.6.18	—	Influenza on the increase amongst Army Veg. Return for this of isolation. On Sick - 2 Cases in personnel front - investigation of these cases shows no connection between them. (Both cycled 1 postman & 1 orderly) contact to be used to prevent Influenza outbreak amongst Army Veg.	
"	23.6.18	—	2 Influenza Cases amongst personnel of unit — S.M. Cooke RAC awarded Meritorious Conduct Service Medal — London Gazette 17.6.18	
"	24.6.18	—	Nothing	
"	25.6.18	—	Influenza spreading in unit in field. All precaution 5 fresh cases Captain GRAHAM granted Special Confidential Leave 25.6. to 9.7.18.	
"	26.6.18	—	Began Rectal Inoculation of 4000 turn out twice daily for all. Sent 3 men — On Sick Convalescent this daily. Major Barlin M.C. + B Section Complete departs for Mer MOUTIER Station notice of 78 American Army Sanitary Trains then & to Collect the Eastern half of the 78th Division — The Ambulance to	

Army Form C. 2118.

WAR DIARY
or
INTELLIGENCE SUMMARY.
(Erase heading not required.)

Instructions regarding War Diaries and Intelligence Summaries are contained in F. S. Regs., Part II. and the Staff Manual respectively. Title pages will be prepared in manuscript.

Place	Date	Hour	Summary of Events and Information	Remarks and references to Appendices
BOURNONVILLE	26.6.18	—	Collecting & evacuating the sick B.Ms to 78th American Divisn. Clothing put an area about 20 square miles — 9 large cars of 39th Divisn American attached t'enable to work the area	
"	27.6.18	—	Captain Nott admitted to F.A. with Influenza —	
"	28.6.18	—	Only one influenza case in unit today	
"	29.6.18	—	Received instructions from O.M. 2nd Army Gen Hosp. Lt. G. FOSTER Motor Proceded *ABBEVILLE & drew Motor Lorrie for 303 Van hein with Ordnance store Motor Ambulances that were couplete for 2 FOURIARDIN	
"	30.6.18		arrived for 303 Van hein	

[signature] I.A.M.C
COMMANDING No 44 FIELD AMBULANCE

WAR DIARY

44 FIELD AMBULANCE

JULY 1918

Army Form C. 2118.

WAR DIARY
or
INTELLIGENCE SUMMARY.
(Erase heading not required.)

Instructions regarding War Diaries and Intelligence Summaries are contained in F.S. Regs., Part II. and the Staff Manual respectively. Title pages will be prepared in manuscript.

Place	Date	Hour	Summary of Events and Information	Remarks and references to Appendices
BOURNONVILLE	1/7/18		Routine	
	2/7/18		Motor ambulances of 132nd & 134th Field Ambulances returned to their units. Major Burton & Beecher rejoined from VIEIL MOUTIER. Collection of sick handed over to 311th Field Hospital, U.S. Army.	
	3/7/18		Routine	
	4/7/18		Routine	
	5/7/18		93509 Pte F.T. Barrett awarded 28 days' F.P. No 2 per (1) Insubordinence (2) 0.2041 attempting to give forbidden information to an unauthorised person.	
		5 pm	At 5.6pm, 3rd U.S. Div. Rank Order No H1 received — sides to be handed over to 303rd Sanitary Train, U.S. Army	
	6/7/16	1.30 am	At 1.30 am Attention to stores received — but to move to RÉTY.	
		9.30 am	Left BOURNONVILLE and came under administration of 89th Division.	
		3.8 pm	Arrived RÉTY and came under administration 34 Division	
RÉTY	7/7/8		Routine	
	8/7/18		Lieut W.H. MORGAN, R.A.M.C. U.S.A. reported arrival for duty & taken on strength.	
	9/7/18		O.O. No 4 of 41st Brigade received — unit to move to CANCHY and LE BREUIL	
	10/7/18		Left RÉTY at 9.30 am. Arrived CANCHY Headquarters and LE BREUIL at 3.0 pm	

WAR DIARY
or
INTELLIGENCE SUMMARY.
(Erase heading not required.)

Army Form C. 2118.

Instructions regarding War Diaries and Intelligence Summaries are contained in F. S. Regs., Part II. and the Staff Manual respectively. Title pages will be prepared in manuscript.

Place	Date	Hour	Summary of Events and Information	Remarks and references to Appendices
LE BREUIL	10/7/18	9.30 p.m.	Received O.D. t/i 91st Infantry Brigade - unit to move to LA PANNE on 11/7/18.	
		11.0 p.m.	Destination changed to HELVELINGHEM	
	11/7/18		Left billets at 7.45 a.m. arrived HELVELINGHEM at 11.0 a.m.	
			Capt. D.S. GRAHAM returned from leave to U.K.	
HELVELINGHEM	12/7/18		Left at 2.0 p.m. & arrived HATTEN at 4.0 p.m. Opened D.R.S.	
HATTEN	13/7/18		Constructive work on D.R.S.	
"	14/7/18		Major T.C. BRITTON and Capt. A. SCOTT and C section moved to HEIST and opened up relief D.R.S. Medical Centre	
	15/7/18		Routine	
	16/7/18		Routine	
	17/7/18		12 O.R.'s reinforcements received	
	18/7/18		Routine.	
	19/7/18		Received 3 O.R. reinforcements	
			7830.2 pte: H.A. HALL R.A.M.C. Graules Special leave to ENGLAND 18.7.18. 3 E.O	
		6.45 p.m.	G.O.C. 14th Div: inspects Unit.	
	20/7/18		Attended by on B.R.C.S. for stores for Recreation	

WAR DIARY
or
INTELLIGENCE SUMMARY.
(Erase heading not required.)

Army Form C. 2118.

Place	Date	Hour	Summary of Events and Information	Remarks and references to Appendices
WATTEN	20/7/18	—	16053 Pte W. A. M. S. HAWTHORNE R.A.M.C. awarded 14 days F.P. No.1 under A.C.I. 717 of 1917 as from March 16th 1918.	
"	21/7/18		Poulins - Officers returned from five days Gas Refresher from Horse "'Poulins - Officers returned from ADMS to New Captain Scott R.A.M.C. proceed	
"	22/7/18		Major Hawthorne from ADMS to New Captain Scott R.A.M.C. proceed to Boursin for temp duty with F Bath H.G.C.	
"	23/7/18		Boursin	
"	24/7/18		One supplement received. T/2 3/767 Dr R.H. LAMBERT R.O.C. awarded 5 days F.P.No.2. Captain Scott returned from temp duty with F Bath H.G.C.	
"	25/7/18		Poulins	
"	26/7/18		Poulins	
"	27/7/18		390112 Pte H. YOUNG R.A.M.C. evacuated to No 1 of the thigh K	
"	28/7/18		38337 Sgt SUTTON R.A.M.C. transferred to No 7 Stat'y Hospital	
"			92332 " P. COHEN " arrived from do do in lieu	
"			Returned on the thigh authority DTS 29 Army P6/60 ? 21.7.18	
"	31/7/18		H/284056 Pte W.N. STATER R.A.C. granted 14 days Special Leave to ENGLAND - 30.7.18 — 13.8.18	

Army Form C. 2118.

WAR DIARY
or
INTELLIGENCE SUMMARY.
(Erase heading not required.)

Instructions regarding War Diaries and Intelligence Summaries are contained in F. S. Regs., Part II. and the Staff Manual respectively. Title pages will be prepared in manuscript.

Place	Date	Hour	Summary of Events and Information	Remarks and references to Appendices
WATTEN	30.7.16 – 31.7.16		Routine. 1 O.R. seen for turn of ashes taken in the Shingle	Signed

Vol 40
149/3200

4 4 Field Ambulance

Aug 1918.

War Diary

for Month August 1918

WAR DIARY or INTELLIGENCE SUMMARY

Army Form C. 2118.

Place	Date	Hour	Summary of Events and Information	Remarks and references to Appendices
WARFEN	1918		Postus F	
	2.8.18		Re Reinforcement - H. LINTRON RAMC admitted taken on E. Strongh	
	3.8.18		Re Reinforcement - SickNESS - 2 NCO men Nsowers to Rest Camp (Ii Army)	
	4.8.18		Major BARTON RAMC grants 14 days special contract leave to ENGLAND	
	5.8.18		160.3 Major CN GAWTHORNE RAMC appointed Temp'y R/Colonel from August 1st 1918 (authority H.Q. D.H. 45944 A/D.I. 20.7.18)	
	6.8.18		His Lieut F/Col GAWTHORNE proceeded for duty to N/Ireland (RAMC) taken off the Strength of the Unit - Captain E.W. GOODMAN RAMC posted taken on the Strength - R/Col GAWTHORNE's vacancy. Lieut F.T.K.	
	7.8.18		PCPs grants ordinary leave F.R. UK 31632 Pte E.C.F HUMPHREY & 37589 Pte D CAMERON licensed as authority B.Ronents DDMS No 1 (A.C.D) - the trates unit the Get Syphilis & .... (Rosa) Lance/Corpl/Capstan CPL Bros asked to co for Unit, Such then to be removed hence - 31212 Col CHOWEF	
			Reports to Acting Sanity Officer wish duty -	
			32302 a/c DUGGAN RAMC evacuates sick Shrink by whange	
	8.10-8.16		Routine.	
	11.8.18		Captain SCOTT RAMC grants 14 days leave F.U. Kingston	

Army Form C. 2118.

WAR DIARY
or
INTELLIGENCE SUMMARY.
(Erase heading not required.)

Instructions regarding War Diaries and Intelligence Summaries are contained in F. S. Regs., Part II. and the Staff Manual respectively. Title pages will be prepared in manuscript.

Place	Date	Hour	Summary of Events and Information	Remarks and references to Appendices.
WATTEN	12.8.16	—	Lt THERRIEN H.Q.R.C. reported for duty. Platoon on the Shingle	
"	13.8.16	—	One O.R. reinforcement arrived — G.O.C. inspected the D.R.S.	
"	14.8.18		Private Sims sick Influenza evacuated to Base	
"	15.8.18		Handed over Surplus Medical Equipment to A.D.M.S. 50/50 in accordance with D.G.M.S. 12.9.11 consisting of 1 pair F.M. Panniers, 1 pair F.P. ", 14 Surg. Haversacks, 3 F. Fracture boxes, 2 Medical Companions —	
			40359 Pte J. Matheson R.A.M.C. sent for Camp & duty with 1st Cohort. 3 O.R.s sent to 9nd Aux Res Camp & 1st Cohort for Private TROW (57442) R.A.M.C. sent to 1st Cohort for Duty & Shiner R.A to Shingle	
	16.8.18			
	17.8.18		40352 Pte Matheson R.A.M.C & 30325? Pte J.M. Gordon R.A.M.C	
	18.8.18		A.D.M.S. administered D.M.S. 94 reviewed — moving to 11 Corps area on the 20th inst. (ST. JAN TER BIEZEN)	

WAR DIARY
or
INTELLIGENCE SUMMARY.

(Erase heading not required.)

Army Form C. 2118.

Instructions regarding War Diaries and Intelligence Summaries are contained in F. S. Regs., Part II. and the Staff Manual respectively. Title pages will be prepared in manuscript.

Place	Date	Hour	Summary of Events and Information	Remarks and references to Appendices
WATTEN	18.6.17	—	Lt. H.H. MORGAN RAMC. lent for surgical duty with 41st Fld Amb Unit.	
			41st Brigade order No.9 received.	
			Received information from M'lle GERMAINE HOEYPERT a French subject living at WATTEN that No.3966 Private A. SUTCLIFFE	
	19.6.17		12 Roy L.I. alias of this unit assaulted her whilst intending [blank]	Q
			Places. Private SUTCLIFFE under close arrest. Remainders been to trial by F.G.C.M.	Q
		8am	All the hospital in charge of Captain GRAHAM RAMC left for this area.	
			Col. EDWARDS (330 d/s) books for study 5"29" F.A.	
	"	3pm	Summary of evidence taken in case of Pvte SUTCLIFFE. Charge under Section 41. AA "When on active service striking striking staff Medical Officer" M'lle GERMAINE HOEYPERT a French subject	
	"		Major BARTON RAMC returned from leave to U. Kingdom	Q

WAR DIARY
or
INTELLIGENCE SUMMARY.
(Erase heading not required.)

Army Form C. 2118.

Place	Date	Hour	Summary of Events and Information	Remarks and references to Appendices
WATTEN	22.6.18		Advance Party of 1st F.A. returns to take over site & B.O.'s & O.R's Whalebone Habous & O.R's	
"	23.6.18 9 P.M.	9 P.M.	Units unhurried for this area & arrived at Ambulance Farm 97 F.25 DSC at 1.30 p.m. found the hospital already taken	
AMBULANCE FARM.	24.6.18		8/18.10 Off/c F.G. CHALKE Remd huspita taken off/c from the 10.6.18 inst. Authority ADMS — Unit (Coys) were told — only Collecting Post J. 24 1st Bgde. Group — All ocr Movable unless unused to FCC.S @ D.D. 23. F.A.	
"	24.6.18 23.3.18		Preparing Camp & supplying troops w/ Lieut W. Egan proceeded to Admr's Office for temporary duty during absence of Lieut Kay Campbell on leave & Major Bolsouth assumed command of unit	
"	24.6.18 25.6.18 26.8.18		Pitching tents Capt. Scott returned from leave. One O.R. confinement received Pte Randall E.L. wounded (at duty)	

WAR DIARY
or
INTELLIGENCE SUMMARY.
(Erase heading not required.)

Army Form C. 2118.

Instructions regarding War Diaries and Intelligence Summaries are contained in F. S. Regs., Part II. and the Staff Manual respectively. Title pages will be prepared in manuscript.

Place	Date	Hour	Summary of Events and Information	Remarks and references to Appendices
Antelaouse Down	29/8/18		Major W.H. Morgan M.C. R.E. V.R. reported for temporary duty to Highlands Service Br. reinforcements training Adm. administrative when No 36. received orders to take over I Coho Reg. Station, one section stake over broad pick bellephony transport & other Capt G.W. Guilleman until the lea. Capt for duty with other sections and is struck off strength. 8 a.m. Transport left. 9 a.m. Bearer under Captain Scott & Lt Fitz. 2.30 pm Personnel left. The Scottes M.T. with ambulances & 3 Dingson, I.T. Co, Sir Brown remained as No 2 Section. No Coy to others in strength. I Coho. Revd Station. 30th August 1918. E.R.A.M.C. assumed duties from 103 - Field ambulance.	VOS VOS
BOLLEZEELE G5A	30/8/18		No 66550 Pte Briggs was placed on 93rd Field hold [?] bund [?] Head, Dr Bailey M.B. on R 2994/39 u/c 27/8/18 heaf. ph. / Aust Aust 5.R. R 2994/39 u/c 27/8/18 Pte R. Bailey M.B. was reported arrived with Sunbeam motorcar and is taken on strength. Major T.C. Brifton admitted to No 36. Cas. Cdg.	VOS
"	31/8/18		Inspection by B. Arms. I Coho at 3.30 p.m.	VOS VOS

R.H.Roberts Major R.A.M.C.
O/C 46 FIELD AMBULANCE.

WAR DIARY.

of

44th Field Ambulance.

From :- 1/9/18.
To :- 30/9/18
****

Army Form C. 2118.

WAR DIARY
or
INTELLIGENCE SUMMARY.
(Erase heading not required.)

Instructions regarding War Diaries and Intelligence Summaries are contained in F. S. Regs., Part II. and the Staff Manual respectively. Title pages will be prepared in manuscript.

Place	Date	Hour	Summary of Events and Information	Remarks and references to Appendices
BOKEZEELE	1/9/18		Major T.C. Britton evacuated sick from 36 C.C.S. One OR reinforcement received	
	2/9/18		Routine	
	3/9/18		Twelve bearers sent from B section for duty with 42nd Field Ambulance	
	4/9/18		No 39609 Pte. A. Sutcliffe tried by Field General Court martial + acquitted	
	5/9/18		One OR reinforcement received, rifted OR returned from the base struck	
			off the strength	
	6/9/18		Lieut. W.M. Morgan, M.O R.C. U.S.A. posted to 2nd Middlesex + struck off strength	
	7/9/18		Routine	
	8/9/18		Lt. Col. Egan returned from temporary duty as ADMS	
	9/9/18		Routine	
	10/9/18		Routine	
	11/9/18		Routine	
	12/9/18		Received orders from D.D.M.S. to close Cpls Rest Station + move to LEBBE FARM on 15/9/18	
	13/9/18		Routine	

Army Form C. 2118.

WAR DIARY
or
INTELLIGENCE SUMMARY.
(Erase heading not required.)

Place	Date	Hour	Summary of Events and Information	Remarks and references to Appendices
BOXLEZEELE	14/9/18		All patients, except one Officer + three O.R. returned to duty. Twelve O.R. returned from 42nd Field Ambulance	AppI
	15/9/18		Lt. Col. M. Egan D.S.O. granted leave to U.K. 16/9/18 – 30/9/18.	AppII AppIII
L'EBBE FARM	6/9/18		Unit left by train at 6.12 a.m., transport marching by road. Four O.R. sent to Advance Aid Post + three O.R. to Harbison and Post	AppIV AppV
27/F 29 B 9.4	7/9/18		One N.C.O. + ten men sent to u/s 2nd Field Ambulance; three O.R. to Aid Post at POPERINGHE Town Hall.	AppVI AppVII
			Raining.	
	18/9/18		The Major Mutton granted sick leave to U.K. from 8/9/18 – 27/9/18.	
	19/9/18	9am	Capt. Graham, Lieut. Trevor Hope + bearer subdivision marched to VIJVERHOEK and bivouacked near A.D.S. from 139th Field Ambulance	
		9.15am	Capt. Scott + rest subdivision marched to VLAMERTINGHE MILL + reported for duty at M.D.S. with 105th Field Ambulance. Parties sent on 16th + 17th September withdrawn.	AppVIII
	20/9/18		Raining.	AppIX
	21/9/18	9am	Thirty bearers left for A.D.S.	AppX
		11am	Headquarters left for Vlamertinghe Mill	
		1.30pm	Transport + remainder of unit left for HALLHOEK. Twelve O.R. of 122nd Field Amb. reported on duty at H.Q.	AppXI

(A8001) D. D. & L., London, E.C. Forms/C2118/14
Wt. W.1771/M.2931 750,000 5/17 Sch. 32

Army Form C. 2118.

WAR DIARY
or
INTELLIGENCE SUMMARY.
(Erase heading not required.)

Instructions regarding War Diaries and Intelligence Summaries are contained in F.S. Regs., Part II. and the Staff Manual respectively. Title pages will be prepared in manuscript.

Place	Date	Hour	Summary of Events and Information	Remarks and references to Appendices
WAHERTINGHE MILL	23/5/18		Capt Shephard, MM (S.R.) & Capt Pozes, SA.T (T.C.) posted March & taken on strength	
OUDERDOM	24/5/18	9.30am	Headquarters & Field Subdivision moved to LONG BARN 28 C 30 d 57 Remainder of unit less transport moved from Strubick to Long Barn. Fifty bearers from #2 & #3 Field Amb. reported for duty at MDS. Long Barn Transport moved to White Farm 27 c 25 d 52.	
	25/5/18		Fifty bearers from #2 & #3 Field Amb reported for duty.	
	26/5/18		Major Conroy RSO, NCC, Capt Webster, MC, hand Reserve Park - Lieut Henmmers joined reported for duty, also thirty two OR. 9 & 10 Field Ambulance. Personnel posted to duties & taken on -	
	27/5/18		M.D.S. 7 Officers 81 other ranks Grascombe 1 Officer 5 other ranks A.R.S. 2 Officers 30 other ranks Walking Wounded Collecting Post 2 Officers + 12 Other ranks One Officer in charge of 4 with other ranks detached w/ R.A.P.'s relays + post in reserve at A.D.S. + bearers 28 H 33 & 49 - 101 Other ranks	

Army Form C. 2118.

WAR DIARY
or
INTELLIGENCE SUMMARY.
(Erase heading not required.)

Instructions regarding War Diaries and Intelligence Summaries are contained in F.S. Regs., Part II. and the Staff Manual respectively. Title pages will be prepared in manuscript.

Place	Date	Hour	Summary of Events and Information	Remarks and references to Appendices
Oudezoom	28/9/18	5.30am	Zero.	Appx S
	29/9/18 4.30pm		Major Grover kind Medical kind Browning + 18 OR returned to 4 & 29. Two officers + 146 other ranks formed month (mostly) Field Ambulance on 28 + 29 15/5/18. Capt. Webster + remainder of personnel of 42 + 143 Field Ambulances returned.	Appx S / Appx S
	30/9/18		All officers & men of unit withdrawn from ADS. & forward zone, with the exception of relieving parties of 1 N.C.O. + 3 men at ADS. + two men at collecting post VOORMEZEELE.	Appx S

B M Barton
Major RAMC
O/C No. 44 FIELD AMBULANCE
c/o RAMC No. 44 FIELD AMBULANCE

WAR DIARY
for month
OCTOBER 1918.

442 Field Ambulance

WAR DIARY or INTELLIGENCE SUMMARY

Army Form C. 2118.

Place	Date	Hour	Summary of Events and Information	Remarks and references to Appendices
LONG BARN	1.10.16		Holding Baths at #10 Pt POPERINGHE. Withdrawn. Troops 1st moved to Headquarters.	
"	2.10.	-	Lt. THERRIEN, Hon C. Capt. to duty with 47 Bge. 8F.A. + Lt Col. J.F. McHugh 19th Corps returned – Lt Col. WEGAN returned from leave in U.K. Admin Commissioner's order 29 received. Still throws on 8th and 15 –	
28.S.17.a.5.9	3.10.16 12.15		NEUVE-EGLISE aaa Unit moved to 28.S.17.a.5.9. Leave a small holding party at LONG BRON. 1 NCO + 2 men sent to BAILLEUL Asylum a.o.a holding Party – Admin Orders No. 30 received –	
"	4.10.16	-	2 Sections in charge of Major BARTON M.C. proceed to HOAT FARM. VLAMERTINGHE, block A.5 4.2.r + 8.3.r by "2" Brigades. Admin order 31 received – whole unit throws 5th boat.	
"	5.10.16	-	FARM. Stud.– Routine.–	
HOAT FARM	6-8 10.16		Routine Collection J Sick.	
"	9.10.16		Captain HAYES RAMC went 15.43 F.A. for temp. duty	

WAR DIARY
or
INTELLIGENCE SUMMARY.

(Erase heading not required.)

Army Form C. 2118.

Instructions regarding War Diaries and Intelligence Summaries are contained in F. S. Regs., Part II. and the Staff Manual respectively. Title pages will be prepared in manuscript.

Place	Date	Hour	Summary of Events and Information	Remarks and references to Appendices
HQ^{rs} 4th FA Bn	10.10.18	—	Training other ranks with Newve Eglise area - left two machine teacher rifle sections	—
"	11.10.18		O.R.s issued for Captain Hayes R.A.M.C. to succeed Lt. St Pierre	—
28 I/33 C 43	12.10.18		Major Barton & advanced party arrived at 10am at new area.	—
"	13.10.18 7pm		Unit left Mont Noir. Train arrived at Stringto from 12.0.T. Captain Hayes struck off strength duty with 4 F.A. Captain Stephens attached for temp. duty with 4 F.A.	—
"	14.10.18		4 Brigade OO No 410 Orders OO. R. received. 8/88 Pte EATON awarded 14 days F.P.No 2 for using stays [?] for overstaying his leave 3 days -	—
"	15.10.18		One NCO + 15 ORs sent for temp. duty with 4 B.F.A. Army O.O. 16 Recvd - training other ranks of these of Eleven to	—
"	16.10.18		O.O. 17 (Army) Received - other ranks of Eleven to 28 T.N. Central (MOY etc) sent from B.F.A. for temp. duty.	—

WAR DIARY
or
INTELLIGENCE SUMMARY.

Army Form C. 2118.

Place	Date	Hour	Summary of Events and Information	Remarks and references to Appendices
HESSIN[ES]	17.10.18		Unit arrived at Hessines - closed -	
	18.10.18	8.30 am	Unit moved b. 28 V 12 a 9.9 out of area	
			west of the forward area.	
		16.00	Advance party in charge of Captain Graham proceeded to Le Barre	
			Four received orders to evening station in the school there.	
	19.10.18	7 pm	Unit moved to LEBLANC FOUR	
		11.00	Unit moved to WATTRELOS + received A.D.S. to the Fabrique ou près	
WATTRELOS			25. Has A. l'Hivrochi - Relieved all the bearers in the forward areas	
	20.10.18		Major Barton & Captain Graham proceeded to 3/S	
			9a 24 + shows Car Collecting Post. Divisional front	
			to line of D'EOCAULT R.A.P. are situated as follows	
			R.A.P. B[...] 87C 13 a 9.2	
			R.A.P. Right 37 B 12 & 8? (a ford Car + works there)	
			Captain Shephard returned from 4 B.F.A.	
	27.10.18		The following have been awarded Military Medals 3/6/15 Lt. HATHEP. D.	
			8/7/62 " JOHNSTON E H	

WAR DIARY
or
INTELLIGENCE SUMMARY.

(Erase heading not required.)

Army Form C. 2118.

Instructions regarding War Diaries and Intelligence Summaries are contained in F. S. Regs., Part II. and the Staff Manual respectively. Title pages will be prepared in manuscript.

Place	Date	Hour	Summary of Events and Information	Remarks and references to Appendices
WATTRELOS	22 AM	Noon	Lieut A.D.L. Steward at 37.B.90.34 with Major BARTON. /c accompanied by Cpl Laine GRAHAM.	
"	"	4pm	Handed over F.D.L. at WATTRELOS to 43 F.A. as a A.D.S. Headquarters pencil. Remain at WATTRELOS. (Adml. Admin. Order 84)	
"	23.b.		Very few casualties passing through.	
"	26-10.18		Relief of bearers & a.d.s. party. Forward area party (52) in charge of Captain HOPPER, SHEPHERD events by Captain SCOTT.	
"	27.10.18		R.O. 81. 42nd Infy. Brigade resumed. Brigade H.a. slip north Tourcoing & 2 Battr. front North of the ESPIERRE Canal. During the Night 27/28. Medical arrangement etcs. as following. R.A.P. Regts 29/U 26 c 80.— R.A.P. left 29/U 22 2 12 Relay Post 29/U 21 a 06.— Car Collecting Post 29/U 20 a 76. R.A.P. artillery.— 37/B 575-3	
"	28.10.18 29.10.18 30.10.18 31.10.18		Routine. Notification received that Major T. BRITTON to the Sheets of WINGFIELD — electric wire rifle for H.Q. at 37 B5-625.—	

R.A.M.C.
COMMANDING No. 4 FIELD AMBULANCE.

WAR DIARY

44 FIELD AMBULANCE

NOVEMBER 1918

WAR DIARY
or
INTELLIGENCE SUMMARY.

(Erase heading not required.)

Army Form C. 2118.

Instructions regarding War Diaries and Intelligence Summaries are contained in F. S. Regs., Part II. and the Staff Manual respectively. Title pages will be prepared in manuscript.

Place	Date	Hour	Summary of Events and Information	Remarks and references to Appendices
WATTRELOS	1.11.18	—	57403 Pte W. HOLDEN R.A.M.C. awarded the Military MEDAL — 68899 Pte T.H. BURLEIGH do	E
"	2.11.18	—	74739 Pte H BURGESS awarded 7days F.P.No 2 for for'bid 10days Rev. Wrishipp loss 1day	
			77847 Pte A.J. MARTIN " 14 " " " " 2days	
			73/024499 L/C W.A. BULL PTE HT (under 26) for trial by F.G.C.M for misslaying Lens 2days	E
	3-5 11.18	—	Routine duties —	
"	6.11.18		31776 Pte G.A. BURKHARDT awarded 14days F.P.No 2. 6days 6 7days pay. Wrishipp 1day 2days	E
"	7.11.18		Routine	
"	8.11.18		30111693 Pte Pte C.S. F.G.C.M in 73/024499 L/C 61days Pay	E
			Referred to the sent of corpomal & four 1 awarded 7days F.P.No 2 7days 6 7days pay	
			39609 Pte J. RATCLIFFE Loy — 1 awarded. Have H 2 harbe	
			About making rung hears larfrage sir	
	9.11.18		39608 Ratcliff's aw'rded 14days F.P.No 2 for rung Mears larfrage sir	E
			Unit moved to Chateau ESPIERRES Superior forces	
Chateau ESPIERRES	10.11.18	14	Captain (A/Major) Dykartes M.C. keep of duty with X Brigade R.G.A	E

WAR DIARY
or
INTELLIGENCE SUMMARY.

Army Form C. 2118.

Place	Date	Hour	Summary of Events and Information	Remarks and references to Appendices
Chateau ESPIERRES	10.11.18		9500 Pte N GEARY RAMC transfd to actg (Yeo) with 8 Ambulance	
"	11.11.18	2.30 pm	GHQ wire received - "Hostilities cease at 11.00 Nov 11"	
"	12.11.18	—	39606 Pte E.S EARLEY RAMC awarded 7days F.P. No 2 for Feb - 1 days pay Under Rev. for misobeying his Sers one day.	
"	13.11.18		Captain SHEPHERD RAMC posted to 1/2 Div. Re-attach of the Shrigh [15.11.18]	
			Captain D.F. RIDDELL MC RAMC reported arrival taken Shrigh [15.11.18]	
			Captain SCOTT A/barles for duty only with 1/8 Manchesters	
			45804 Pte J. ANDERSON + T/1005 Dr A CATTELL each awarded 7days No 2 F.P. forfeit one days pay under K.R's for misobeying bars one day.	
			40R sent to CROIX for truck light later motichom	
"	14.11.18	—	ADMS. D.O. No 93 received. Must some with 43" Brigade to Tourcoing 43 Brigade OO No 43". As Must moves on 15.11.18 with Brigade Group Received instructions from ADMS to move H.Q. daily to WATTRELOS start after civilian population from the left week	

Army Form C. 2118.

WAR DIARY
or
INTELLIGENCE SUMMARY.
(Erase heading not required.)

Place	Date	Hour	Summary of Events and Information	Remarks and references to Appendices
TORCOING	15.11.18		Unit moved to Torcoing to billets in the Town.	
"	16.11.18		Routine collection & evac of Brigade group & Army Corps troops in the vicinity	
"	17.11.18		One Officer Rank Reinforcement arrived	
"	18.11.18		32142 A/C ATKINSON. R.A.M.C. H/Commander 7 days. 8 days pay fined. R/D for temp overstaying his pass 2 days	
"	19.11.18		Routine.	
"	20.11.18		22074 Pte Short. R. H.L.I. alt 6 awards. 7days F.P. No 2 & forfeit 10 days pay under R.W. for overstaying his leave one day	
"	21.11.18		Captain SCOTT returns from B.E.F. Manchester. D.M.S. 2nd Army. Major Genl GUISE MOORES inspects the Unit. 26191 T.S. Major. E.A. SHILLING. R.A.M.C. assumes Station Sergeant. 10744. Pte J. SHEEHAN. R.A.M.C. awarded 7days F.P. No 2 for forfeit 7 days pay in all R/D for disobeying his leave one day	
"	22.11.18		Routine	
"	23.11.18			
"	24.11.18		Sgt FREEBORN (88852) R.A.M.C. evacuated Albert by the sheriff	

Army Form C. 2118.

WAR DIARY
or
INTELLIGENCE SUMMARY.
(Erase heading not required.)

Instructions regarding War Diaries and Intelligence Summaries are contained in F. S. Regs., Part II. and the Staff Manual respectively. Title pages will be prepared in manuscript.

Place	Date	Hour	Summary of Events and Information	Remarks and references to Appendices
TORCOING	24.11.16	-	Captain RIDDEL & Apsarles for duty & Duty with 170 H.L.I. Routine duties	
"	26.11.16	-	34129 Pte T.W.JONES R.W.F. awarded Mayor F.O.No 2 of 7.11.16 & 145 Pay for misbehaving his bart stay	
"	27.11.16	-	147/16-2166 Pte M.Cost AOC MT awarded Mayor F.O.No 2 of 7.11.16 & 14p Pay ways Con for misbehaving his drank stay	
"	28.11.16		Routine	

Major [signature]

WAR DIARY

DECEMBER 1915

44 FIELD AMBULANCE

Army Form C. 2118.

WAR DIARY
or
INTELLIGENCE SUMMARY.
(Erase heading not required.)

Instructions regarding War Diaries and Intelligence Summaries are contained in F. S. Regs., Part II. and the Staff Manual respectively. Title pages will be prepared in manuscript.

Place	Date	Hour	Summary of Events and Information	Remarks and references to Appendices
TURCOING	1.12.18 to 2.12.18		Routine collection from 403rd Brigade Group also Corps Rotary Tropo.	Q
"	3.12.18		391.29 Pt. McLUEL I.A. RAMC sent to Transylvania Tropo Reinfort	Q
			One Reinforcement (Sgt. Bryant) received	
			Detail Liquidation Circulars Nun Barrium No 2 received	
			Schize of Continuous Sentence	Q
"	4.12.18 5.12.18		Routine Collection of Sick	Q
"	6.12.16		112/05 0° 213 Pt. D.H.R Nicholas A.o.C.H.T. awards to the Cross	Q
			de Guerre. Authority 14 Div. Routine Orders 4.12.18.	
"	7.12.18		74/09/402 Dr. H.E Dot. 9HIN R.O.C. H.T. awarded Mayo 70	Q
			1020 for Stick. 1 days pay under Kings for overstaying his	
			Leave 1 day	
			Captain D.F RIDDELL MC Kent D'Inglais struct off to strength	Q
"	8.12.18		Routine	Q
"	9.12.18		Routine	Q

WAR DIARY
or
INTELLIGENCE SUMMARY.
(Erase heading not required.)

Army Form C. 2118.

Instructions regarding War Diaries and Intelligence Summaries are contained in F. S. Regs., Part II. and the Staff Manual respectively. Title pages will be prepared in manuscript.

Place	Date	Hour	Summary of Events and Information	Remarks and references to Appendices
TOURCOING	10.12.18		Major B.M. Barton M.C. left for England & Visits RHQ. Strength	
	11.12.18		Captain Scott RAMC returned from Leave & duty with 78th Bty	
			Demobilisation float numbers began	
	12.12.18		Lt F. J. THERRIEN MORL Struck off duty taken on the	
			Strength	
	13.12.18		78187 Gr F HOLLAH (married) 7 days No. 2 F.P. (Appx 16) 14 days	
			Pay for misplaying his tins in the Bay.	
	14.12.18		Demobilisation continued Juniors as far as Balmuenos 220	
	15			
	15.12.18			
	16.12.18		Posting —	
	20.12.18			
	21.12.18		72011 Dr M A Willis RAMC cut shore for transfer to ENGLAND	
"	22 - 24.12.18		Dr Compassionate Grounds	
	25.12.18		Routine	
	26.27.12.18		Xmas day	
			Routine	

Army Form C. 2118.

WAR DIARY
or
INTELLIGENCE SUMMARY.
(Erase heading not required.)

Place	Date	Hour	Summary of Events and Information	Remarks and references to Appendices
Pour Rein	28.12.18		First postal van Amerikaties. Mr Norris (a policeman)	
"	29.12.18		Officers Conference reports sent to H. q. Div. S.	
"	30-31.12.18		Routine L.	

14th DIVISION.

WAR DIARY ----- 44th Field Ambulance.

1st January 1919 , ------ 30th January 1919.

WAR DIARY
or
INTELLIGENCE SUMMARY.
(Erase heading not required.)

Army Form C. 2118.

Place	Date	Hour	Summary of Events and Information	Remarks and references to Appendices
TOURCOING	1.1.19	-	Routine Collection Relief.	
"	2.1.19	-	No. 61056 Pte H. Bishop R.A.M.C. sent to G.H.Q. Schools Cat- School to report ff the strength	
"	3&4.1.19	-	41st Infy Brigade changed over with 45th Infy Brigade Routine Collection Relief -	
"	5&6.1.19	-	32176 Pte H Dougherty R.A.M.C. awarded 14 days F.P. No 2	
"	7.1.19	-	11299 " E.H. Homes " " 7 days F.P. No 2	
"	8.1.19	-	Major Graham R.A.M.C. granted 4 days leave to U.K. from 9.1.19 - 23.1.19 -	
"	9&10.1.19 10.1.19 11&12.1.19	-	Routine - Lt W.H. Morgan M.O.R.C. reports for duty. Routine	
"	13.1.19	-	Captain Welch R.A.M.C. reports for duty. attacks 38609 Pte A. Sutcliffe awarded 7 days F.P. No 2	

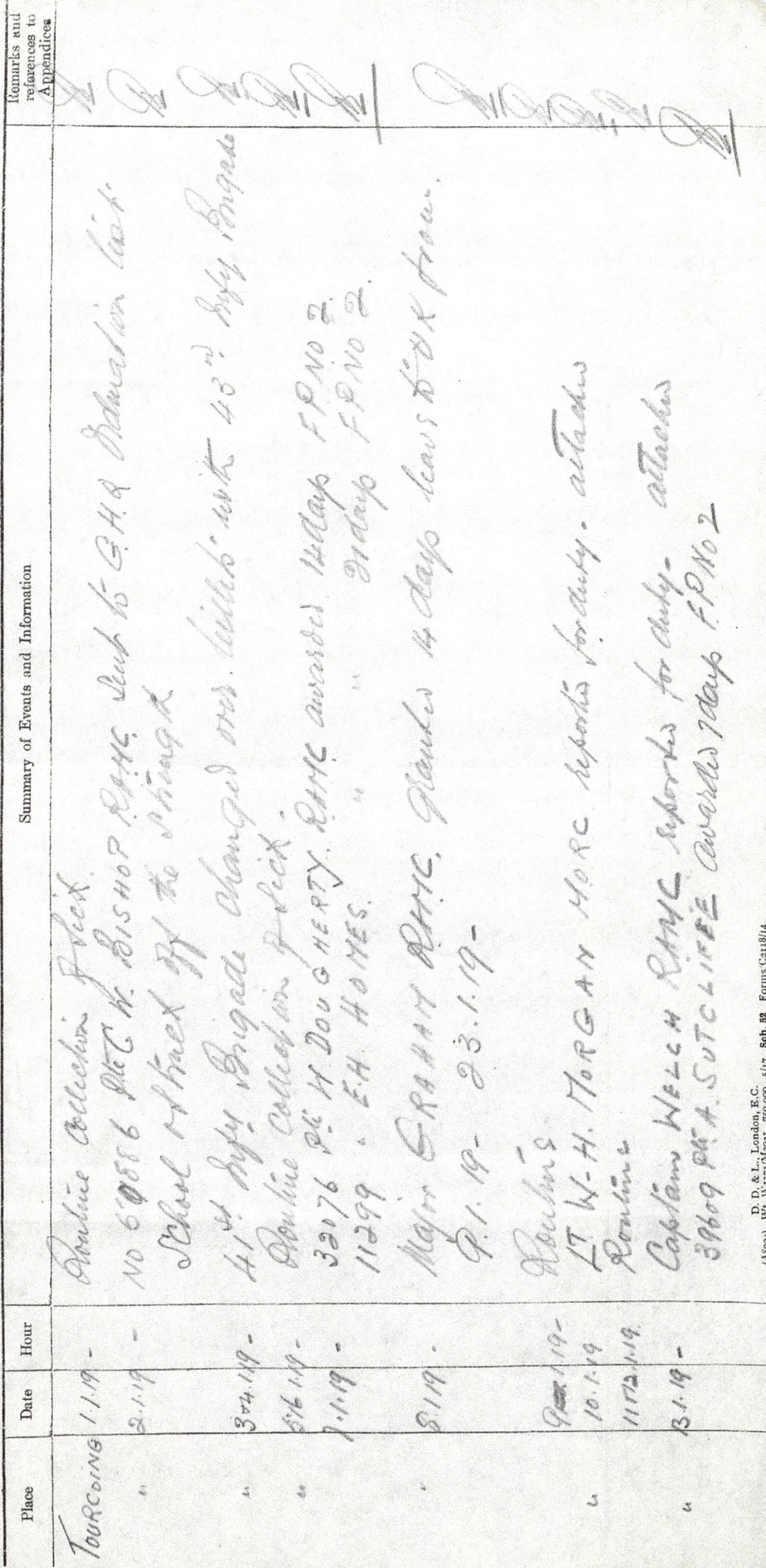

WAR DIARY
or
INTELLIGENCE SUMMARY.
(Erase heading not required.)

Army Form C. 2118.

Place	Date	Hour	Summary of Events and Information	Remarks and references to Appendices
TOURCOING	13.1.19 –		76191 S.H. Skilling RAMC cert to England on demobilization. Struck off strength	
"	16-17.1.19		Routine – Demobilization of RAPC staff	
"	18.1.19		No 62145 Sgt. K.C. Hell RICH RAMC cert to Officers Commanding Reinforcements ETAPLES to trick off the strength (authority DAG – CR No 5728 P3/852/1 – dt 2.1.19)	
"	"		Number of RAPC Nurslip SR to week ending 18.1.19 = 12 20 RS proceeded on leave to ENGLAND	
"	19.1.19 "		Routine collection of sick	
"	20.1.19			
"	25.1.19		Number of O.R's demobilized for week ending 25.1.19 = 23. from WR. proceeded to England on leave 8	
"	26.1.19		No me 54570 Pte Wright J.H awarded the meritorious service medal. A.S.C.M.T.	

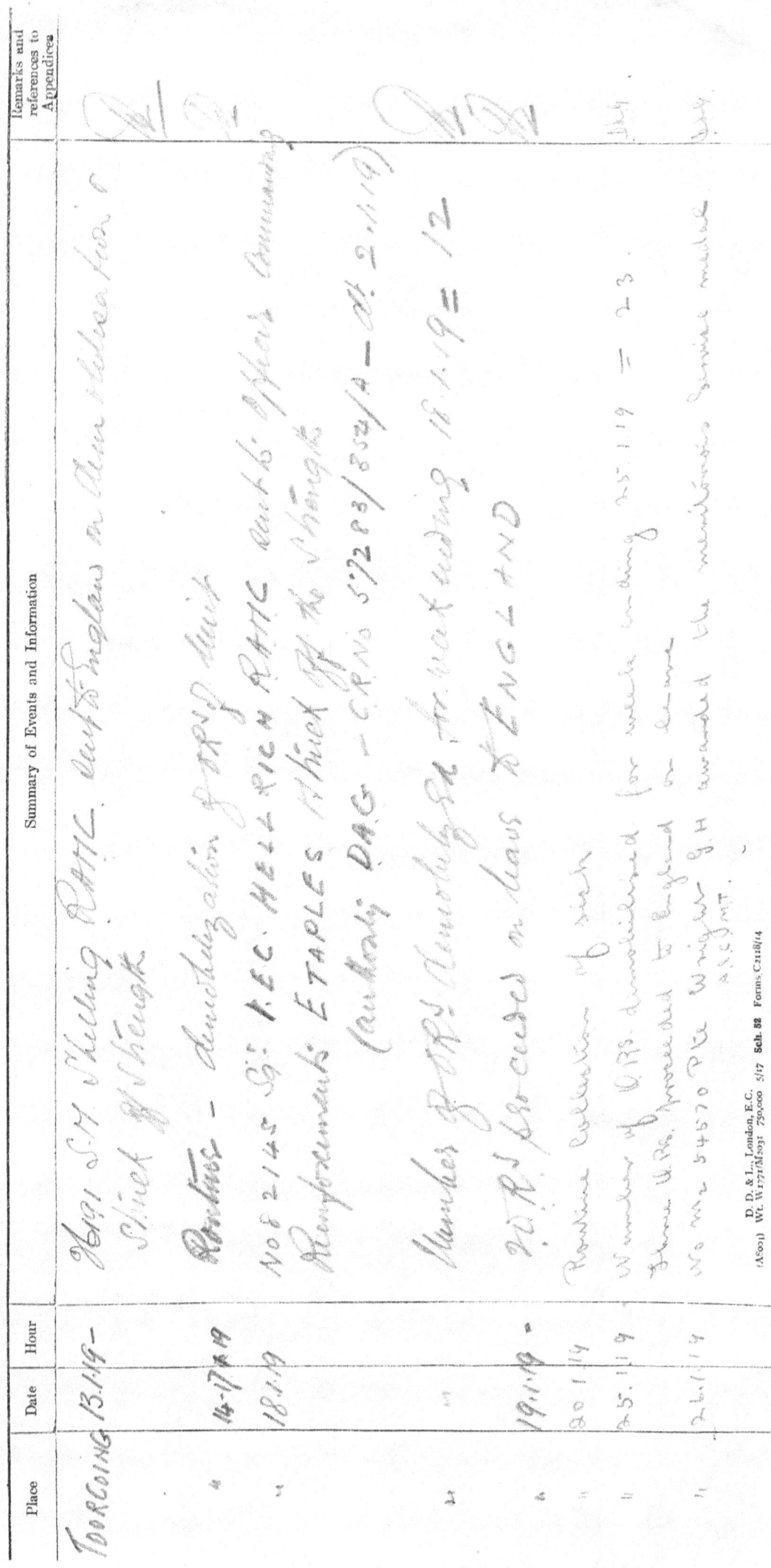

Army Form C. 2118.

WAR DIARY
or
INTELLIGENCE SUMMARY.
(Erase heading not required.)

Instructions regarding War Diaries and Intelligence Summaries are contained in F. S. Regs., Part II. and the Staff Manual respectively. Title pages will be prepared in manuscript.

Place	Date	Hour	Summary of Events and Information	Remarks and references to Appendices
Saumur	27.1.19		Lieut Morgan W.H. M.R.C. proceeded to 102nd Field Ambulance for temporary duty.	OC 4
"	28.1.19.		Capt A Scott Rame Proceeded on leave to U.K. 27.1.19 — 10.2.19. Routine.	
"	29/29.1.19		R/F Col A. W. Egan D.S.O. Rame proceeded on leave to U.K. 29.1.19 — 12.2.19. Major O.S. Fisher assumes command of the unit from above date.	4/4
"	30.1.19		Routine collection of sick. 1 O.R. invalided to U.K. in hours.	9/4

O. S. Fisher
Major R.A.M.C.
COMMANDING No. 44 FIELD AMBULANCE

14th DIVISION.
****

WAR DIARY ----- 44th Field Ambulance.

Period:- 1/2/19 - 28/2/19.

Army Form C. 2118.

WAR DIARY
or
INTELLIGENCE SUMMARY.
(*Erase heading not required.*)

Instructions regarding War Diaries and Intelligence Summaries are contained in F.S. Regs., Part II. and the Staff Manual respectively. Title pages will be prepared in manuscript.

Place	Date	Hour	Summary of Events and Information	Remarks and references to Appendices
January	1-2-19		Routine work continuing	
"	2-2-19		Temporary Capt. a. Light appointed Advr. M.gor mtder orders of field ambulance from 25-12-18.	
"	3-2-19		Routine work continuing	
"	4-2-19		WO 31888 Pte H Elliot Ranne wounded 7.4 pm F.P. No 2 captive no leg by R.V. whilst evacuated dies leave from 11.10 hrs 2-2-19 to 05.10 hrs 3-2-19 (10 hrs)m	
"	6-2-19		Capt. P. Lachani S.M.S. reported his arrival a taken on our strength	
"	7-2-19		Routine sick collecting	
"	8-2-19		Routine. Number of men demobilised during week nothing significant over 6 shown	
"	10-2-19		Numbers of men proceeding on leave – two. WO. T9/3456 S.S. J.C. Wolfe R.a.s.c proceeded to 131 F.A. for employment Lt. W.H. Monger. M.R.C. reported from H.H.M F.A. for duty with this unit	
"	11-2-19		WO. 33617 Pte (a/sgt) H.E. Brunswick Ranne is promoted to sgt (substantive) from 9-12-18 WO. 31215 Pte (a/cpl) F.B. Clarke Ranne promoted to W.S/substantive 9-12-18	

WAR DIARY or INTELLIGENCE SUMMARY

Army Form C. 2118.

Place	Date	Hour	Summary of Events and Information	Remarks and references to Appendices
Jemining	17-2-19		W.O.3/867 Pte (cpl a/s) Bomar E. to W Cpl = 16-1-17. W.O 31873 Pte (a/s cpl) Elar T/J to A. Cpl = 24-3-18. W.O 31494 Pte (a/s Cpl) Perry C.W. to a/s Sgt. 25-3-18	
"	18-2-19		W O 8214 S Sgt. Stevens N.E.S. returned from Base dept C/wing 9"	
	19-2-19		Kick on the storage	
"	19-2-19		Routine and collecting etc dispersing	
	20-2-19		Routine not active	
	21-2-19		Routine week ended.	
	22-2-19		No of men demobilised during the week was 14. No of men on leave 5.	
	23-2-19		Sample motor cycle man from the Garage	
	24-2-19		Capt A. St. Johnston posted to duty from the 14th A.+ S.H. Lt E.T. Thurion M.R.C. was discharged hospital 24-2-19 and resumed duties with this unit the same day. Notification received from A.D.M.S. that Major D.S. Gradon relinquished the acting rank of Major from 22/2/19.	
	25-2-19		Capt D.S. Gradon proceeded to U.K. on expiration of extension (L.S.H./1/14) vacancy kept D.C. Walsh also proceeded to U.K. for demobilisation.	
			Routine	
	26-2-19		Lt Col W. Egan returned from leave and resumed command of unit.	
	27-2-19			
	28-2-19		Routine. No of men demobilised during week 8. No of men on leave — nil.	

CONFIDENTIAL.

WAR DIARY

- of -

44th FIELD AMBULANCE.(R.A.M.C.)

From: 1st April, 1919.
To: 30th April, 1919.

Army Form C. 2118.

WAR DIARY
or
INTELLIGENCE SUMMARY.
(Erase heading not required.)

Instructions regarding War Diaries and Intelligence Summaries are contained in F. S. Regs., Part II. and the Staff Manual respectively. Title pages will be prepared in manuscript.

Place	Date	Hour	Summary of Events and Information	Remarks and references to Appendices
TOURCOING	1/4/19		Routine	
	2/4/19		Routine	
	3/4/19		No. T4/049101 Sr. A. Solfern R.A.S.C. M.T. reversion his 3d Stripe Undated rank	
	4/4/19		Routine	
	5/4/19		Routine	
	6/4/19		No. 9292 Pte Harmer A.E. awarded 3 days C.B. for being in town without pass, and not wearing a belt	
	7/4/19		No. 14197 Pte Hallah F.E. awarded 3 days C.B. for being without pass on parade, warm riding breeches, contrary to orders	
	8/4/19		Routine	
	9/4/19		Routine	
	10/4/19		No. 368397 Pte Rae G.T. R.A.M.C. evacuated sick to 62 C.C.S.	
	11/4/19		No. M2/219418 Pte Foakly H.S. and No. M380286 Pte Hawker W.J. R.A.S.C. M.T. transferred with ambulance cars to 9th M.T. Vehicle reception park	
	12/4/19		Routine	
	13/4/19		Major E.W. Goodman M.C. U.S.A. granted leave to U.K. from 14th to 23rd April 1919.	
	14/4/19		No. 53906 A/Cpl F. Southwell, No. 305104 Pte Leehot and No. 88014 Pte Whelan A.R.C. of proceeded to N.2 Convalescent camp, St ANDRE for ambulance	
			Capt T.O. Robins R.A.M.C. proceeds for temporary duty in unit of Major Goodman from 14th	
			Field Ambulance	
	15/4/19		Routine	

Army Form C. 2118.

WAR DIARY
or
INTELLIGENCE SUMMARY.
(Erase heading not required.)

Instructions regarding War Diaries and Intelligence Summaries are contained in F. S. Regs., Part II. and the Staff Manual respectively. Title pages will be prepared in manuscript.

Place	Date	Hour	Summary of Events and Information	Remarks and references to Appendices
WAMBRECHIES	16/4/19		Routine. Inform received that 116 Field Amb at WAMBRECHIES	
	17/4/19		Routine	
	18/4/19		Routine	
	19/4/19		No of men on leave during week – 3.	
	20/4/19		Routine	
	21/4/19		Routine	
	22/4/19		Routine	
	23/4/19		Routine	
	24/4/19		Routine	
	25/4/19		Capt T.D.C.Bow R.A.M.C. proceeded to 60 Field Amb for temp duty	
	26/4/19		Routine. No of men on leave during week ended 26th – 4.	
	27/4/19		Routine	
	28/4/19		Routine	
	29/4/19		Routine	
	30/4/19		Routine	

J.S.T.T.
Major R.A.M.C.
COMMANDING No 44 FIELD AMBULANCE

CONFIDENTIAL.

WAR DIARY

- of -

44th FIELD AMBULANCE (R.A.M.C.)

1 - 31st March, 1919.

Army Form C. 2118.

WAR DIARY
or
INTELLIGENCE SUMMARY.
(Erase heading not required.)

Instructions regarding War Diaries and Intelligence Summaries are contained in F. S. Regs., Part II. and the Staff Manual respectively. Title pages will be prepared in manuscript.

Place	Date	Hour	Summary of Events and Information	Remarks and references to Appendices
TOURCOING	1.3.19		Roach's lecture - Vet. - Demobilisation proceeding	2.
"	2.3.19		Received two Lorries - visits etc to training area at Lutrain POWs	2.
"	4.3.19		lifts to Roubaix -	2.
"	5.3.19		Roubaix	2.
"			Sg. Cohen RAMC (Anderson) vacancy vet to CCS.	2.
"			7/o 26147 Sg. F.J. HANSELL RoCHF sick to trains from No 1 OR	2.
"	6.3.19		Hair to complete Cadre.	
"			Qt. MACHIN. W. to 31 ADH & b. No 31 ADH OSb for duty. Which	2.
"			Pt. King R - Pt. Gillespie J. returns from ADH etc.	2.
"	7.3.19		Roubaix	2.
"	8.3.19		Re G. P. D's demobilizers awaiting movement. - 11 - No on leave - 1	2.

WAR DIARY
or
INTELLIGENCE SUMMARY.

Army Form C. 2118.

Place	Date	Hour	Summary of Events and Information	Remarks and references to Appendices
TOURCOING	9.3.19	—	All stores & transport taken up to H.Q. 2 F.A. (outlining area) in Charge of Major Scott RAMC — Captain Foster Pratt accompanying transport. Officers & O.R.s Billet as Grant).	
"			Relieving of Pt. arrived on systems driving motor lorries — Private HASLETT RAMC (385710) of Scots Guards Cd. L 2.10.0	
			1 Public servant of 17-10-0	
"	10.3.19 11.3.19 12.3.19		Received orders to proceed to United Kingdom for service in India pending Major Alec Scott RAMC Handed over unit	
	13.3.19		Capt Panzani J.M.S returned from Michelham Home at MENTONE and was taken on the strength	a/s
	14.3.19		Routine	a/s
	15.3.19		Lt W.H. Morgan M.R.C U.S.A. proceeded to report to D.M.S. 2nd Army at Cologne for duty	a/s

WAR DIARY or INTELLIGENCE SUMMARY

Army Form C. 2118.

(Erase heading not required.)

Instructions regarding War Diaries and Intelligence Summaries are contained in F. S. Regs., Part II. and the Staff Manual respectively. Title pages will be prepared in manuscript.

Place	Date	Hour	Summary of Events and Information	Remarks and references to Appendices
TOURCOING	16.3.19		Routine	
	17.3.19		Routine	
	18.3.19		Routine. Rgt. was demobilised during week – B. No on leave – 1	
	19.3.19		Major E.W. Goodman M.R.C. U.S.A. reported for duty and taken on the strength. M.O.R's sent to No.17 C.C.S., DUREN.	
	20.3.19		Routine	
	21.3.19		1 O.R. sent to No.62 C.C.S. for duty	
	22.3.19		Routine	
	23.3.19		Routine. Two O.R. men demobilised during week – Y. M. in Base – Nil	
	24.3.19		Routine	
	25.3.19		Capt. E. THERRIEN M.R.C. U.S.A. proceeded to United Kingdom for a course of instruction. Claimed Madame at KNOTTY ASH, Liverpool and struck off strength	
	26.3.19		No. 32067 Pte A French R.A.M.C. 44 Field Ambulance awarded the Decoration Medaille 2nd Class Croix de Guerre, Belgium	
	27.3.19		Routine	
	28.3.19		Routine	
	29.3.19		Under instructions received from D.M.S. 3rd Army, only one officer per value of a Field Ambulance was retained after this date. The following two officers were accordingly struck off the strength of this unit – Major E.W. Goodman M.R.C. U.S.A and Capt. P. Farthern Y.M.S.	
	30.3.19		Routine	
	31.3.19		The unit is now down to Cadre strength and no more men have been demobilised	

O. Scott Major R.A.M.C.

C O N F I D E N T I A L.

W A R   D I A R Y

- of -

44th FIELD AMBULANCE.

From: 1st May, 1919.
  To: 31st May, 1919.

Army Form C. 2118.

WAR DIARY
or
INTELLIGENCE SUMMARY.

(Erase heading not required.)

Instructions regarding War Diaries and Intelligence Summaries are contained in F. S. Regs., Part II. and the Staff Manual respectively. Title pages will be prepared in manuscript.

Place	Date	Hour	Summary of Events and Information	Remarks and references to Appendices
	1/5/19		Routine	
	2/5/19		Routine	
	3/5/19		Routine. No of men granted leave to U.K. cleary accept it.	
	4/5/19		Routine	
	5/5/19		Rectin E.W. Gordon m.g USAV returned home leave	
	6/5/19		Major E.W. Gordon arrived from leave	
	7/5/19		Routine	
	8/5/19		Routine	
	9/5/19		Rest	
	10/5/19		Rested S men parties doing salvage work	
	11/5/19		Major E W Gordon permitted to join the Bureau	
	12/5/19		Routine	
	13/5/19		No Tg/9/2969 Se 165.SC. No 1/3746 S.Peruvia	
	14/5/19		R.O 517. Demand No. 2.85.S Aug. Hand over	
	15/5/19	T4/89452 S.Sapper Tg/94075 S god home	
	16/5/19		Home transport (6).	
	17/5/19		Handed over the Unit to Capt. Foster Russell.	

G. Lutt
Capt. QM

Army Form C. 2118.

WAR DIARY
or
INTELLIGENCE SUMMARY.
(Erase heading not required.)

Place	Date	Hour	Summary of Events and Information	Remarks and references to Appendices
Tourcoing	16.5.19			

WAR DIARY or INTELLIGENCE SUMMARY

Army Form C. 2118.

44 M Coy

Place	Date	Hour	Summary of Events and Information	Remarks and references to Appendices
Tourcoing	1.6.19		Routine	
	2.		Routine	
	3.		M2/155215 Cpl. Pickring, M2/162166 Pte Cook, M2/055213 Pte Nicholls & M2/054570 Pte Wright. Transferred to 36th Div M.T. Coy for demobilisation	
	4.		The undermentioned 14,000+ men forming the cadre of the unit proceeded to St Andre on route for U.K. 32150 S/Sgt Cook, 31094 Sgt Pratt, 31140 Sgt Storm, 30615 A/S/Sgt Norman, 32142 Pte Ackroyd, 32447 Pte Burg, 31766 Pte Burkhardt, 435327 Pte Fletcher, 31173 Pte Gee, 4346 Pte Gillespie, 31810 Pte Heselyn, 354452 Pte Munday, 34129 Pte Jones Wm, 31415 Pte King, 31371 Pte McEnery, 37561 Pte Millward, 34429 Pte Randall and 39655 Pte Ratcliff. Sgt Major Cryle transferred to M.T. Coy 14th Div. Train & struck off strength of T/497 St 392.78 on withdrawal of Cadre for duty	
5.		Routine	Number of men on leave 3	
6.		Routine		
7.		Routine		
8.		M/461596 Pte O'Neill transferred to 36th Div M.T. Coy for demobilisation	
9.		M2/114604 Pte Simmons reported for duty	
10.			
11.		Routine	
12.		Routine	
13			

Army Form C. 2118.

WAR DIARY
or
INTELLIGENCE SUMMARY.

(Erase heading not required.)

Instructions regarding War Diaries and Intelligence Summaries are contained in F. S. Regs., Part II. and the Staff Manual respectively. Title pages will be prepared in manuscript.

Place	Date	Hour	Summary of Events and Information	Remarks and references to Appendices
Fowey	15/7		S/SS Bolton sent to Avonmouth for drafts	
	16"		Routine	
	17"		Routine SS Bolton with 760 R.D. 1 SS 200 R.D.H. Entrained	
	18"		Routine	
	19"		Entrained at Avonmouth with Equipment 9 P.m. 1 Officer & other ranks	
	20"		Wings at Antwerp docks at 7.20 a.m. Detrained and parked vehicles	
	21"		Routine	
	22"		Routine	
	23"		Routine	
	24"		Routine	
	25"		Routine	
	26"		Routine	
	27"		This day loaded SS Kenyon's shipment in Reg'd RD 16 in route for Antwerp	
	28"		Routine	
	29"		Entrained 5.00 p.m. for Demobilization Camp, Boulogne	
	30"		Arrived at Boulogne 2.05 p.m.	
	1/8		Routine	
	2"		Equipment Guard proceeded to U.K. for demobilization	

(Signed) John Dugg. O.M. S. Lieut.
O.C. Depot

www.ingramcontent.com/pod-product-compliance
Lightning Source LLC
Chambersburg PA
CBHW080810010526
44113CB00013B/2355